D1293873

VERSATILE VEGETABLES

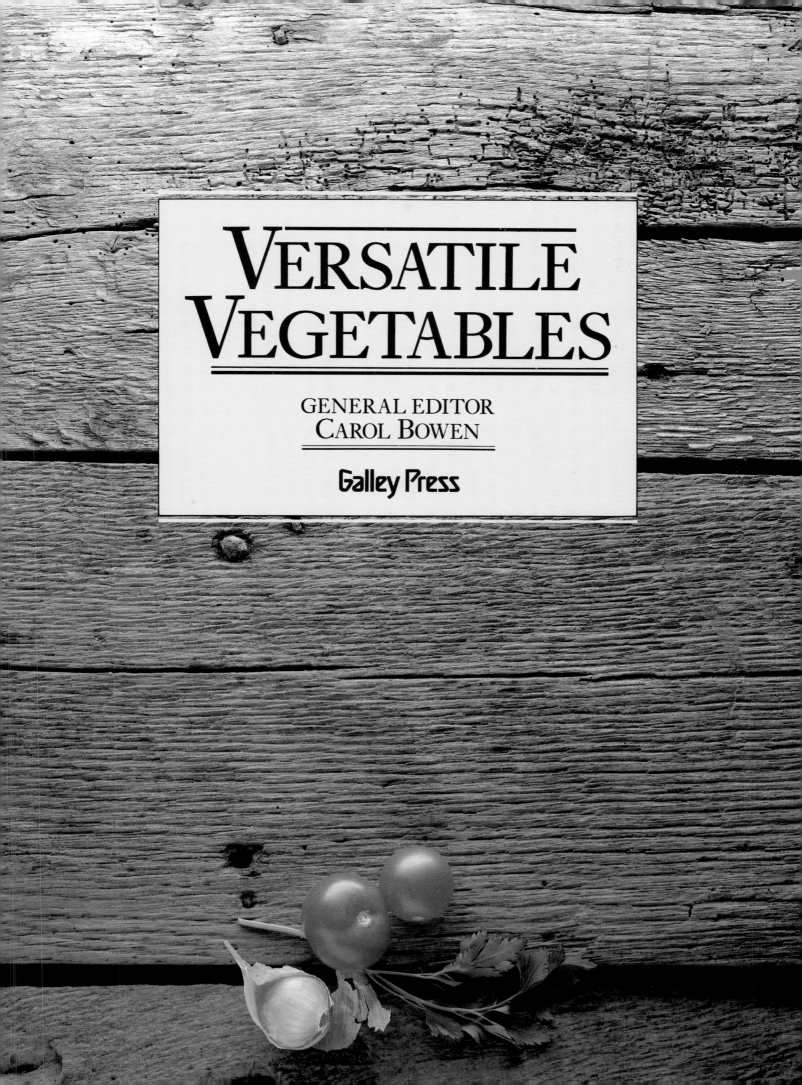

VERSATILE VEGETABLES

GENERAL EDITOR
CAROL BOWEN

Galley Press

First published 1984 by
Octopus Books Limited
59 Grosvenor Street, London W1

© Octopus Books Limited 1984

This edition published 1988

ISBN 0 86136 611 5

Printed in Hong Kong

CONTENTS

General Editor: Carol Bowen
Photography by Paul Williams

INTRODUCTION

The range of vegetables available in Britain today is extensive and nature ensures the virtue of variety throughout the year – from the early pale green hues of home-grown celery to the golden autumn corn on the cobs. Indeed there is a vegetable for every month of the year, every occasion from the simple to sumptuous and to suit every appetite. Rarely a meal goes by without their inclusion from the traditional and basic 'meat and two veg' or crispy crunchy salad to the fashionable all-vegetable main meal dish.

NUTRITION

Including vegetables as a staple ingredient in any diet makes good nutritional sense. Vegetables provide a good source of protein, carbohydrate, some fat, many vitamins and an abundance of minerals. Vegetable proteins are described as incomplete because they lack a few of the essential amino acids but when combined with other foods rich in those amino acids they provide complete proteins that are hard to beat. For example – when cereals, such as rice and corn, are eaten together with certain vegetables, they supplement each other's amino acids to provide complete proteins.

Although each kind of vegetable has its own nutritional characteristics, as a group they are rich in Vitamins C, A, B_1 and folic acid. Vegetables are particularly valuable for the dietary fibre they provide. Because of their high water content and low fat content, most vegetables are also low in calories, making them extremely useful for slimmers.

Broccoli and Brussels sprouts are the best sources of Vitamin C, apart from oranges and strawberries. Peppers, cauliflower, spinach and peas are good too. Excellent sources of folic acid are broccoli, spinach, Brussels sprouts, peas, cauliflower and spring cabbage. Root vegetables, especially carrots, are a particularly good source of Vitamin A. The best sources of dietary fibre are peas, broad beans, haricot and red kidney beans. Pulses are also a particularly good source of protein.

Nutritional value will however vary, sometimes drastically, with the age of the vegetable, conditions under which it has been grown and stored, and its preparation – especially cooking. As a general rule, young but not immature vegetables that have been stored out of direct sunlight and extreme heat or cold, and cooked for the minimum amount of time have the highest nutritional value.

SELECTING FOR QUALITY

In line with a desire for a more healthy diet most people are turning to vegetables for variety at the expense of meat, fish and eggs and suppliers are rewarding their demands with an increasing supply of unusual and often forgotten vegetables. An increasing number of supermarkets are now providing more shelf space for unusual vegetables like kohlrabi, chayote, endive, radicchio and scorzonera.

As a general guide to purchase there are a few golden rules to follow: the most important is to let your eyes and nose judge the freshness and quality of a vegetable; buy in season wherever possible for flavour and economy; and avoid vegetables that are sold as first of the crop – generally the price will be exorbitant and the vegetables may have been harvested prior to full maturity.

Wash and thoroughly drain all vegetables before using and don't prepare too well ahead or overcook – or you'll lose flavour and nutritional value. Beyond this, check the specifics in the A to Z section of each chapter.

With the growing list of fresh, frozen, preserved and dried vegetables finding their way to our tables, there should be no

SEASONAL AVAILABILITY OF FRESH VEGETABLES

VEGETABLE	AVAILABILITY	VEGETABLE	AVAILABILITY
ARTICHOKES – globe	June–October	CELERIAC	All Year Round: October–November*
– Jerusalem	October–November	CELERY	All Year Round: September–April*
ASPARAGUS – white	May–June		
– French	May–July	CHAYOTE	December–March
AUBERGINES	All Year Round: July–October*	CHICORY	All Year Round: December–March*
BEANS – broad	May–July		
– French	June–October	CHILLIS	All Year Round: June–September*
BEANSPROUTS	All Year Round		
BEETROOT	All Year Round: September–March*	CHINESE CABBAGE	All Year Round: September–November*
BROCCOLI – sprouting	March–May	COURGETTES	All Year Round: July–August*
– calabrese	August–October	CRESS/WATERCRESS	All Year Round: May–July*
BRUSSELS SPROUTS	September–April	CUCUMBERS	All Year Round: August–September*
CABBAGE – summer	August–September		
– autumn/winter	October–February	DANDELIONS	January–March
– Savoy	September–May	ENDIVE – curly	September–October
– spring	April–May	– Batavian	October–December
– red	September–May		
CARDOON	October–February	FENNEL	All Year Round: August–September*
CARROTS	All Year Round: July–October*		
CAULIFLOWERS	All Year Round: May–July*	GARLIC	All Year Round: March and September*

NOTE: The homegrown season or best time to buy is indicated by an asterisk where applicable.

excuse for vegetable variety. Choose from the pages that follow, prepare carefully according to instructions, spice up with a sprinkling of herbs or exotic spices and you have the makings of many nourishing and memorable meals.

FREEZING

The season for most vegetables can, even at best, be short and ill-timed and it is for that reason that freezing has found increasing popularity as a form of preserving most vegetables. Peas, runner beans and sweetcorn, can ring the changes in a usual winter diet of Brussels sprouts, cabbage or broccoli. However to ensure excellent results in freezing it is essential to follow the rules on preparation, packaging, labelling or coding and finally storage:
* Freeze only fresh food in perfect condition – vegetables cannot be improved by freezing.
* Freeze vegetables as soon as possible after buying or gathering and initial preparation.
* Pick or buy only as much produce at one time as can be prepared and frozen without delay.
* Blanch vegetables before freezing (see Vegetable Freezing Chart – – overleaf).
* Cool hot foods quickly before freezing.
* Pack the prepared food into moisture-proof and vapour-proof bags or containers for freezing.

* Pack vegetables in meal-size quantities whenever possible.
* Exclude as much air as possible from the packs before sealing.
* Label the packs clearly, with the date of freezing, and keep a separate freezer record.
* Freeze packs until solid in the coldest part of the freezer.
* Follow the freezer manufacturers' instructions on setting the temperature guage or fast freeze button.
* In most cases cook vegetables from frozen for the best results.
* Never refreeze vegetables unless they are cooked first.

Most vegetables can be frozen with the exception of a few salad leafy type vegetables whose high water content renders them unsuitable. Prepare vegetables for freezing in much the same way as for cooking. After preparation, most vegetables must be blanched before freezing to preserve their quality in the freezer. Blanching is necessary to retard the activity of natural enzymes present in vegetables; if it is not carried out the enzymes will continue to work in the freezer with consequent deterioration of colour, texture, flavour and nutritive value.

To blanch vegetables: fill a blanching basket with no more than 500 g/1 lb prepared vegetables. Immerse in a large pan containing about 4 litres/7 pints rapidly

boiling water. Return quickly to the boil, then calculate the blanching time accurately, from the moment the water returns to the boil.

Immediately the blanching time is complete, remove the basket from the pan and plunge into a bowl of iced water to refresh the vegetables – for the same length of time as blanching. Drain and pack – in convenient quantities. The blanching water can be used for up to 6 to 7 batches of the same vegetable. It must then be replaced with fresh boiling water.

Vegetables can be frozen as a solid block or, more popularly open frozen for free-flow results. To open freeze vegetables, line a tray with foil or greaseproof paper, then spread out the individual items on it so that they are not touching each other. Freeze, using the fast-freeze control until solid. Remove from the tray, using a palette knife, then pack, seal and return to the freezer.

BOTTLING

Of the alternative methods of preserving vegetables to freezing, bottling is no longer recommended. This is because it is now generally recognised that the temperatures reached in home bottling cannot be guaranteed to be high enough to kill the bacteria in vegetables in order to render them safe to eat. This is true even if a pressure cooker is used.

VEGETABLE	AVAILABILITY	VEGETABLE	AVAILABILITY
HORSERADISH	October–February	POTATOES	All Year Round: September–October*
KALE	December–April	PUMPKIN	September–November
KOHLRABI	All Year Round	RADICCHIO	September–April
LEEKS – summer	May–August	RADISHES	All Year Round: June–September*
– winter	November–March		
LETTUCE – cabbage	All Year Round	SCORZONERA	October–March
– Cos	All Year Round: October–February*	SHALLOTS	July
– Iceberg	All Year Round	SORREL	June–September
– Lamb's	All Year Round: October–April*		
MARROWS	May–August	SPINACH	May–July and September–November
MORELS	April–June		
MUSHROOMS – cèpes	August–October	SPRING ONIONS	All Year Round: July–September*
– chanterelles	July–December		
– cultivated	All Year Round	SWEDES	October–April
– field	August–October	SWEETCORN	August–September
– wild	July–December		
ONIONS	All Year Round	SWEET POTATOES	All Year Round: November–April*
OKRA	July–October	TOMATOES	All Year Round: June–October*
PARSNIPS	September–February	TRUFFLES	Autumn
PEAS	June–August	TURNIPS	October–December
PEPPERS	All Year Round: July–September*	VINE LEAVES	June–December (rarely available)

VEGETABLE FREEZING CHART

Those vegetables not mentioned are considered unsuitable for freezing.

VEGETABLE	SELECTION	PREPARATION FOR FREEZING	BLANCHING TIME	STORAGE TIME
ARTICHOKES – globe	Small young chokes that are not fully open.	Remove coarse outer leaves. Trim stalk level with base. Cut off pointed top and spiky tops to leaves. Freeze whole or as hearts. Cook hearts before freezing.	whole: 5 to 7 minutes hearts: no need	12 months 6 months
– Jerusalem	Choose firm tubers.	Scrub, peel thinly and slice or dice.	2 minutes	3 months
ASPARAGUS	Choose young tender stalks. Reject any with woody or withered stems.	Grade according to thickness. Trim off thick end and any scales. Sort into equal bundles.	2 to 4 minutes	12 months
AUBERGINES	Choose firm ripe fruits with smooth shiny skins.	Slice or cube according to later use. Degorge and rinse.	cubes: 4 minutes slices: 3 minutes	9 months
BEANS – broad	Small young pods.	Shell or if very young leaves whole.	$1\frac{1}{2}$ to 2 minutes	12 months
– French	Choose small tender beans not longer than 10 cm (4 inches).	Top and tail. Slice if large.	whole: 3 minutes slices: 2 minutes	12 months
– runner	Young crisp beans.	Top and tail, remove strings. Leave whole or slice.	whole: 3 minutes slices: 2 minutes	12 months
BEETROOT	Select small beetroot about 7.5 cm (3 inches) in diameter.	Twist off leaves. Wash carefully. Cook before freezing.		6 months
BROCCOLI	Bright green, purple or white compact heads with tender stalks.	Grade for size and cut into even-sized pieces.	2 to 4 minutes	12 months
BRUSSELS SPROUTS	Choose small very firm and tight buds.	Wash, trim the base and remove any outer damaged leaves. Grade according to size.	$1\frac{1}{2}$ to 3 minutes	12 months
CABBAGE – summer, autumn, winter, Savoy and red	Select firm heads with a good colour and firm texture.	Remove and discard outer leaves. Cut into quarters and remove woody triangles at base. Shred finely.	1 minute	12 months
– spring	Young dark green leaves.	Separate leaves. Trim away any hard ends. Leave whole or cut into strips.	$1\frac{1}{2}$ minutes	6 months
CARROTS	Choose young spring carrots of even shape.	Remove tops and scrub or peel thinly. Freeze whole or sliced.	3 minutes	12 months
CAULIFLOWERS	Choose white, firm cauliflowers with green leaves and fresh appearance.	Divide into florets about 5 cm (2 inches) in diameter. Grade according to size.	2 to 3 minutes	6 months
CELERIAC	Choose firm small roots.	Peel and wash then cut into cubes, thick slices or grate.	cubes and slices: 1 to 2 minutes grated: 1 to $1\frac{1}{2}$ minutes	12 months
CELERY	Select firm large heads that are fresh and green.	Scrub and slice into 5 cm (2 inch) lengths.	3 minutes	9 months
CHICORY	Choose conical, tightly-packed heads.	Trim bases and remove any outer damaged leaves.	4 minutes	5 months
CHILLIS	Firm, shiny chillis without wrinkles.	Cut in half, remove stalks and seeds. Open freeze on trays. Double wrap.	—	12 months
COURGETTES	Small young courgettes.	Trim the ends and leave whole, slice or cube.	whole: 2 minutes slices or cubes: 1 minute	9 months
CUCUMBERS	Firm straight cucumbers.	Peel, chop and purée. Freeze leaving 2 cm ($\frac{3}{4}$ inch) headspace.	—	2 months
FENNEL	Choose firm, tight heads with white leaf bases.	Trim and cut each head into quarters.	3 to 5 minutes	6 months
HORSERADISH	Young roots that show no signs of woodiness.	Trim, clean thoroughly then grate. Sprinkle with wine vinegar. Pack in rigid containers.	—	6 months

VEGETABLE	SELECTION	PREPARATION FOR FREEZING	BLANCHING TIME	STORAGE TIME
KOHLRABI	Choose small stems with a firm texture.	Remove leaves and peel thinly. Slice or leave small whole.	whole: 3 minutes slices: 2 minutes	12 months
KALE	Choose young leaves with a good bright green colour.	Pull the leaves from the stems like spinach. Wash.	3 minutes	12 months
LEEKS	Choose firm, young leeks with a fresh green colour.	Trim away root and the topmost green leaves. Wash thoroughly and leave whole or slice.	3 to 4 minutes	6 months
LETTUCE	Select tight lettuce hearts that are crisp and firm.	Remove any damaged or wilted leaves.	2 minutes	6 months
MARROWS	Choose only small to medium marrows.	Peel if liked. Halve and scoop out seeds. Cut into 2.5 cm (1 inch) dice.	2 minutes	6 months
MUSHROOMS & FUNGI	Choose firm undamaged mushrooms with no trace of damp.	Wipe and trim stalks if necessary. Leave raw or sauté in butter. Open freeze whole uncooked mushrooms. Pack sautéed mushrooms into rigid containers.	—	whole uncooked: 1 month sautéed: 3 months
ONIONS	Firm onions of all varieties with crisp, papery skins.	Trim, top, tail and peel. Grade according to size. Leave whole or slice.	whole, button or shallots: 2 to 4 minutes sliced: 1 to 2 minutes	6 months 6 months
OKRA	Small pods about 5 cm (2 inches) long.	Trim the stems.	3 minutes	12 months
PARSNIPS	Young parsnips that are crisp and bright in colour.	Trim and wash. Peel thinly and core and slice.	4 minutes	12 months
PEAS – podded – mangetout	Young and tender pods. Flat shiny pods.	Shell. Top and tail.	1 minute ½ to 1 minute	12 months 12 months
PEPPERS	Firm shiny peppers without wrinkles.	Core, deseed and slice or chop. No need to blanch for 6 months storage.	3 minutes	12 months
POTATOES	Undamaged tubers without signs of decay or disease.	Scrub *new potatoes* and remove skins. Cook until tender. Freeze. For *chips* – cook in hot oil for 2 to 3 minutes. Drain and open freeze.	12 months 3 months	
PUMPKIN	Choose firm fruit without too many blemishes.	Peel and remove seeds. Cut into chunks and cook until soft. Drain and mash. Pack in rigid containers leaving 2 cm (¾ inch) headspace.	—	12 months
RADISHES – winter	Choose firm undamaged roots.	Trim, scrub and peel thinly then grate or dice.	2 minutes	6 months
SALSIFY & SCORZONERA	Choose firm young roots that are fresh in appearance.	Trim off leaves and scrub but do not peel. Blanch for 2 minutes then remove skins. Cut into 7.5 cm (3 inch) pieces.	—	6 months
SPINACH	Young fresh green crisp yet tender leaves.	Snap off stalks, wash each leaf individually.	2 minutes	12 months
SWEDES	Small roots that show no signs of woodiness.	Top, tail and peel thinly. Cut into 2 cm (¾ inch) dice.	2 minutes	12 months
SWEETCORN	Choose cobs that are just ripe with plump, pale-coloured kernels which are even-sized.	Pull away leaves and silks. Trim stems level with base of cobs. Alternatively remove kernels after blanching.	2 to 6 minutes	12 months
TOMATOES	Choose firm, medium-sized ordinary tomatoes, under rather than over ripe.	Prepare whole or as purée. Pack in rigid containers leaving a 2 cm (¾ inch) headspace.	—	12 months
TURNIPS	Choose small to medium turnips that have bright green tops.	Top and tail then peel thinly. Leave small whole or cut into 2 cm (¾ inch) dice.	2 to 3 minutes	12 months

PICKLING

Pickling, by contrast to freezing, is a more traditional form of preservation based on using vinegar to keep out and prevent the growth of micro-organisms and so maintain foods in prime condition. It is important to use a good quality vinegar with an acetic acid content of at least 5%. When making sharp pickles the vegetables are usually brined beforehand. This removes any surplus water that would weaken the vinegar. There are two methods of brining – wet and dry.

With dry brining the vegetables are prepared then layered in a bowl with salt, allowing 1 tablespoon salt to 500 g/1 lb vegetables. Cover and leave overnight. Dry brining is suitable for cucumber, marrow, tomatoes and red cabbage.

Wet brining, for cucumber and onions, involves soaking the vegetables in a brine solution. Dissolve 50 g/2 oz salt in 600 ml/1 pint water to 500 g/1 lb vegetables. Cover and keep immersed overnight.

After brining, rinse the vegetables well in cold water and pack into pickle jars. Pour spiced vinegar over and cover securely with either a metal cap with a vinegar-proof lining, greaseproof paper and then a round of muslin dipped in melted fat or paraffin wax, or a preserving skin or vinegar-proof paper. Leave 2 to 3 months to mature in a cool, dark place. The exception is red cabbage which loses its crisp texture after 2 to 3 weeks.

Chutneys and relishes offer another way of preserving vegetables. To prepare vegetables for chutneys finely mince, chop or slice. Simmer to a pulp with vinegar, sugar, spices and salt. The chutney is ready when no excess water remains, taking from 1 to 4 hours.

To prepare a relish, chop the vegetables in chunks and cook for a shorter time to keep the ingredients shape. Pour the hot mixture into clean, dry, pre-heated jars and cover as for pickles. Allow to mature for 2 to 3 months before eating.

DRYING

Most vegetables are best preserved by freezing, brining or making into relishes. However, a reasonable amount of success can be obtained by drying mushrooms, peas, onions and beans. Prepare peas, onion slices and beans as for freezing, including blanching. Dry on a towel, then in a cool oven until quite hard. Cool, then pack in airtight tins to store. Soak in cold water for 12 hours to reconstitute. Mushrooms can also be dried by threading the caps onto string and hanging in an airing cupboard with the door ajar for about 2 days. Onion slices or rings can also be dried. Blanch in boiling water for ½ minute. Dry, then place in a cool oven to dry with the door ajar for about 3 hours until crisp and dry. Cool, then pack in airtight jars.

THE FINISHING TOUCH

Suitable garnishes for vegetable dishes can lift an ordinary dish to the luxury class. They should complement the dish in colour and flavour. Choose one that not only suits the food but the setting and the serving dish too. Here are a few suggestions:

Spring Onion Curls: Trim the spring onion tops. Thinly slice the remaining green part lengthways to the bulb. Chill in iced water to curl.

Celery Curls: Cut celery sticks into 7.5 cm (3 inch) lengths. Slice each piece into narrow strips, almost to the end. Chill in iced water to curl.

Vegetable Shapes: Thinly slice a peeled turnip, carrot, swede or pepper crossways and cut out shapes with canapé cutters or with a sharp knife. Interesting shapes include flowers, hearts, fish, moons and stars.

Cucumber Twists: Cut the cucumber across into thin slices. Using a sharp knife, cut each slice from the edge to the centre. Open the cut and twist each slice in opposite directions. Decorate the centre with a sprig of herbs if liked.

Cucumber Wheels: Using a paring knife, thinly pare the cucumber along its length at regular intervals. Thinly slice crossways to make notched slices that resemble wheels.

Tomato Rose: Using a sharp knife, carefully cut away the skin from the tomato in one piece. Roll up to form a rose and secure with a cocktail stick.

Carrot Curls: Scrape raw carrots and slice them lengthways and paper thin, using a vegetable peeler. Roll up, fasten with a cocktail stick and immerse in iced water to curl. Serve on or off the cocktail sticks.

Gherkin Fans: Make lengthwise cuts almost to the end of each gherkin, from the 'flower' end. Spread out carefully to form an open fan.

Radish Roses: Cut off a narrow slice from the root end of each radish, then cut thin 'petals' from stem to root. Put into iced water until the cuts open to form petals.

Radish Water Lilies: Make 4 to 8 small deep cuts, crossing in the centre of the radish at the root end, and leave in iced water to open out.

Cucumber Butterflies: Cucumber slices cut in half and in turn cut again from the outside peel edge almost into the centre will open to form butterfly shapes.

Herb Bows and Bundles: Stems or sprigs of herbs look very attractive if held together either at the base or in the middle by a stem of the same herb or a contrasting one.

Bundles or bouquets of chives, dill and fennel look most attractive held this way.

Pepper Rings: Slice away the cap from the pepper. Remove and discard the core and seeds. Slice horizontally into thin rings to use as a garnish.

Hollow Shells: Hollow shells of tomato or pepper make decorative cases to hold herbs and savoury fillings. Hollowed-out pumpkins also make good containers for soups.

Cucumber Bows: Remove a 5 cm (2 inch) piece of cucumber from the stem end. Cut at regular intervals vertically almost to the base. Fold and tuck in every alternate slice to make a cucumber bow.

Pepper Lattice: Core, deseed and thinly slice red, green or yellow peppers and arrange over food to make a colourful lattice.

Sliced Olives: Pimiento-stuffed olives look very attractive if sliced horizontally to show their colourful red centres.

Vegetable Nest: Finely shredded lettuce, cabbage or Chinese leaves, small young beans or mangetout make an attractive edge to a salad dish.

Chicory Wheel: Carefully separate the leaves from chicory, rinse and drain. Arrange on a plate to radiate from the centre of the dish like the spokes of a wheel.

Striped Courgettes: Using a paring knife, cut thin strips along the length of each courgette at regular intervals. Slice horizontally to cook.

Herb or Vegetable Butter Shapes: Mix 125 g (4 oz) butter with 1 to 2 teaspoons chopped fresh herbs or very finely chopped vegetables. Spread onto a sheet of greaseproof paper, place another sheet of paper on top and, with a rolling pin, roll out to a thickness of about 5 mm ($\frac{1}{4}$ inch). Refrigerate until firm. Remove the top sheet of paper and cut out shapes from the firm butter with petit-four or small biscuit cutters. Chill until required.

Tomato or Pepper Baskets: Make two parallel cuts from the top down to just above centre of the tomato or pepper, leaving a strip 5 mm ($\frac{1}{4}$ inch) wide between the cuts (this forms the handle). Cut in at right angles to meet the base of the cuts and remove the two wedge-shaped pieces. Remove the core and seeds with a teaspoon. Fill with herbs or cooked vegetables.

Pepper Bundles: Core and deseed the pepper then remove one small slice horizontally from one end to make a pepper ring. Thinly slice the remaining peppers and gather together in a bundle. Push through the pepper ring to hold and secure.

Pepper rings also make colourful 'holders' for bundles of asparagus, green beans and julienne strips of most vegetables.

Cucumber Boats: Halve a cucumber lengthways and scoop out the seeds with a teaspoon. Cut into 5 cm (2 inch) lengths and serrate the long unpeeled edges.

Cucumber Chains: Thickly slice an unpeeled cucumber. Using a sharp knife, remove the centre seeds. Cut one edge of each slice and lock the hollowed-out slices together to make a chain.

Vegetable Knots: The thinly pared peel or skin of cucumbers, carrots and courgettes for example, can be cut into thin strips and knotted in the centre to make an attractive garnish.

Tomato Beak or Arrow: Cut a slice off the side of the tomato so that it will stand firmly. On the side directly opposite, using a sharp knife, cut a small V into the tomato without going right down to the base. Leave the cut piece in place. Now cut two more larger V's outside the first. Push the pieces forward to make a 'beak' or arrow.

Tomatoes Van Dyke: Using a sharp knife, cut small zig-zag lines around the circumference of a tomato to meet at either end. Pull apart to separate into water lily shapes.

LEAFY VEGETABLES

Feathery light, crisp, mostly green and fragrant, leafy vegetables are often considered the salad family. Quite justly so for its members, lettuce, chicory, cress, dandelion, endive, radicchio, sorrel, spinach and vine leaves can be used in a host of salads and hors d'oeuvres. They also make tasty soups, light vegetable dishes and moist wrappings for savoury mixtures.

All need careful handling during preparation and will not tolerate extreme temperatures, lengthy storage or long cooking times. For optimum flavour they must be cooked in the minimum amount of stock or water, for a short time.

Choose leafy vegetables when they are at their best – young and tender. Older specimens will prove bitter and coarse and are only suitable for soups, hot pots and braised dishes. Look for shiny leaves that are unblemished and reject any that are limp. The vegetable must be crisp and firm for peak freshness.

CHICORY

Origin: Chicory (*Cichorium intybus*), as we know it today, is the cultivated and much developed form of wild chicory, the plant whose root was first used as a coffee substitute, or for adding to coffee. In its primitive form it was native to Europe and west Asia. Cultivated chicory was first raised by the Belgian gardener Brézier in the 19th century, who discovered, by chance, that chicory roots stored in the dark put out pale green shoots in winter, which formed a conical head of crisp, white, faintly bitter leaves up to 20 cm/8 inches long. It quickly became a popular vegetable.

Perhaps this gives rise to one of the most famous confusions between chicory and endive. In Britain we call such conical chicons, chicory, but in France they call them endive or Belgian endive. To confuse further, the French name what we call endive, chicory.

Availability: Belgium is still the main growing and exporting centre, but now chicory is also grown in France, Holland, England and America.

Chicory is available all year round, but is at its best in season, between December and March.

Buying: Chicory, although bought in heads, is sold by weight. There are three varieties in general cultivation: Red Verona, a pink tinged chicory; Witloof, a Belgian chicory also called Brussels Chicory; and Sugar Loaf, a variety that produces delicious hearts during the summer months.

Preparation and serving: Prepare chicory by removing the outer leaves, trim the root end clean, then scoop out any bitter core with a sharp-pointed knife. The heads can then either be separated into whole single leaves, left whole or sliced into thin strips or rings. Place in a sieve, rinse and drain.

The centre of a chicory head can be bitter, becoming more so with age. To reduce this, blanch in boiling water with lemon juice added for 2 minutes. Plunge into cold water then drain thoroughly.

Chicory is delicious in any number of mixed or green salads, especially those with citrus fruits. Its leaves are also tasty for dunking in dips and sauces. When preparing chicory as a cooked vegetable, leave the heads whole and simmer in stock or water for 15 to 20 minutes, depending upon size. Alternatively, braise in butter over a low heat until cooked, about 20 minutes. Never use an iron pan for cooking chicory, it will discolour and darken the vegetable. Traditionally, cooked chicory is served with melted butter, béchamel, mornay or hollandaise sauce.

Always store chicory in a cool, dark place, the salad drawer of a refrigerator is ideal; it will keep for up to 1 week.

Nutritional value: Chicory is a good source of Vitamin C, and contains only 9 Calories (40 kj) per 100 g/3½ oz.

CRESS AND WATERCRESS

Origin: Cress, or salad cress as it is also known, and watercress are both members of the Cruciferae family. Salad cress (*Lepidium sativum*) originated in the East and was used as a medicinal plant, helping to cure stomach upsets.

Like cress, watercress (*Nasturtium officinale*) is usually eaten raw as a salad and has a pleasant pungent flavour.

Availability: Cress is cultivated throughout the United Kingdom. It is available all year round but the supply peaks from May to July, coinciding with the salad season. Salad cress, unlike watercress, is extremely easy to grow on cotton wool or compost and is often seen growing on window sills. Mustard is a similar crucifer plant and is often sown together with cress and sold as 'mustard and cress'.

Watercress however, needs a supply of pure running water. For this reason one should not be tempted to pick and eat wild watercress unless you are very sure of the purity of the water supply.

Buying: Cress is easily perishable so look out for a supply with crisp green leaves and fresh appearance. Avoid any with yellow or wilted leaves.

Salad cress, or mustard and cress, is generally sold in punnets. Choose one with a damp compost. It will continue to grow until you are ready to cut it, up to 2 weeks after purchase.

Watercress is sold by the bunch. Select bunches that are fresh, bright and clean. Sort and discard any damaged leaves from the bunch as soon as possible after purchase.

Preparation and serving: To prepare salad cress, snip off the cress with scissors close to the soil, place in a sieve, rinse and drain thoroughly.

Watercress stems should be trimmed and sorted, placed in a sieve, rinsed and drained thoroughly. Watercress will keep best if placed in a loose plastic

DANDELION

WATERCRESS

CRESS

bag in the refrigerator until required.

Cress is a useful ingredient in green and mixed salads. It makes a tasty ingredient for dips and sauces and is especially useful as a colourful and attractive garnish for grills, sandwiches and other savoury dishes.

Watercress is excellent in salads, where its dark green colour adds contrast to other salad vegetables. Chopped and simmered with stock and seasonings it makes a tasty soup; blended with mayonnaise it makes a delicious salad dressing or sauce for fish.

Nutritional value: Cress and watercress are valuable sources of Vitamins A and C, as well as calcium and iron. They contain about 10 Calories (43 kj) per 100 g/3½ oz.

DANDELION

Origin: The dandelion (*Taraxacum officinale*) is a member of the Compositae family. It is regarded as a common weed by most gardeners, especially when it invades a lawn. It has green toothed leaves and bright yellow flowers that are in full bloom in late spring and early summer.

As a food plant, dandelion has rather gone out of fashion since its hey day in Victorian times. Its leaves today are mainly gathered for rabbit food. Dandelion leaves however, make a tasty and healthy salad ingredient.

Availability: Dandelions grow wild in almost every country lane and meadow, if given the chance. Only occasionally are they sold in greengrocers' shops or on market stalls, and those you do find for sale are generally sold as long plants complete with roots.

Buying: In this case we generally mean picking! Dandelions are best harvested in the winter and spring months while the leaves are still young. Older, coarser leaves are too bitter to eat. If you should decide to grow your own as a salad vegetable then the best flavour is obtained if young plants are forced in a cellar or covered by a box in the garden to prevent sunshine reaching them. This gives the leaves a pale green colour and a beautifully fresh flavour.

Preparation and serving: Hand-pick the dandelion leaves and sort so that only the young leaves are used. Place in a sieve, rinse and drain thoroughly. Tear any large leaves into small pieces.

Dandelion leaves are delicious in a mixed green salad or alone with just a well-flavoured vinaigrette dressing. Tasty combinations include dandelion with watercress or crisp fried bacon.

Cook dandelion leaves as a vegetable as for spinach, with very little water in a pan with a tight-fitting lid. Dandelion

CHICORY

BATAVIAN ENDIVE

leaves can also be infused to make a 'tea', fermented to make a wine or the root can be used for a ginger type beer.

Nutritional value: Dandelions are rich in Vitamins A and C. They contain 18 Calories (77 kj) per 100 g/3½ oz.

ENDIVE

Origin: The endive (*Cichorium endivia*) is a member of the Compositae family. It probably originated as a herb growing wild in southern Europe or the East; the ancient Egyptians and Greeks were known to use it. The first endive was brought to England by the Romans, and endives have been grown here since the 16th century.

There are two main varieties of endive: winter endive, often called curly endive because of its curly leaves; and Batavian endive, often called escarole or scarole, which has broader, smooth leaves. Before they mature, both curly and Batavian endive have their leaves tied together to blanch the centres. This blanching produces light-coloured, tender, deliciously crisp inner leaves or heart to the endive.

Availability: Curly endive is sown in June and July to provide supplies from September to November, while Batavian endive is sown in August providing endives in winter. They can therefore be bought from September to early April, although supplies are sometimes scarce.

Endive is grown in most European countries. Homegrown supplies are boosted by imports from Europe.

Buying: Endive is usually bought by the head rather than by weight. Choose one with crisp, bright leaves. Avoid any that look limp, withered or damaged, they will have already lost a lot of their flavour and nutritional value. Wrap in a damp cloth and store in the refrigerator until required, up to about 3 days.

Preparation and serving: To prepare endive for use in salads, remove any coarse or damaged outer leaves. Trim away and discard the root end, separate the leaves into single spears, small sprigs or shred into strips. Place in a sieve, rinse and drain thoroughly. A salad basket, spinner or a soft cloth can be used to dry the leaves.

Serve endive as a salad, simply tossed in a piquant dressing. To serve cooked, trim away and discard the root end, leave the endive whole, cut into quarters or tear into large sprigs. Place in a sieve, rinse and drain thoroughly. Cook in boiling salted water for 12 to 15 minutes with a little lemon juice. Drain and serve with melted butter or a savoury sauce.

Nutritional value: In common with other leafy green vegetables, endive is a good source of Vitamins A and C. It also contains iron, calcium, sodium and phosphorus. Endive contains only 11 Calories (47 kj) per 100 g/3½ oz.

LETTUCE, CABBAGE

Origin: The cabbage lettuce (*Lactuca sativa* var. *capitata*) is a plant of the Compositae family, and is a cultivated form of the wild lettuce native to the south of the Caucasus. It was popular with the Romans and Greeks as early as the 4th century BC, but may have been grown much earlier in the Far East.

Cabbage lettuce was a popular vegetable in Britain by the 16th century but it was eaten cooked rather than as a salad vegetable. It was not until varieties forming round hearts were cultivated that people began serving lettuce as a fresh salad vegetable – the most popular and usual way that it is eaten today.

Availability: Regular supplies of cabbage lettuce are available all year round. They are grown in large quantities in the United Kingdom, both out of doors and under glass. Cabbage lettuces are also imported from Holland.

Buying: Cabbage lettuces are sold individually, not by weight. Look out for varieties like Avon Defiance, Buttercrunch or Webbs Wonderful with good solid hearts. Avoid any with withered leaves; they will have a poor flavour and a low nutritional value.

Preparation and serving: Always use a cabbage lettuce while at its freshest, or it will quickly lose its crispness and fresh green colour.

Prepare by cutting away the root and removing and discarding the coarse outer or damaged leaves. Separate the leaves, leaving the heart whole, place in a sieve, rinse and drain thoroughly. A salad basket, spinner or soft cloth will all help to dry the leaves. Alternatively, leave in the air to dry, but never in direct sunlight. Tear, rather than cut, any large leaves into smaller bite-sized pieces or shred coarsely.

It is essential to use a cabbage lettuce crisp. However, a tired limp lettuce can sometimes be revived quickly by standing it in a bowl of iced water, with the cut surface of the stem downwards.

Always make up a lettuce salad at the very last moment or just before serving and, ideally, do not toss in its dressing until served. Use just enough dressing to coat rather than drench the leaves for perfect mouth-watering results.

Cabbage lettuce has a vast number of culinary uses. Its leaves can be used whole for lining a dish, while shredded lettuce makes a good base for shellfish cocktails. It can be used in many salads and sandwich fillings.

Although chiefly used in salads, cabbage lettuces can be used to make soups. Their leaves can also be used to wrap around and enclose savoury fillings and stuffings and they make good braised vegetables in their own right.

Nutritional value: Cabbage lettuce contains a good supply of Vitamin A, phosphorus, some calcium and sodium and a little iron. With only 12 Calories (51 kj) per 100 g/3½ oz, it is a useful vegetable in any slimming diet.

LETTUCE, COS

Origin: The cos lettuce (*Lactuca sativa*) is a plant of the Compositae family. It is also known, especially in America, as romaine lettuce. It is easy to recognise by its long, narrow, bright green, leaves and loaf-shaped head. It can grow up to 35 cm/14 inches long and weigh up to 625 g/1¼ lb.

It is thought to have originated in ancient Egypt where it was valued as an aphrodisiac, but did not gain popularity throughout Europe until the Middle Ages.

Availability: Cos lettuce is at its best in prime season, from early October to early February. It is commercially grown in England, America and all the Mediterranean countries. Imports come from Israel.

Buying: Choose a cos lettuce that has a full, closely-bunched head with crisp, dark green outer leaves. Discard those with a limp texture, damaged appearance or yellowing leaves.

Choose from three main varieties: Paris White, a self-folding variety; Little Gem, a lettuce halfway between a cos and a cabbage with a solid little crisp heart; and Salad Bowl, with a profusion of leaves but no heart.

Preparation and serving: Prepare cos lettuce by cutting away the root and removing and discarding any coarse outer or damaged leaves. Separate the leaves, leaving the heart, if any, whole. Place in a sieve, rinse and drain

COS LETTUCE

WEBBS WONDERFUL

thoroughly. Dry the leaves, using a salad basket, spinner or soft cloth. Leave whole or tear the leaves into smaller bite-sized pieces.

Cos lettuce is served raw in salads where it can be dressed with any number of different dressings, vinaigrette or French being the most popular. It is also delicious served hot as a soup, gratin dish or braised vegetable entrée or side dish with melted butter.

Nutritional value: Cos lettuce has the same value as cabbage lettuce (opposite).

LETTUCE, ICEBERG

Origin: Iceberg lettuce (*Lactuca sativa*) is a member of the Compositae family. It is an American-bred variety of lettuce. It gets its name from the old method of storage under which it was kept, namely under layers of crushed ice. Today it is popular throughout Europe as well as America for its solid head of crisp, pale green leaves, very densely packed and curly at the ends. It is generally about the same size as a cabbage, weighing about 350 g/12 oz.

Availability: Iceberg lettuce can be found almost all year round, although supplies are often scarcer or less regular in the summer months. It is grown extensively in America. From December to March most of the crop comes from California and Arizona. As the hotter weather approaches, supplies come from Colorado, New York, New Jersey and the mid-western states. Iceberg lettuce is now also grown, on a small scale, throughout Europe.

Buying: Iceberg lettuce is sold by the head rather than by weight. Look out for heads that are round and well-formed with fresh-looking green outer leaves. Avoid any with heavy whitish heads, they are usually over-mature and bitter.

Preparation and serving: Iceberg lettuce, because it is so compact, will go a long way. A whole head will serve 6 to 10 people adequately. If you only need enough to serve 1 to 2 people then it is advisable to halve or quarter the lettuce before preparing for use. The remainder can be stored, wrapped in cling film, in the refrigerator until required, up to 1 to 2 weeks.

To prepare, trim away and discard the root end and any coarse outer or damaged leaves. Separate the leaves or shred coarsely. Place in a sieve, rinse and drain. Dry the leaves, using a salad basket, spinner or soft cloth.

Use in salads or sandwiches or braise as a vegetable and serve with melted butter or a sauce. Cooked with stock and seasonings, iceberg lettuce also makes a good soup.

Nutritional value: It has the same value as cabbage lettuce (opposite).

LETTUCE, LAMB'S

Origin: Lamb's lettuce (*Valerianella locusta*), also called corn salad, is a member of the Valerianaceae family. Its name derives from the fact that the leaves are at their greenest and most flavoursome when lambing begins.

It is a native European wild plant, but it was certainly cultivated at the time of the Roman Empire. It was introduced to the United Kingdom from the Low Countries about 400 years ago. It is generally sown as an autumn or winter crop for use when other salad vegetables are scarce.

Availability: Lamb's lettuce is available throughout the year, but is mainly in season from mid-October to the end of April. Most is locally grown but imports do come from Europe to the United Kingdom.

Buying: Choose lamb's lettuce that is crisp, green and clean. Pre-packed lamb's lettuce will generally have been cleaned. Since lamb's lettuce grows close to the ground, home-grown or non pre-packed bunches will need careful sorting and rinsing before use. Lamb's lettuce is sold either by the bunch or by weight.

Preparation and serving: Remove and discard any coarse outer or damaged leaves then leave in small sprigs or shred coarsely. Place in a sieve, rinse and drain thoroughly.

Use in green salads but avoid mixing with very strongly flavoured ingredients that will overwhelm its delicate flavour. The leaves are mildly aromatic and appreciate a vinaigrette, yogurt or soured cream dressing. Lamb's lettuce also blends well with the flavour of eggs, citrus fruits, cold meats and other green leafy vegetables.

Nutritional value: Lamb's lettuce has one of the highest vitamin values of all green leafy vegetables. It contains plenty of Vitamins A and C, as well as phosphorus and calcium. It has only 15 Calories (65 kj) per 100 g/$3\frac{1}{2}$ oz.

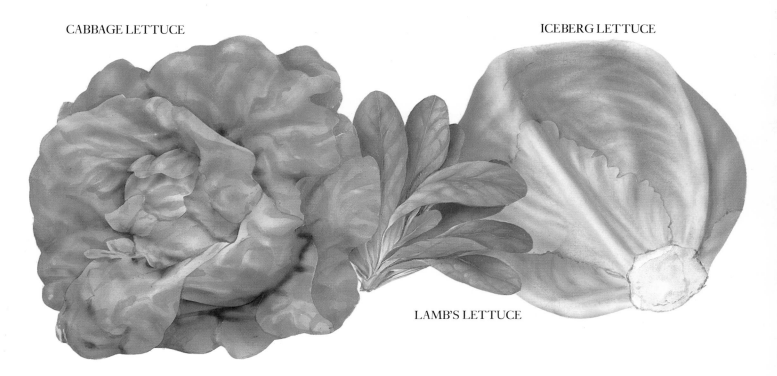

CABBAGE LETTUCE

ICEBERG LETTUCE

LAMB'S LETTUCE

RADICCHIO

Origin: Radicchio (*Cichorium intybus*), also known as red chicory and *rosso di Treviso*, has an early history the same as chicory, to which it is related. It is a small leafy vegetable, ranging in colour from deep purple to light red or pink, that has only recently become popular in the United Kingdom. The leaves, sometimes compact, often loose, are occasionally streaked white. According to the variety, the flavour may be mild, slightly bitter or decidedly bitter, but very aromatic.

Availability: Radicchio is in season from mid-September to the beginning of April. It is cultivated throughout southern Europe. The main growing area is the Italian province of Treviso, and many Italians call it simply Treviso, an officially recognised name throughout the country. Most of our radicchio is imported from Italy.

Buying: Radicchio is generally sold by weight but can be bought per head. Each head weighs about 125 g/4 oz. Look for heads that are crisp, colourful and value for money. Wrap in cling film, a damp cloth or foil and keep in the refrigerator for up to 4 days.

Preparation and serving: It is essential to remove the small root from a radicchio because it is very bitter. Separate the leaves or leave the head whole. Place in a sieve, rinse and drain thoroughly. Tear any large leaves into smaller bite-sized pieces. The bitter taste can be reduced by blanching radicchio in boiling water for 2 minutes or by soaking in lukewarm water for 20 minutes before use.

Radicchio can be used in just the same way as chicory. It makes a colourful and flavoursome salad ingredient. It can also be served hot, baked, stuffed or braised in a casserole.

Nutritional value: Radicchio is valuable for its Vitamin C. It contains about 20 Calories (86 kj) per 100 g/3½ oz.

SORREL

Origin: Sorrel (*Rumex actosa*) is a member of the Polygonaceae family. It is a perennial plant native to Europe and Asia.

There are two main varieties of sorrel: wild sorrel (*Rumex acetosa*); and French sorrel *(Rumex scutatus)*. Often regarded as a herb, sorrel has been especially popular through the centuries in France and Russia, mainly as a medicinal herb and salad vegetable.

As a plant it grows to a height of about 45 cm/18 inches, and bears green, arrow-shaped, spinach-like leaves which taste sharp and slightly sour.

Availability: Sorrel is available mainly during the summer months. It grows wild in the countryside but is grown commercially and is available from specialist stores and shops. Imports to the United Kingdom mainly come from France where it is eaten in abundance.

Buying: Sorrel is generally sold by weight. Choose sorrel stems that are crisp and dark green. Avoid any that are limp or where the leaves are damaged or turning yellow.

Preparation and serving: Sorrel stems are inedible so the leaves must be stripped from the stems before use. Tear from the stems, place in a sieve, rinse and drain thoroughly. Tear any larger leaves into smaller bite-sized pieces or shred coarsely.

Sorrel can be used raw in salads, cooked as a purée rather like spinach, as a herb in sauces and stuffings and, many consider best of all, as a soup.

Nutritional value: Sorrel is valuable for its Vitamin C, iron and potassium. It is low in calories containing about 20 Calories (86 kj) per 100 g/3½ oz.

SPINACH, SPINACH BEET, ORACHE AND SWISS CHARD

Origin: Spinach (*Spinacia oleracea*), a member of the Chenopodiaceae family, is a native of the Orient, thought to have been brought to Europe by the Crusaders. It has been cultivated in Europe since the Middle Ages.

There are two types of true spinach: the round-seeded type, generally harvested in summer; and the prickly-seeded variety, grown for use in winter and spring. In addition there are several other leafy vegetables that resemble spinach: Spinach beet (*Beta vulgaris*) which is also known as perpetual spinach; Swiss chard (*Beta vulgaris*) or Seakale beet; and Orache (*Atriplex hortensis*), sometimes called wild spinach.

True spinach leaves range from the very delicate and smooth kind to large, curling rather tough leaves. Spinach beet, Swiss chard and orache have larger, ribbed, slightly curly leaves. Their flavour is similar but milder than that of spinach and they can be prepared in the same way. There are red- and green-leaved forms of orache.

Spinach is very popular in Turkey, France and Italy.

Availability: Fresh spinach is available in season from May to July and from September to November, sometimes in April too. Forced spinach is often available during the remainder of the year.

Most of the spinach we eat has been grown in Britain but imports come from Italy, Belgium and Holland.

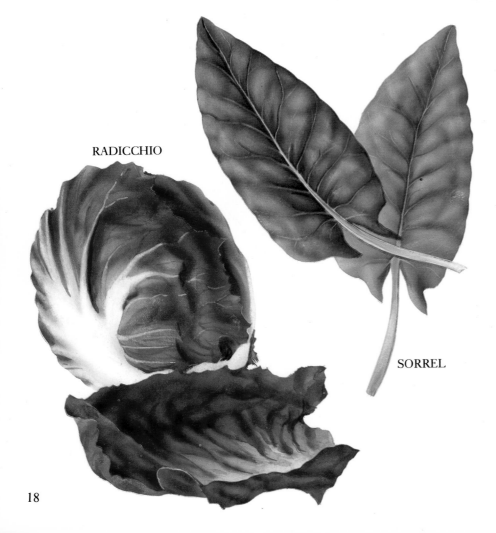

RADICCHIO

SORREL

Buying: Spinach deteriorates quickly after picking so buy and use as quickly as possible. Choose crisp green stems. It is best to buy spinach as required since it rarely stores well, even in the refrigerator. Spinach is sold by weight.

Preparation and serving: Strip the leaves from the stems and immerse in cold water. Rinse, drain and repeat with fresh water. Repeat as many times as necessary until the water is clean.

As spinach has a high water content, it does not need additional water for cooking. Simply place the leaves in a pan with just the water clinging to the leaves from washing. Sprinkle lightly with salt, cover tightly and cook, over a gentle heat, for 7 to 10 minutes. Drain thoroughly and chop or purée as liked.

Spinach is delicious served raw as a salad vegetable. Cooked spinach goes well with cheese, mushrooms, pine kernels, flaked almonds, cream, nutmeg and anchovies. It also makes a tasty soup, soufflé or stuffing for omelettes, pancakes and pasties.

Nutritional value: Spinach is considered, not unjustly, to be an extremely healthy vegetable, although its iron content was over-estimated for many years. It contains plenty of Vitamin C and B, a good supply of potassium, calcium, magnesium, iron, iodine and phosphorus. Low in calories it provides 18 Calories (77 kj) per 100 g/3½ oz.

VINE LEAVES

Origin: The vine leaf (*Vitis vinifera*) originally came from the Mediterranean region, but it is now found in other areas. It is very popular in Greek, Turkish and Middle Eastern cooking.

Availability: Vine leaves are available fresh only in their country of origin, but they are available in the United Kingdom both canned in brine or vacuum-packed. Most of our imports come from Greece and Turkey.

Buying: Stuffed vine leaves and loose vine leaves can sometimes be bought individually in good delicatessen shops. Canned or vacuum packs are easier to obtain; they are generally sold in 4 serving quantities.

Preparation and serving: Canned vine leaves are often marinated in a flavoured oil or brine. Soak them in water for about 20 minutes before use.

Serve vine leaves stuffed as the Greeks and Turks do, with sweet and savoury mixtures. Serve as a starter, main dish or vegetable accompaniment.

Nutritional value: Fresh vine leaves are valuable for their Vitamin C, most of which is lost during canning and preserving. Vine leaves have about 20 Calories (86 kj) per 100 g/3½ oz.

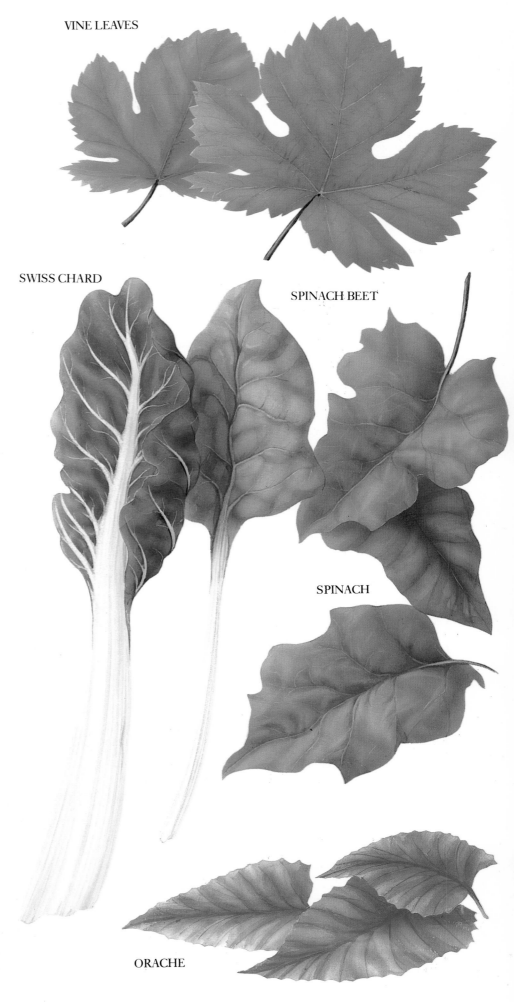

VINE LEAVES

SWISS CHARD

SPINACH BEET

SPINACH

ORACHE

Chilled Watercress Soup

25 g/1 oz butter
2 leeks, thinly sliced
1 small onion, chopped
250 g/8 oz potato, diced
2 bunches of watercress
600 ml/1 pint light stock
salt
freshly ground black pepper
300 ml/½ pint milk
croûtons to garnish (see note)

Melt the butter in a pan, add the leeks and onion and fry for 5 minutes, without browning. Add the potato and cook for 3 to 4 minutes.

Meanwhile, remove the tough stalks from the watercress and roughly chop the leaves. Add to the pan with the stock, and salt and pepper to taste. Bring to the boil, then cover and simmer for 10 minutes.

Sieve or work in an electric blender until smooth. Pour into a bowl and stir in the milk. Chill for several hours before serving.

Serve garnished with croûtons.
Serves 4 to 6

NOTE: To make croûtons, cut bread into 1 cm/½ inch cubes, or use small pastry cutters to make fancy shapes like stars, hearts etc. Fry these in a little butter until crisp and golden all over. Drain on kitchen paper.

Sorrel Soup

625 g/1¼ lb sorrel
15 g/½ oz butter
750 ml/1¼ pints chicken stock
2 egg yolks
150 ml/¼ pint double cream
pinch of grated nutmeg
pinch of cayenne pepper
salt

Place the sorrel leaves in a sieve, rinse and drain thoroughly, then chop roughly. Melt the butter in a pan, add the sorrel and cook for 2 to 3 minutes. Add the stock and simmer over a low heat for about 10 to 12 minutes.

Beat the egg yolks with the cream. Remove the soup from the heat and allow to cool slightly. Add the cream mixture gradually, stirring constantly. Reheat gently but do not allow the soup to boil; it will thicken slightly. Season to taste with nutmeg, cayenne pepper and salt. Serve immediately.
Serves 4 to 6

Lettuce Soup with Mint

25 g/1 oz butter
1 onion, chopped
2 large heads lettuce, shredded
2 tablespoons plain flour
750 ml/1¼ pints milk
pinch of grated nutmeg
salt
freshly ground black pepper
2 egg yolks
120 ml/4 fl oz double cream
1 tablespoon chopped mint

Melt the butter in a large pan. Add the onion and lettuce, cover and cook over a gentle heat for 6 to 8 minutes. Stir in the flour. Bring the milk to the boil, then gradually add to the lettuce mixture, stirring constantly. Add the nutmeg and season with salt and pepper to taste. Cover and simmer for 15 to 20 minutes.

Allow the soup to cool slightly, then place in an electric blender and blend for 1 minute.

Beat the egg yolks and the cream together in a bowl, then stir in 150 ml/¼ pint of the soup. Return the remaining soup to the pan. Stir in the egg mixture and bring to just below the boil, stirring; do not allow to boil or the soup will curdle. Immediately remove from the heat and pour into a warmed soup tureen. Serve hot sprinkled with the chopped mint.
Serves 6

Gourmet Chicory Soup

2–3 heads chicory
2 tablespoons duck or goose fat or oil
salt
freshly ground black pepper
1½ teaspoons wine vinegar
750 ml/1¼ pints chicken stock
150 ml/¼ pint double cream
cayenne pepper
1 tablespoon finely chopped parsley

Rinse and drain the chicory, remove the thick stems and cut the leaves into rings. Heat the fat or oil in a pan, add the chicory rings and cook for 2 to 3 minutes. Season to taste with salt and pepper, add the wine vinegar and stock. Simmer over a low heat for about 20 minutes.

Add the cream and reheat gently. Season to taste with cayenne pepper and serve sprinkled with parsley.
Serves 4 to 6

Lettuce soup with mint; Gourmet chicory soup; Chilled watercress soup

Californian Iceberg Lettuce Salad

½ iceberg lettuce
2 hard-boiled eggs, shelled and
    quartered
2 tablespoons salad cress
2 tablespoons mayonnaise
120 ml/4 fl oz soured cream
few stuffed olives, sliced
1 tablespoon chopped onion
1 tablespoon chilli sauce
salt
tomato wedges to garnish

Cut the lettuce into wedges or tear the leaves into large strips. Place in a sieve, rinse and drain thoroughly. Arrange in a salad bowl. Mix in the egg and cress.

To make the dressing, mix the mayonnaise with the soured cream, olives, onion, chilli sauce, and salt to taste. Pour the dressing over the salad and serve immediately, garnished with tomato wedges.
Serves 4

Chicory Salad with Roquefort Dressing

2–3 heads chicory
1 stick celery, chopped
1 small onion, peeled and sliced into
    fine rings
50 g/2 oz Roquefort cheese, crumbled
5–6 tablespoons salad oil
1 clove garlic, peeled and crushed
juice of 1 lemon
1 teaspoon salt
pinch of freshly ground black pepper
1 teaspoon sugar
chopped summer savory to garnish
    (optional)

Rinse and drain the chicory, remove the thick stem and cut the leaves into strips. Arrange in a serving bowl with the celery and onion rings.

Reserve a little Roquefort to garnish. Place the oil, garlic, lemon juice, salt, pepper, sugar and remaining Roquefort in a bowl and beat with an electric whisk to make a smooth dressing.

Pour the dressing over the chicory salad and toss well. Leave to stand for 10 minutes before serving to allow the flavours to develop. Sprinkle the reserved Roquefort and savory, if using, on top.
Serves 4

Cos Lettuce with Yogurt Dressing

1 cos lettuce
3–4 tablespoons natural yogurt
1 clove garlic, peeled and crushed
1 teaspoon tomato purée
1 scant teaspoon sugar
salt
freshly ground white pepper

Separate the lettuce, place the leaves in a sieve, rinse and drain well. Tear into pieces and place in a salad bowl.

To make the dressing, mix the yogurt with the garlic, tomato purée, sugar, and salt and pepper to taste, until smooth. Pour the dressing over the lettuce and toss thoroughly to coat. Serve immediately.
Serves 4 to 6

Radicchio and Fish Salad Sylvester

325 g/11 oz white fish fillet (halibut,
    perch, sole, etc)
300 ml/½ pint light stock
2 tablespoons mayonnaise
4 tablespoons soured cream
1 head radicchio
1 large orange
1 apple, peeled, cored and chopped
1 hard-boiled egg, shelled and sliced, to
    garnish

Poach the fish fillet very gently in the light stock in a shallow pan for about 5 to 8 minutes until tender; do not allow the stock to boil. Remove the fish from the stock and leave to cool. Reserve 2 tablespoons of the stock.

Meanwhile beat together the mayonnaise, cream and reserved fish stock for the dressing.

Separate the radicchio and use some of the leaves to line a serving dish. Peel and segment the orange, removing all of the pith. Cut the remaining radicchio into fine strips.

Break the cooled fish into pieces and place in a salad bowl, with the fruit and radicchio. Pour on the dressing and fold in thoroughly, but carefully, to avoid breaking up the fish. Cover the bowl and leave the salad to stand in the refrigerator for several hours before serving. Garnish with the egg slices to serve.
Serves 4

NOTE: This unusual salad makes a delicious starter. It looks most attractive arranged in grapefruit shells.

Watercress Mayonnaise

1 bunch watercress
1 egg yolk
¼ teaspoon salt
¼ teaspoon freshly ground white pepper
¼ teaspoon mustard powder
150 ml/¼ pint olive oil
1 teaspoon wine vinegar
2 tablespoons corn oil
2 large sprigs parsley, roughly chopped
2 large sprigs mint, roughly chopped
2 tablespoons double cream

Trim the watercress stems and sort the leaves, place in a sieve, rinse and drain thoroughly. Chop the watercress.

Beat together the egg yolk and seasonings in a bowl until thickened. Add the oil drop by drop, beating constantly. As the mixture thickens, add the vinegar. Continue beating adding the remaining oil in a steady stream.

Heat the corn oil in a frying pan, add the watercress, parsley, and mint, and fry stirring, for 10 minutes. Drain, then rub the mixture through a nylon sieve or work to a purée in an electric blender or food processor.

Leave to cool. Mix the watercress mixture into the mayonnaise with the cream. Serve chilled.

Makes 300ml/½ pint

NOTE: This mayonnaise is particularly delicious served with hard-boiled eggs or any egg salad, and cold fish dishes.

ABOVE: *Radicchio and fish salad Sylvester; Chicory salad with Roquefort dressing; Californian iceberg lettuce salad*

23

Lamb's Lettuce with Tomatoes and Egg

150 g/5 oz lamb's lettuce
1 clove garlic, peeled and halved
½ onion, peeled and chopped
2 tablespoons wine vinegar
salt
freshly ground black pepper
pinch of sugar
3 tablespoons oil
2–3 tomatoes, sliced
2 hard-boiled eggs, shelled and chopped

Separate and sort the lamb's lettuce, place in a sieve, rinse and drain thoroughly. Rub the inside of a large salad dish with the garlic. Place the lamb's lettuce in the bowl.

To make the dressing, beat the onion with the vinegar, salt and pepper to taste, sugar and oil. Pour over the lamb's lettuce and toss well to coat.

Arrange the tomato and chopped egg around the outside of the dish and season with salt and pepper to taste.
Serves 4

NOTE: This is a delicious salad to serve with quick-fried meats, such as steak or lamb chops. Watercress may be used in place of lamb's lettuce.

Iceberg Lettuce Malibu

½ iceberg lettuce
1 orange
25 g/1 oz fresh dates, stoned
120 ml/4 fl oz soured cream
1 tablespoon lemon juice
salt
freshly ground white pepper
pinch of caster sugar
pinch of grated nutmeg

Slice the lettuce crosswise into strips or cut into individual portion wedges. Place in a sieve, rinse and drain thoroughly. Arrange in a salad bowl.

Peel and segment the orange, removing all of the pith. Halve the segments. Cut the dates into strips and add to the lettuce with the orange pieces.

Beat the soured cream with the lemon juice, salt and pepper to taste, sugar and nutmeg to make a well-seasoned dressing. Pour over the salad and mix thoroughly, then leave to stand for a few minutes before serving to allow the flavours to develop.
Serves 4 to 6

NOTE: This delicious salad may be served in grapefruit shells or on salad plates as an hors d'oeuvre or accompaniment.

Radicchio with Garlic Dressing

2 heads radicchio
3 cloves garlic, peeled and finely
    chopped
1 tablespoon shredded basil leaves
salt
freshly ground white pepper
1 tablespoon grated Parmesan cheese
4–5 tablespoons olive oil
1 tablespoon wine vinegar

Remove the outer leaves from the radicchio and cut away the thick stems. Separate the leaves, tearing larger leaves into pieces. Place in a sieve, rinse and drain thoroughly. Arrange in a salad bowl.

To make the dressing, beat the garlic with the basil, salt and pepper to taste, cheese, oil and vinegar. Pour over the radicchio and toss lightly. Leave to stand for a few minutes before serving to allow the flavours to develop.
Serves 4 to 6

NOTE: Serve this delicious simple salad as a starter to cheese fondue, or as an accompaniment to spaghetti dishes, lamb chops or cheese on toast.

Chicory and Mandarin Salad

2–3 heads chicory
1 box salad cress
50 g/2 oz cooked ham, chopped
150 g/5 oz button mushrooms, thinly
    sliced
3 tablespoons canned mandarin oranges,
    drained
1 tablespoon chopped nuts (hazelnuts or
    walnuts, for example)
1 tablespoon mayonnaise
2–3 tablespoons canned mandarin juice
salt
freshly ground black pepper

Rinse and drain the chicory and remove the thick stems. Set aside a few leaves for garnish; cut the remainder into fine rings. Snip off the cress with scissors close to the soil, place in a sieve, rinse and drain thoroughly.

Place the chicory rings in a serving bowl with the ham, mushrooms, mandarin oranges and half of the cress. Toss well to mix. Sprinkle with the chopped nuts.

To make the dressing, mix the mayonnaise with the mandarin juice and salt and pepper to taste. Pour over the salad and toss thoroughly to coat all of the ingredients.

Arrange the reserved chicory leaves around the edge of the salad bowl. Garnish the salad with the remaining cress before serving.
Serves 4 to 6

NOTE: This is an excellent salad to serve with a wide variety of meat and fish dishes, particularly freshwater fish.

Chicory and mandarin salad; Lamb's lettuce with tomatoes and egg; Iceberg lettuce malibu; Radicchio with garlic dressing

Watercress and Radicchio Salad

1 bunch watercress
2 heads radicchio
juice of 1 lime or ½ lemon
1 tablespoon chopped onion
pinch of sugar
freshly ground black pepper
½ clove garlic, peeled and crushed with
   salt
120 ml/4 fl oz soured cream

Trim the watercress stems and sort the leaves, place in a sieve, rinse and drain thoroughly. Remove the stems from the radicchio, place in a sieve, rinse and drain thoroughly. Cut into thick strips and mix with the watercress in a bowl.

To make the dressing, mix the lime or lemon juice with the onion, sugar, pepper to taste and garlic. Fold into the cream and leave to stand for a few minutes to allow the flavours to develop.

To serve, pour the dressing over the watercress and radicchio. Toss thoroughly and serve immediately.
Serves 4 to 6

NOTE: This salad is ideal for serving with fish or pasta dishes.

Radicchio Rosette

1 head radicchio
2–3 tablespoons Italian dressing
½ fennel bulb, cut into fine julienne
   strips
2 teaspoons lemon juice
6–8 black olives, stoned (optional)

Rinse and drain the radicchio without removing the thick stem. Carefully prise the leaves apart with your fingers to form a rosette, being careful not to break the leaves off the stem.

Holding the radicchio firmly by the stem, dip the leaves into the Italian dressing several times to coat. Carefully cut away the stem and place the radicchio rosette in a serving bowl.

Toss the fennel in the lemon juice to prevent discoloration. Fill the middle of the radicchio rosette with the fennel and olives, if using. Sprinkle the remaining fennel on top to serve.
Serves 4

Lettuce Heart Salad

1–2 cos lettuce (depending on size)
1 teaspoon made mustard
dash of brandy
120 ml/4 fl oz whipping cream
salt
freshly ground black pepper
50 g/2 oz cooked ham, finely chopped
2 hard-boiled eggs, shelled and finely
   chopped

Discard any coarse lettuce leaves. Remove the outer leaves from the lettuce and cut the hearts into halves or quarters. Place in a sieve, rinse and drain thoroughly. Use the outer leaves to line a salad bowl. Arrange the lettuce hearts in the bowl.

To make the dressing, add the mustard and brandy to the cream and season with salt and pepper to taste. Stir well and pour over the lettuce hearts. Sprinkle with the chopped ham and egg. Serve immediately.
Serves 4 to 6

RIGHT: *Chicory and liver salad; Lettuce salad*
BELOW: *Radicchio rosette; Lettuce with hazelnuts*

Iceberg Lettuce with Hazelnuts

1 small iceberg lettuce
1 carrot, peeled and grated
2–3 tablespoons coarsely chopped
   hazelnuts
3 tablespoons salad oil
2 tablespoons lemon juice
1 teaspoon made mustard
salt
freshly ground black pepper
TO GARNISH:
few avocado slices (sprinkled with
   lemon juice) or cucumber slices

Tear the lettuce into large pieces or strips, place in a sieve, rinse and drain thoroughly. Arrange in a serving bowl. Top with the grated carrot and hazelnuts.

To make the dressing, beat the oil with the lemon juice, mustard, and salt and pepper to taste, until smooth. Pour the dressing evenly over the salad. Cover and leave to stand in the refrigerator for a few minutes before serving, to allow the flavours to develop.

Garnish with avocado or cucumber slices before serving.
Serves 4

Chicory and Liver Salad

125–150 g/4–5 oz calf's liver
salt
freshly ground black pepper
25 g/1 oz butter
2 oranges
½ cucumber, sliced
2–3 heads chicory, cut into fine strips
3 tablespoons Italian or garlic dressing
1 tablespoon lemon juice
1 tablespoon mixed chopped fresh herbs
   (chives, parsley, thyme)

Season the calf's liver with a little salt and pepper. Heat the butter in a frying pan, add the liver and fry for about 4 minutes each side. Leave to cool, then chop into bite-sized pieces.

Peel and segment the oranges, discarding all pith, and chop roughly. Line a salad bowl with the cucumber slices. Mix the liver with the chicory and orange.

To make the dressing, beat the Italian or garlic dressing with the lemon juice and herbs. Add to the liver mixture and toss well to coat. Spoon into the cucumber-lined bowl and serve immediately.
Serves 4 to 6

NOTE: This delicious salad can be served as a snack, a supper dish or as a tasty starter.

Fresh Lettuce Platter

1 lettuce
250 g/8 oz tomatoes, sliced
salt
freshly ground black pepper
1 small onion, peeled and finely chopped
1 tablespoon finely chopped basil
250 ml/8 fl oz soured cream
basil sprigs to garnish

Remove the outer leaves from the lettuce and keep to one side for garnish. Cut the lettuce heart into wedges. Place in a sieve, rinse and drain thoroughly.

Arrange the lettuce heart in a salad bowl or in individual serving dishes, and surround with the tomato slices. Season the tomato liberally with salt and pepper to taste.

To make the dressing, stir the onion and basil into the soured cream and season with salt to taste. Pour over the lettuce just before serving.

Shred the reserved lettuce finely and sprinkle in the centre of the salad. Serve immediately, garnished with basil sprigs.
Serves 4

Endive Salad Catalan

1 small head endive
1 clove garlic, peeled and crushed with
  ½ teaspoon salt
2 tablespoons vinegar
1 tablespoon ground almonds
1 bottled or canned pimiento, finely
  chopped
5 tablespoons olive oil

Separate the endive leaves and cut into small strips. Place in a sieve, rinse and drain thoroughly. Place in a serving bowl.

To make the dressing, beat the garlic with the vinegar, ground almonds,

pimiento and olive oil. Pour over the salad and toss to mix.

Cover and leave to stand in the refrigerator for at least 30 minutes before serving to allow the flavours to develop.
Serves 4

Radicchio Salad Supreme

1 radicchio
3–4 medium tomatoes, cut into wedges
125 g/4 oz Camembert cheese, cubed
1 teaspoon made mustard
120 ml/4 fl oz whipping cream
salt
freshly ground black pepper
3 teaspoons chopped parsley
½ onion, peeled and chopped

Remove the outer leaves from the radicchio and keep to one side for garnish. Separate the heart, tearing larger leaves into pieces. Place in a sieve, rinse and drain thoroughly. Place in a mixing bowl. Add the tomatoes and cheese and mix well.

To make the dressing, beat the mustard with the cream, salt and pepper to

taste, and 2 teaspoons parsley. Fold in the onion and pour over the salad. Toss lightly and leave to stand for a few minutes to allow the flavours to develop.

Line a salad bowl with the reserved radicchio leaves and fill with the salad. Sprinkle with the remaining parsley.
Serves 4

Iceberg Lettuce with Mushrooms

1 small iceberg lettuce
150 g/5 oz mushrooms, finely sliced
juice of 1 lemon
1 clove garlic, crushed
1 tomato, chopped
salt
freshly ground black pepper
3 tablespoons Italian dressing
1 tablespoon chopped parsley

Cut the lettuce into 8 wedges, place in a sieve, rinse and drain thoroughly. Arrange in a large salad bowl.

Sprinkle the mushroom slices with the lemon juice and garlic. Add the chopped tomato and season to taste with salt and pepper.

Fold the Italian dressing and parsley into the mushroom and tomato mixture. Leave to stand for a few minutes to allow the flavours to develop, then arrange in the centre of the lettuce wedges to serve.
Serves 4

Endive and Mushroom Salad

½ head endive
150 g/5 oz mushrooms, finely sliced
1 tablespoon lemon juice
½ onion, peeled and finely chopped
120 ml/4 fl oz soured cream
dash of Tabasco sauce
salt
freshly ground black pepper

Separate the endive leaves, cut into fine strips, place in a sieve, rinse and drain thoroughly. Place in a serving bowl. Sprinkle the mushroom slices with the lemon juice and add to the endive; toss thoroughly.

To make the dressing, beat the onion with the soured cream, Tabasco sauce and salt and pepper to taste. Pour over the salad and toss well to mix. Serve immediately.
Serves 4

Piquant Dandelion Leaves

625 g/1¼ lb dandelion leaves
knob of butter
2 tablespoons chopped back bacon
½ onion, peeled and chopped
2 hard-boiled eggs, shelled and chopped
freshly ground black pepper

Remove the dandelion leaves from their stems, place in a sieve, rinse and drain thoroughly. Place in a bowl.

Heat the butter, add the bacon and fry until just crisp. Add the onion and cook for 2 to 3 minutes. Remove from the heat, add the chopped egg and moisten in the pan juices. Season with pepper and pour the warm sauce over

the dandelion leaves.

Toss the salad ingredients together and serve immediately.
Serves 4 to 6

Fresh lettuce platter; Radicchio salad supreme; Endive and mushroom salad; Iceberg lettuce with mushrooms

Radicchio and French Bean Salad

350 g/12 oz French beans, trimmed
salt
1 head radicchio
1 onion, peeled and sliced into rings
2 cloves garlic, peeled and crushed
4–5 tablespoons olive oil
2–3 slices white bread, crusts removed

Parboil the French beans in boiling salted water for 2 minutes; rinse and drain. Cut into 5 cm/2 inch lengths.

Separate the radicchio, place the leaves in a sieve, rinse and drain thoroughly. Tear into large pieces and place in a salad bowl with the French beans and onion rings.

To make the dressing, beat the garlic with the olive oil and a pinch of salt. Pour two-thirds of the dressing over the salad and mix thoroughly.

Cut the bread into cubes. Heat the remaining dressing in a frying pan over a high heat, add the bread cubes and fry until golden brown. Drain on kitchen paper. Sprinkle the bread cubes over the salad and serve immediately.
Serves 4 to 6

NOTE: Serve this delicious salad as a snack or to accompany an informal meal or as part of a buffet spread.

Dandelion Salad

350–400 g/12–14 oz dandelion leaves
½ onion, peeled and finely chopped
2 tablespoons Italian dressing
120 ml/4 fl oz single or soured cream
salt
freshly ground black pepper
2 hard-boiled eggs, shelled and sliced
caviar or lumpfish caviar to garnish
　(optional)

Remove the dandelion leaves from their stems, place in a sieve, rinse and drain thoroughly.

To make the dressing, mix the onion with the Italian dressing. Fold in the cream and season to taste with salt and pepper. Leave the dressing to stand for a few minutes for the flavours to develop.

Place the dandelion leaves in a bowl and pour over the dressing. Place a ring of sliced egg around the bowl, season with salt and pepper to taste and garnish with caviar, if liked.
Serves 4

American Spinach Salad

250 g/8 oz leaf spinach
150 g/5 oz bacon rashers, rinds
　removed
2 hard-boiled eggs, shelled and sliced
½ onion, peeled and chopped
1 tablespoon herb-flavoured wine
　vinegar
salt
freshly ground black pepper
1 tablespoon dry sherry
3 tablespoons oil

Sort the spinach, cut away any thick woody stems, place in a sieve, rinse and drain thoroughly. Grill the bacon or fry in its own fat, until crisp. Drain on kitchen paper, then chop the bacon. Place the spinach in a large serving bowl, add the bacon and egg slices and toss lightly.

To make the dressing, mix the onion with the vinegar, salt and pepper to taste, sherry and oil. Pour over the

salad and leave to stand for about 30 minutes before serving to allow the flavours to develop.
Serves 4

NOTE: Spinach salad makes an excellent starter to a main fish course.

Cos Lettuce 'Poco'

1 small cos lettuce
1 small box salad cress or 1 small bunch
　watercress
1 shallot or 1 small onion, peeled and
　sliced into fine rings
125 g/4 oz cooked chicken, diced
150 g/5 oz Roquefort cheese, crumbled
4 tablespoons olive oil
2 tablespoons lemon juice
1 clove garlic, peeled and crushed
salt
freshly ground black pepper
1 teaspoon made mild mustard
dash of Worcestershire sauce
TO GARNISH:
2 hard-boiled eggs, shelled and
　quartered

Separate the lettuce leaves, place them in a sieve, rinse and drain thoroughly. Snip off the cress with scissors close to the soil, or trim and sort the watercress. Place in a sieve, rinse and drain thoroughly.

Place the lettuce, cress, shallot or onion rings and chicken in a bowl and mix thoroughly. Sprinkle with the Roquefort cheese.

To make the dressing, beat together the olive oil, lemon juice, garlic, salt and pepper to taste, mustard and Worcestershire sauce. Pour over the salad and toss to mix. Season the egg quarters with salt and pepper to taste and use to garnish the salad.
Serves 4

NOTE: Cos Lettuce 'Poco' can be served as a vegetable dish or with French bread and red wine as a supper dish or substantial snack.

Cos lettuce 'Poco'; Radicchio and French bean salad; American spinach salad; Dandelion salad

Caesar's Salad

2 cloves garlic
6 tablespoons olive oil
3 slices bread, crusts removed
2 tablespoons lemon juice
salt
freshly ground black pepper
50 g/1¾ oz can anchovies, drained
2 eggs, par-boiled for 1 minute
1 large cos lettuce
4 tablespoons grated Parmesan cheese

Place the garlic and the olive oil in a jug and leave to soak for 3 to 4 hours, then strain the oil, discarding the garlic.

Cut the bread into 5 mm/¼ inch cubes. Heat 4 tablespoons of the oil in a small frying pan, add the bread cubes and fry until golden, then remove and drain on kitchen paper.

Mix the remaining oil with the lemon juice and salt and pepper to taste. Chop the anchovies and add to the dressing. Break the eggs into the bowl, scraping out the partly set egg white, and mix thoroughly to combine the egg with the dressing.

Tear the lettuce into a bowl, add the dressing and toss well. Add the cheese and croûtons and give a final toss before serving.
Serves 6

Watercress and Egg Salad

2 bunches watercress
120 ml/4 fl oz soured cream
1 clove garlic, peeled and crushed with salt
1 tablespoon chopped parsley
1 tomato, skinned and chopped
2 hard-boiled eggs, shelled and chopped
freshly ground black pepper
TO GARNISH:
1 tomato, cut into wedges
1 hard-boiled egg, shelled and sliced

Trim the watercress stems, sort the leaves, place in a sieve, rinse and drain.

To make the dressing, mix the soured cream and garlic together. Fold in the parsley, tomato and chopped egg. Season with pepper to taste.

Arrange the watercress in a serving bowl and top with the egg and tomato dressing. Garnish with the tomato wedges and the sliced egg.
Serves 4

NOTE: For a special Easter variation, fill a bowl with watercress marinated in a vinaigrette dressing. Top with halved hard-boiled quail's eggs or hard-boiled eggs in their shells, coloured by soaking in beetroot juice.

RIGHT: *Watercress with orange and nuts; Lettuce with warm bacon cubes*
BELOW: *Watercress and egg salad; Caesar's salad*

Endive Salad with Yogurt Dressing

1 head endive
3 tablespoons drained canned mandarin
    oranges
1 clove garlic, peeled and crushed with
    salt
2–3 tablespoons canned mandarin juice
freshly ground black pepper
1 tablespoon chopped fresh herbs
150 ml/¼ pint natural yogurt

Separate the endive leaves and cut into very fine strips. Place in a sieve, rinse and drain thoroughly. Place the endive in a serving bowl and fold in the mandarin oranges.

To make the dressing, mix the garlic, mandarin juice, pepper to taste and herbs with the yogurt. Beat well, pour over the salad and mix thoroughly.

Leave the endive salad to stand for a few minutes before serving to allow the flavours to develop.
Serves 4

NOTE: Replace the canned mandarin orange segments with fresh ones when they are in season. Add a pinch of sugar to the dressing.

Watercress with Orange and Nuts

1 bunch watercress
1 large orange
2 tablespoons chopped hazelnuts
120 ml/4 fl oz natural yogurt
½ clove garlic, peeled and crushed with
    salt
pinch of sugar
2 teaspoons chopped parsley
freshly ground black pepper

Trim the watercress stems, sort the leaves, place in a sieve, rinse and drain thoroughly. Place in a large serving bowl. Peel and segment the orange, removing all pith, then chop roughly. Add the orange and hazelnuts to the watercress.

To make the piquant dressing, beat the yogurt with the garlic, sugar, pars-

ley and pepper to taste. Pour over the watercress and toss well. Leave to stand for about 30 minutes before serving to allow the flavours to develop.
Serves 4

NOTE: This salad is ideal for serving in individual portions in grapefruit or orange shells as an hors d'oeuvre.

Lettuce with Warm Bacon Cubes

1 large lettuce
juice of ½ lemon
1 tablespoon finely chopped onion
1 tablespoon chopped parsley
pinch of sugar
2 tablespoons water
salt
freshly ground black pepper
50 g/2 oz thick cut bacon, diced

Separate the lettuce and tear roughly; place the leaves in a sieve, rinse and drain thoroughly. Leave the lettuce to dry in the air (not in direct sunlight), then place in a serving bowl.

To make the dressing, beat the lemon juice with the onion, parsley, sugar, water and salt and pepper to taste. Pour over the lettuce and toss

thoroughly to mix.

Fry the bacon in its own fat in a small frying pan until crisp and golden. Sprinkle over the lettuce and serve immediately.
Serves 4

Lettuce Rolls

1 large cabbage lettuce
15 g/½ oz butter
2 tablespoons fresh white breadcrumbs
1 clove garlic, peeled and crushed with
    salt
300 g/10 oz pork sausage meat
WHITE SAUCE:
25 g/1 oz butter
25 g/1 oz plain flour
300 ml/½ pint milk
salt
freshly ground black pepper
TOPPING:
2 tablespoons grated Parmesan cheese

Separate the lettuce, place the leaves in a sieve, rinse and drain thoroughly. Blanch for a few seconds in boiling salted water. Plunge into cold water then drain in a sieve.

Melt the butter in a pan. Add the breadcrumbs and fry until golden. Add the garlic and sausage meat. Fry over a moderate heat until cooked, about 8 to 10 minutes.

Divide the mixture evenly between the lettuce leaves, placing it across the centre. Roll up and place in an oven-proof dish.

To make the sauce, melt the butter in a pan, stir in the flour and cook for 1 minute. Gradually stir in the milk and cook, stirring, for 2 to 3 minutes.

Season with salt and pepper to taste.

Pour the white sauce over the lettuce rolls and sprinkle with the Parmesan cheese. Cook in a preheated hot oven (220°C/425°F, Gas Mark 7) for 10 to 15 minutes or until the topping is golden and bubbling.
Serves 4

NOTE: Serve this unusual supper dish with boiled potatoes, rice or crusty French bread.

Braised Sorrel

750–800 g/1½–1¾ lb sorrel
15 g/½ oz butter, melted
pinch of grated nutmeg
4 tablespoons beef stock
salt
freshly ground black pepper
1 tablespoon cream (optional)
1 hard-boiled egg, shelled and chopped

Sort the sorrel, place in a sieve, rinse and drain thoroughly. Melt the butter in a pan. Add the sorrel and cook over a low heat for about 5 minutes, stirring occasionally. Add the nutmeg, stock and salt and pepper to taste and cook for a further 5 to 8 minutes. Stir in the cream, if using.

Just before serving, sprinkle with the egg. Serve with veal, chicken or fish.
Serves 4

Spinach Soufflé

400 g/14 oz fresh leaf spinach, rinsed
    and drained
15 g/½ oz butter
1 clove garlic, peeled
1 small onion, peeled and finely chopped
salt
grated nutmeg
3 egg yolks
2 tablespoons double cream
1 tablespoon grated Parmesan cheese
3 egg whites
1 teaspoon lemon juice

Squeeze the spinach to remove as much moisture as possible, then chop very finely. Melt the butter in a flameproof casserole, add the garlic and fry until golden brown. Remove the garlic from the pan with a slotted spoon. Add the onion to the pan and cook until softened. Add the spinach and season with salt and nutmeg to taste. Cook for 2 to 3 minutes then remove from the heat.

Beat the egg yolks with the cream and stir into the spinach mixture with the cheese. Whisk the egg whites and lemon juice until stiff, then fold into the spinach mixture with a metal spoon.

Spoon into a greased 1.2 litre/2 pint soufflé dish and cook in a preheated moderately hot oven (200°C/400°F, Gas Mark 6) for about 30 minutes, until golden, well risen and just firm to the touch. Serve immediately.
Serves 4

Spinach soufflé; Greek vine leaves with savoury filling

NOTE: Serve with meat, fish and poultry dishes, or as an hors d'oeuvre.

Greek Vine Leaves with Savoury Filling

1 × 425 g/15 oz can vine leaves
250 ml/8 fl oz oil
150 g/5 oz minced beef or lamb (or a
    mixture of both)
1 large onion, peeled and finely chopped
¼ fennel bulb, grated
2 cloves garlic, peeled and crushed
150 g/5 oz cooked long-grain rice
1 tablespoon chopped dill
1 teaspoon dried oregano
salt
freshly ground black pepper
300 ml/½ pint dry red wine

Place the vine leaves in a sieve, rinse and drain thoroughly. Heat 1 tablespoon of the oil in a large frying pan, add the minced meat, onion, fennel and garlic and fry, stirring, until cooked, for about 8 to 10 minutes. Stir in the rice, dill, oregano and salt and pepper to taste. Spread the mixture evenly over the vine leaves. Fold the long sides of the vine leaves over and roll up securely from the shorter edge to make neat parcels.

Mix the remaining oil and the red wine in a pan, add the stuffed vine leaves, cover and cook over a gentle heat for about 20 minutes. Remove with a slotted spoon to serve.
Serves 4

NOTE: Stuffed vine leaves make a delicious starter; they will add variety to any buffet table spread or, with fresh crusty bread, they make a tasty supper dish.

In Greece, where this dish originated, these stuffed vine leaves are called *dolmas* and are made with a variety of sweet and savoury fillings. You can, for example, replace the minced meat stuffing with a mixture of currants, pine nuts and cooked rice.

Chicory in Mustard Sauce

4 heads chicory
150 ml/¼ pint salted water
juice of 1 lemon
15 g/½ oz butter
scant 1 tablespoon plain flour
150 ml/¼ pint meat stock
2–3 tablespoons single cream
scant 2 tablespoons made mild mustard
1 teaspoon sugar
1 tablespoon chopped dill

Rinse and drain the chicory and remove the thick stems. Bring the water and lemon juice to the boil. Add the chicory heads, lower the heat and cook for about 10 minutes. Drain, reserving the cooking liquid.

Melt the butter in a small pan, stir in the flour and cook until golden. Gradually add the reserved cooking liquid and meat stock, stirring constantly.

Add the cream, mustard and sugar and bring to the boil, stirring constantly. Add the par-cooked chicory and cook for a further 10 minutes over a very low heat until just tender.

Transfer to a warmed serving dish and sprinkle with the chopped dill. Serve immediately, as a delicious accompaniment to grilled meat or fish.
Serves 4

Spinach Pancakes

625 g/1¼ lb fresh leaf spinach
15 g/½ oz butter
1 small onion, peeled and chopped
salt
grated nutmeg
25 g/1 oz plain flour
2 eggs
250 ml/8 fl oz water
1 tablespoon single cream
pinch of salt
oil for shallow frying
75 g/3 oz Emmenthal cheese, grated

Sort the spinach, place in a sieve, rinse and drain thoroughly. Squeeze to extract excess moisture. Melt the butter in a pan. Add the spinach, onion, salt and nutmeg to taste. Cook over a low heat for about 12 minutes.

Meanwhile, beat the flour with the eggs and half of the water. Gradually stir in the remaining water, then the cream and salt to make a smooth batter. Heat a 20 cm/8 inch frying pan and add a few drops of oil. Pour in a quarter of the batter and tilt the pan to coat the bottom evenly. Cook until the underside is brown, then turn over and cook

for 10 seconds. Remove and repeat with the remaining batter to make four pancakes, stacking the pancakes between greaseproof paper as they are cooked.

Spread the spinach mixture evenly over a quarter of each pancake. Fold in half and in half again to make fans. Place in a greased ovenproof dish and sprinkle with the cheese. Cook in a preheated hot oven (220°C/425°F, Gas Mark 7) for 10 to 15 minutes, or under a preheated hot grill for 3 to 4 minutes, until the cheese is bubbling and golden.
Serves 4

Spinach with Flaked Almonds

1 kg/2 lb leaf spinach, spinach beet or
    orache
25 g/1 oz butter
½ onion, peeled and finely chopped
salt
grated nutmeg
2 egg yolks
4 tablespoons double cream
50 g/2 oz flaked almonds

Sort the spinach, place in a sieve, rinse and drain thoroughly. Tear the leaves into manageable pieces. Melt the butter in a large pan, add the onion and cook for 2 to 3 minutes until softened. Add the spinach, a little at a time, turning it in the butter to coat. Season with salt and nutmeg to taste. Cook over a low heat for 10 to 15 minutes, until tender depending upon the thick-ness of the spinach leaves.

Beat the egg yolks with the cream and stir into the spinach mixture. Immediately remove the spinach from the heat and transfer to a warmed serving bowl. Add the flaked almonds to the butter remaining in the pan and fry, stirring, until golden. Fold the almonds into the spinach and serve immediately.
Serves 4

Spinach and Potato Ring

750 g/1½ lb leaf spinach, spinach beet
    or orache
25 g/1 oz butter
salt
grated nutmeg
750 g/1½ lb potatoes, peeled and cubed
120 ml/4 fl oz milk, warmed
1 egg yolk
2 tablespoons grated Parmesan cheese

Sort the spinach, place in a sieve, rinse and drain thoroughly. Chop the spinach finely. Melt half of the butter in a pan, add the spinach and cook over a low heat for 12 to 15 minutes. Season with salt and nutmeg to taste.

Cook the potatoes in boiling salted water for about 15 to 20 minutes until tender. Drain and mash with the milk, remaining butter and a pinch of nutmeg. Season to taste with salt if liked. Beat in the egg yolk, Parmesan cheese and cooked spinach, mixing well. Spoon the mixture into a greased 1.2 litre/2 pint ring mould.

Bake in a preheated moderately hot oven (200°C/400°F, Gas Mark 6) for about 20 minutes until firm to the touch. Loosen the edges of the mould with a knife then turn out onto a large serving plate.
Serves 4

NOTE: Spinach and potato ring is delicious with lamb or pork chops, liver, fish or stewed veal.

ABOVE: *Chicory in mustard sauce; Spinach pancakes; Spinach with flaked almonds*

Endive with Walnut Sauce

1 head endive
600 ml/1 pint salted water
juice of ½ lemon
15 g/½ oz butter or margarine
scant 1 tablespoon plain flour
150 ml/¼ pint double cream
salt
cayenne pepper
2 tablespoons chopped walnuts

Separate the endive leaves, place in a sieve, rinse and drain thoroughly. Tear into large pieces. Bring the water and lemon juice to the boil. Add the endive and simmer, over a low heat, for 12 to 15 minutes. Drain, reserving the cooking liquid. Place the endive in a serving dish and keep warm.

Heat the butter or margarine in a small pan, add the flour and cook for 1 minute, stirring constantly. Gradually add 150 ml/¼ pint of the endive cooking liquid, then the cream, stirring constantly. Season to taste with salt and a little cayenne pepper and fold in the chopped walnuts. Spoon the sauce over the endive and serve immediately.
Serves 4 to 6

Cos Lettuce au Gratin

1 cos lettuce
600 ml/1 pint water
salt
50 g/2 oz butter, melted
2 tomatoes, cut into wedges
2–3 tablespoons grated Emmenthal cheese

Separate the lettuce, place the leaves in a sieve, rinse and drain thoroughly. Bring the water to the boil in a large saucepan, add the lettuce and salt. Bring to the boil, then lower the heat and cook gently for 4 to 5 minutes. Drain and place in an ovenproof dish. Spoon over the melted butter and surround with the tomato wedges.

Sprinkle with the cheese.
Cook in a preheated hot oven (220°C/425°F, Gas Mark 7) for 10 to 12 minutes, or under a preheated hot grill for 3 to 4 minutes, until golden brown.
Serves 4 to 6

NOTE: This is a delicious accompaniment to grilled meat, fish or rissoles.

Spinach with Mushrooms

750 g/1½ lb leaf spinach
200 g/7 oz button mushrooms
1 tablespoon lemon juice
15 g/½ oz butter
50 g/2 oz bacon, derinded and chopped
salt
grated nutmeg
freshly ground black pepper
1 egg yolk

Sort the spinach, place in a sieve, rinse and drain thoroughly. Tear into large pieces. Trim the mushrooms leaving small mushrooms whole but cutting larger ones in half. Sprinkle with the lemon juice.

Melt the butter in a pan, add the bacon and fry until just crisp. Add the spinach, mixing well with the pan juices. Season to taste with salt, nutmeg and pepper. Add the mushrooms and cook over a low heat for 12 to 15 minutes, stirring occasionally.

Beat the egg yolk lightly and stir into the mixture. Cook for 2 to 3 minutes until slightly thickened. Season with pepper to taste. Serve immediately.
Serves 4

Chicory au Gratin

4–6 small heads chicory
juice of 2 lemons
4 tablespoons oil
2 teaspoons chopped basil
salt
freshly ground black pepper
4 tablespoons double cream
150 g/5 oz Mozzarella cheese, sliced

Rinse and drain the chicory, remove the thick stems and cut the heads into thick rings. Sprinkle with the lemon juice and leave for a few minutes.

Beat the oil with the basil and salt and pepper to taste. Fold into the cream and pour over the chicory rings. Turn the chicory to coat with the sauce, then spoon into an ovenproof dish. Sprinkle the cheese evenly over the top. Cook in a preheated hot oven (220°C/425°F, Gas Mark 7) for 15 to 20 minutes.

Serve hot with French bread, or as an accompaniment to gammon steaks.
Serves 4

Spinach with Cheese

1 kg/2 lb leaf spinach, spinach beet or orache
40 g/1½ oz butter
1 clove garlic, peeled and halved
salt
grated nutmeg
pinch of cayenne pepper
125 g/4 oz Bonbel, Gouda or Bel Paese cheese, finely peeled and cubed

Sort the spinach, place in a sieve, rinse and drain thoroughly. Tear into large pieces. Melt the butter in a pan, add the garlic and fry until golden brown. Remove the garlic from the pan with a slotted spoon. Add the spinach and season with salt, nutmeg and cayenne pepper to taste. Cook for about 12 to 15 minutes over a low heat, stirring frequently. About 3 minutes before the end of the cooking time stir two-thirds of the cheese into the spinach mixture.

Spoon into a warmed serving dish and sprinkle the remaining cheese over the top.
Serves 4

Cos lettuce au gratin; Spinach with mushrooms; Chicory au gratin

TUBERS & ROOTS

Tasty and satisfying, tubers and roots are most sustaining vegetables.
From the tender young spring carrots to the crisp summer radishes
through to the autumn and winter earthy parsnips, swedes and turnips, there
seems to be a tuber or root for every season. Potatoes have the virtue
of being suitable to serve at any time of the year and take on
a multitude of guises to afford it – roast, sautéed, creamed, baked or piped into
Duchesse whirls are just a few.

The less well known members of this family include salsify with its long,
creamy root resembling an elongated carrot; celeriac with its gnarled
tough appearance; scorzonera, a black-skinned root which
when peeled reveals a creamy white flesh; and the sweet potato
with its sometimes crimson skin. These unusual roots and tubers
deserve greater recognition for their distinctive
individual flavours.

ARTICHOKES, JERUSALEM

Origin: The Jerusalem artichoke (*Helianthus tuberosus*) is a potato-like tuber that is thought to have originated in Brazil. It does not come from Jerusalem, as the name suggests, but it is thought that the name is a corruption of the word girasole – the Italian name for the sunflower plant to which it is closely related.

There are several varieties including the white, yellow, red and purple – many of which are pear-like in shape. Almost all have the typical bitter-sweet flavour for which they are known.

Availability: Jerusalem artichokes are grown throughout Europe, including Britain, and in South America. Planted in February to March they come into season in Europe for harvesting from October. Supplies are good throughout the winter months.

Buying: Jerusalem artichokes are sold by weight. Look for young tubers that are not too large and bitter in flavour. Only buy as much as you intend to use immediately since they do not store well once harvested.

Preparation and serving: Jerusalem artichokes should be prepared in just the same way as potatoes. Scrub, peel thinly and slice or chop for use. Sprinkle liberally with lemon juice to prevent discoloration. Cook in boiling salted water for 20 to 30 minutes, depending upon size. Drain and toss in melted butter and herbs if liked.

Jerusalem artichokes are delicious served in salads, gratin dishes, or as a vegetable accompaniment in a sauce. They can also be turned into a soup or deep-fried in hot oil.

Nutritional value: Jerusalem artichokes provide Vitamins C and B and small quantities of trace minerals. Reasonably low in calories they provide the slimmer with a tasty alternative to the potato at only 18 Calories (77 kj) per 100 g/3½ oz.

BEETROOT

Origin: The beetroot (*Beta vulgaris* var. *esculenta*) is a member of the Chenopodiaceae family. Native to the Mediterranean, it has been popular in Britain since Tudor times. It was enjoyed by the ancient Romans who liked to serve it pickled. As a root vegetable, it has a brownish red skin and deep red to purple flesh.

Availability: Fresh beetroot is available almost all year round but is in season from late summer to early spring. Beetroot is grown in all European countries, including Britain and extensively in Russia where it is a staple food.

Buying: There are two main types of beetroot on sale. The round globe variety, available in summer and early autumn, and the long-rooted beetroot, available in late autumn and winter. Beetroot is at its best when small, young and tender. Choose roots that are firm and juicy and of fresh appearance.

Beetroot can also be bought ready-cooked, pickled or bottled in brine.

Preparation and serving: To cook beetroot, trim the leaf stalks to about 2.5 cm/1 inch above the root but do not peel. Cook in boiling salted water for 1 to 2 hours, depending upon size. Plunge into cold water, cut away the leaf stalk and rub off the skin. Prepared this way the beetroot will not 'bleed' excessively into the cooking liquid. The beetroot can then be sliced, cubed or cut into julienne strips for serving.

Serve beetroot in a creamy sauce as a vegetable accompaniment; pickled with apple, onion, vinegar and spices as a relish or salad ingredient; or puréed with stock and seasonings to make a delicious soup that looks most enticing if topped with swirls of soured cream.

Nutritional value: Beetroot provides sodium, phosphorus and calcium and small amounts of Vitamins A and C. Cooked beetroot contains 44 Calories (189 kj) per 100 g/3½ oz.

CARROTS

Origin: The carrot (*Daucus carota*) is a member of the Umbelliferae family. It has been known in South-East Asia and Western Asia for centuries but has only really been grown in Europe since the 16th century.

Different types of carrot are found all over the world from the basic white-rooted primitive plant in Asia, small purple-rooted carrot in Egypt, long-rooted carrot in Japan to the more familiar orange-coloured carrot in Europe and the USA.

COOKED BEETROOT

JERUSALEM ARTICHOKES

BEETROOT

CELERIAC

CARROTS

There are numerous varieties of short, medium and long-rooted carrot to choose from, ranging in colour from white through yellow to deep orange and varying in shape from slim to stumpy, cylindrical to tapering and with blunt or pointed roots. With such variety flavour differs enormously too.
Availability: Carrots are available all year round. They are grown extensively throughout Europe. Britain boosts its own production with supplies from Holland.
Buying: Most carrots are sold loose by weight, although occasionally bunches of young carrots complete with their green tops are found. As a popular vegetable in Britain, they are also available canned, frozen and in a juice form.

Choose carrots with a fresh appearance, good clean skin and fresh foliage. The stem end is the most important place to check for quality. If it is blackened or deeply discoloured, the carrot is likely to be old and of poor flavour.
Preparation and serving: Very young new carrots do not need peeling or scraping, simply scrub and rinse them well. Older carrots should be scraped or thinly peeled before use. Leave whole, slice, quarter or cut into thin julienne strips as liked. Cook in boiling salted water for 10 to 30 minutes, according to size and age.

Toss in butter, herbs, cheese or spices after cooking. Alternatively, serve in a Béchamel sauce or toss in cream. Older carrots are also delicious puréed with butter or cream and salt and pepper to taste.

Raw carrot makes a delicious salad vegetable, cocktail dip or crudité ingredient. Fresh carrot juice can also be made from carrots that have been scrubbed and rinsed.

Carrots are also used extensively for their flavour in stews, casseroles, gratin dishes, soups and stocks. They are sometimes even grated for use in cakes.
Nutritional value: Carrots are a very healthy vegetable. They are valuable for their rich supply of Vitamin A. They also supply sodium, calcium and phosphorus. Carrots contain 23 Calories (98 kj) per 100 g/3½ oz.

CELERIAC

Origin: Celeriac (*Apium graveolens*) is a member of the Umbelliferae family, originating from the Mediterranean region. In classical times it was used as both a vegetable and a herb.

It has a flavour similar to that of celery to which it is closely related – so much so that it is sometimes called turnip-rooted celery. Lifted young, celeriac has small light brown or sandy coloured roots with dark green tops. Varieties lifted later are much darker and more swollen in appearance with thicker skins – the tops will generally have been trimmed away before sale. Young celeriac has a delicately aromatic flavour; larger roots will taste much stronger and may even be rather pungent.
Availability: Fresh celeriac is available all year round but is at its best in high season from the end of October to February. It is grown in most European countries, including Britain.

Buying: Celeriac is generally sold by weight but sometimes by the root. Choose roots that are firm and of fresh appearance. Reject any that seem soft or withered. If sold with the tops on then look for crisp, green foliage.
Preparation and serving: Trim away the upper leafy tops – these can be used to make soups, sauces, salads and garnishes if liked. Remove the root end and peel fairly thickly. This is easiest done if the root is halved and quartered first. Slice or chop the white flesh for use. Sprinkle with lemon juice to prevent discoloration. Cook in boiling salted water for 10 to 20 minutes according to size.

Serve in a white sauce, creamed like potatoes, or tossed in butter and herbs. Celeriac is of course delicious eaten raw, rather like celery. Use it also to make tasty gratin dishes, soups and salads.
Nutritional value: Celeriac is valuable for its phosphorus, sodium, calcium and other trace elements. It also has small amounts of Vitamins A, C and E. Low in calories, cooked celeriac contains only 14 Calories (59 kj) per 100 g/3½ oz.

HORSERADISH

Origin: The horseradish (*Armoracia lepathifolia*) is a member of the Cruciferae family. It was originally a native of Southern Europe and Asia but has been grown in more northerly parts of Europe since the 15th century. It was valued mainly as a medicinal plant rather than as a vegetable or herb, for it was considered an excellent remedy for fever and indigestion and a good cure for toothache.

In appearance horseradish looks like a long, light-skinned root speckled with dark markings, complete with a green leafy top. The inner flesh is white and tastes very strong and pungent.

Availability: Horseradish is grown all over Europe, and still grows wild in many parts of Britain. It is in season from October to the end of February but can often be found at other times of the year.

Buying: Horseradish can be bought in many grocers and good supermarkets fresh, ready-grated or as a sauce mixed with cream. The fresh root may be sold whole, in quarters or smaller pieces. Only buy as much as you need at any one time – horseradish will quickly lose its flavour after cutting. Grated horseradish, packed in vacuum sealed jars is generally available in 125 g/4 oz jars for convenient use.

Preparation and serving: Rinse, peel and grate horseradish to use. If possible do this by an open window to prevent your eyes from watering too much from the pungent fumes. Sprinkle with lemon juice to prevent discoloration. Alternatively use the grater attachment on a food mixer or processor for extra speedy results.

Use horseradish raw in sauces, dips, salad dressings and stuffings. As a sauce or relish it is traditionally served with roast beef and smoked trout or mackerel.

Nutritional value: Horseradish is rich in calcium, phosphorus and Vitamin C. It contains 59 Calories (253 kj) per 100 g/3½ oz.

PARSNIPS

Origin: The parsnip (*Pastinaca sativa*) is a member of the Umbelliferae family. It is a very ancient root vegetable that probably originated between the Mediterranean and the Caucasus to the northeast. Its long white root looks like a large, slim radish, of the winter variety, that tapers to a sharp point. It has a unique nut-like flavour.

Availability: Parsnips are grown throughout Europe and Britain grows sufficient for home demand. They are in season from September to February.

Buying: Parsnips are sold by weight. Look for smooth, firm, well-shaped parsnips of small to medium size. Large ones are likely to be bitter and woody.

Preparation and serving: Parsnips are prepared rather like carrots. Cut off the tops and roots and peel thinly. Cut into slices or quarters lengthways. Cook in boiling salted water or stock

for 20 to 25 minutes, depending upon size. Toss in butter and herbs or fold into soured cream.

Parsnips can also be roasted like potatoes to serve with roast meats, fried after parboiling for 5 minutes, served as a purée with butter and grated nutmeg, baked as a gratin dish, mashed with equal quantities of carrots or potatoes, served as a soup or added to casseroles and hotpots.

Nutritional value: Parsnips are valuable in the diet for their Vitamins A and C. They contain 49 Calories (210 kj) per 100 g/3½ oz.

POTATOES

Origin: The potato (*Solanum tuberosum*) is a member of the Solenaceae family. It comes originally from South America, more precisely from the plateaux of Peru. There are many stories and claims of the way in which it first came to Britain – both Columbus and Drake have been credited with its introduction. However, what Drake brought back to Queen Elizabeth I from his voyages was the related sweet potato rather than the ordinary potato as we know it today. It is now generally recognised that Spanish conquistadors introduced the potato to Europe from South America. It is said that Fred-erick the Great of Prussia, in search of cheap nourishing food for his people, made the potato popular, but the first Europeans to grow potatoes on a large scale were the Italians.

The Germans and Russians used to be the greatest potato-eaters in Europe. Today, Britain has the highest consumption per head of population.

Availability: Potatoes are grown in almost all the countries of Europe, including Britain. Supplies are good and regular all year round. New potatoes are imported into Britain during the early spring, and when supplies dwindle, from Cyprus and Egypt. Maincrop potatoes are exported on a large scale from Holland and Italy to the rest of Europe.

Buying: Today there are about 100 varieties of potato to choose from. It would be impossible to remember all of their names but it is important to recognise main varieties – firm, floury, waxy or salad potatoes – to ensure that the best is chosen to suit the method of cooking. Your greengrocer will advise on the best floury, waxy, firm or salad potato in season at any one time.

Never choose potatoes that are wrinkled, damaged in any way, sprouting or with green patches. Look for well-shaped tubers with a fresh appearance, smooth skin and even size.

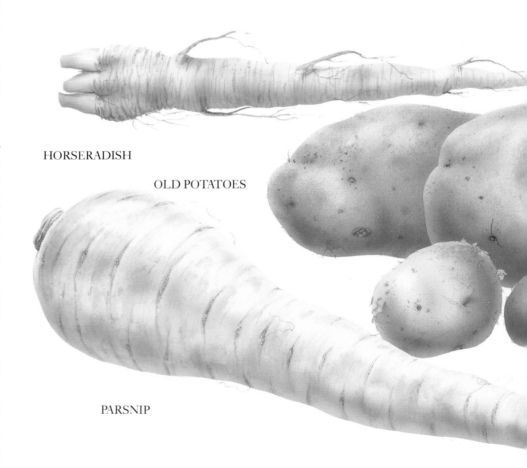

HORSERADISH

OLD POTATOES

PARSNIP

Preparation and serving: There are countless ways in which you can serve potatoes. In most cases potatoes should be peeled thinly before use. For plain boiled new potatoes this is not necessary. Scrub then rinse and cook in boiling salted water for 15 to 20 minutes depending upon size. Floury, firm or waxy potatoes are all suitable for boiling.

After boiling the potatoes may be mashed or creamed with a little butter, cream or milk and seasoning if liked. Floury potatoes are the best variety to choose for this method of serving. If you intend to use cooked potatoes in a potato salad then choose small young waxy potatoes or special salad potatoes that will not break up during cooking. Such firm and waxy potatoes are also ideal for making pommes frites or chips.

Potatoes are also delicious served roasted around a joint of meat. Parboil potatoes for about 5 minutes, drain and place around the joint with a little fat. Cook in a moderately hot oven for about 50 to 60 minutes, turning once during the cooking time.

For sauté potatoes or pan-fried potatoes, peel the potatoes and slice thinly. Cook in hot shallow fat until golden, turn over and cook until golden and cooked through, about 15 minutes.

Potatoes taste delicious if topped with butter and herbs, especially parsley. Such is their versatility that they can be added to casseroles and hot pots, baked in their jackets and served with soured cream and other creamy sauces, cut into thin julienne strips and fried until crisp and crunchy, puréed then piped and baked into elaborate shapes and mixed with other root vegetables like carrot, turnip and swede for a vegetable dish with a difference.

Nutritional value: Potatoes still suffer from the bad reputation of being a fattening vegetable. Served plain nothing could be further from the truth at only 80 Calories (343 kj) per 100 g/$3\frac{1}{2}$ oz. The trouble begins, however, when the potato is fried, mixed with butter, cream or other rich ingredients – so slimmers take care. As a guideline the following values apply to potato dishes:

Mashed potatoes – 119 Calories (499 kj) per 100 g/$3\frac{1}{2}$ oz.

Baked potatoes (with skins) – 85 Calories (364 kj) per 100 g/$3\frac{1}{2}$ oz.

Roast potatoes – 157 Calories (662 kj) per 100 g/$3\frac{1}{2}$ oz.

Chipped potatoes – 253 Calories (1065 kj) per 100 g/$3\frac{1}{2}$ oz.

New boiled potatoes – 76 Calories (324 kj) per 100 g/$3\frac{1}{2}$ oz.

Potato crisps – 533 Calories (2224 kj) per 100 g/$3\frac{1}{2}$ oz.

Calories aside, the potato is a very nutritious vegetable. It provides a rich source of carbohydrate, protein, calcium, phosphorus and potassium. It also has significant amounts of Vitamins A, B$_1$, B$_2$ and C.

RADISHES

Origin: The radish (*Raphanus sativus*) is a member of the Cruciferae family. It was grown by the ancient Egyptians as long ago as 2600 BC and was probably introduced to Britain by the Romans.

There are two main types: the small, summer variety, popular for use in salads; and the large, winter radish which can weigh up to 250 g/8 oz.

There are many varieties of small summer radishes available today. The roots may be round, oval or spindle-shaped and may vary in colour from red to pink, yellow or white. They all have the same peppery taste. There are just as many varieties of large winter radish – there are white, brown, purple and even black radishes, with either carrot-shaped or turnip-shaped roots.

Availability: Forced radishes are available all year round but outdoor radishes are only in season during the late spring and summer. They are grown extensively throughout northern Europe but especially in Britain, Holland and Belgium.

WHITE WINTER RADISH

RED SUMMER RADISHES

NEW POTATOES

SWEET POTATOES

SALSIFY

SCORZONERA

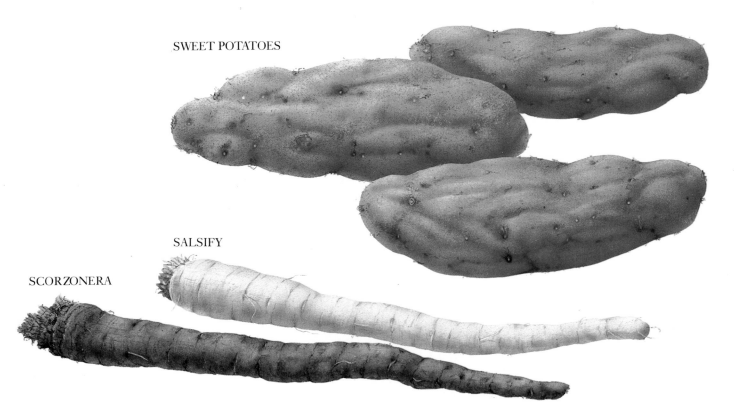

Buying: Large winter radishes are almost always sold individually while small summer radishes are sold in bunches, sometimes pre-packed. Look for radishes with fresh, green, crisp tops and smooth, bright, firm and well-formed roots.

Preparation and serving: Trim away the tops and roots, rinse and dry. Large winter radishes may also need peeling thinly. Leave whole if small or cut into slices or thin spirals.

Radishes are popular sprinkled with salt and served with cheese, in dips, salads and sandwich fillings.

To serve as a vegetable, cook whole in boiling salted water for about 10 minutes. Drain and serve in a Béchamel or cheese sauce.

Radishes also make colourful garnishes cut into fancy shapes like roses.

Nutritional value: Radishes are a good source of Vitamin C. Low in calories they contain only 15 Calories (65 kj) per 100 g/3½ oz.

SALSIFY AND SCORZONERA

Origin: Salsify (*Tragopogon porrifolius*) and Scorzonera (*Scorzonera hispanica*) are members of the Compositae family, and both are native to southern Europe. Scorzonera is also called black salsify, because it is like a black-skinned version of salsify. As the botanical name suggests, the Spanish first cultivated it.

Salsify, which has a creamy white skin, is also called oyster plant because it is supposed to taste like oysters. In appearance salsify and scorzonera roots look like long, rather shrivelled carrots, but under their skins is a soft, succulent, white flesh. Scorzonera tastes a little like asparagus but is more aromatic and astringent in flavour.

Availability: Salsify and scorzonera are in season from October to March. Most supplies are imported from Belgium and Holland.

Buying: Salsify and scorzonera are usually sold by weight. Choose roots that are firm, fresh-looking with well-formed roots and fresh tops. Avoid and reject any that are damaged, soft or diseased in any way.

Preparation and serving: Peel the roots thickly, removing the base and tops. Rinse quickly to remove the thick, milky and slightly sticky juice that will ooze out. Place in water with a little vinegar or lemon juice to prevent discoloration. Leave whole or cut into smaller pieces. Cook in boiling salted water until tender, about 30 to 35 minutes. Toss in a little butter or serve in a sauce.

Salsify and scorzonera can alternatively be baked as gratin dishes, and used to make creamy soups. The young leaves make a delicious salad ingredient. If grated and tossed in a little lemon juice to prevent discoloration, the fresh roots can also be added to winter salad mixtures.

Nutritional value: Scorzonera and salsify contain phosphorus and iron. The cooked vegetables have 18 Calories (77 kj) per 100 g/3½ oz.

SWEDE

Origin: The swede (*Brassica napus* var. *napobrassica*), also known as rutabaga, is a member of the Cruciferae family. This large root vegetable is believed to have originated in Europe as recently as the 17th century, for there are no earlier records. There are purple, white and yellow skinned varieties, all with yellowish flesh.

Availability: Swede is in season from October to April but some may be found during the summer months. Swedes are grown in all European countries, including Britain.

Buying: Swede is sold by weight. Choose young tender ones that are full of flavour, firm to the touch and of fresh appearance.

Preparation and serving: Prepare swedes by cutting a slice from the top and the root end, then peel thickly to reveal the yellow flesh. Rinse and cut into quarters, slices or cubes. Cook in boiling salted water for 30 to 45 minutes, according to size.

Swedes are delicious cooked then mashed with butter, cream and ground nutmeg. They are also tasty roasted with a meat joint. Parboil for 10 minutes, drain and place around the meat roast; cook for 30 to 40 minutes. Swedes are also delicious added to meat and vegetable casseroles, or hotpots.

Nutritional value: Swedes supply calcium, Vitamin C and niacin. Cooked swede contains 18 Calories (77 kj) per 100 g/3½ oz.

SWEET POTATOES

Origin: The sweet potato (*Ipomoea batatas*) is a member of the tropical Convolvulaceae family. It is also known as batata and yam. The sweet potato's origin is uncertain; it could have come from Mexico or eastern Asia. However, sweet potatoes first became popular in Central and South America, and today they are common in Spain and Italy too. They were the first 'potatoes' brought to England from the New World, but the ordinary potato ousted it from favour.

In appearance sweet potatoes are rather long tubers with purplish or sand-coloured skins and an orange flesh. The ends of the tubers are pointed and curved. The flavour is sweet and sometimes aromatic and the texture slightly sticky. They can be rather floury if boiled but less so if baked, roasted or fried.

Availability: Sweet potatoes are available all year round but are best in high season from November to April. Sweet potato supplies are lowest from the beginning of June to early August.

They are grown in all hot, tropical countries, but especially on the American continent. Most imports come to Britain from America.

Buying: Choose small or medium sweet potatoes that taper at both ends.

Look for firm, fresh-looking ones with smooth young skins. Sweet potatoes are usually sold by weight although some supermarkets pre-pack them in convenient quantities.

Preparation and serving: Like potatoes, sweet potatoes can be cooked in many different ways. At the very simplest they can be peeled, chopped and cooked in boiling salted water for 15 to 20 minutes. However, they are tastier if boiled in their jackets, then the flesh removed before eating or serving. They can also be fried, creamed, puréed, candied or served as a kind of sweet pudding.

Nutritional value: Sweet potatoes are rich in carbohydrate, Vitamin A and Vitamin C. They are a high calorie vegetable containing 91 Calories (387 kj) per 100 g/3½ oz.

TURNIPS

Origin: The turnip (*Brassica rapa*) is a member of the Cruciferae family. It has been a popular vegetable since Roman times, especially in France where it is used extensively in casseroles, hotpots and vegetable dishes.

Availability: Main crop turnips are at their best in season during the autumn and winter, although summer harvested supplies are often available from July to October.

They are grown in all European countries. Britain sometimes boosts its own production with supplies of baby turnips from France.

Buying: Turnips are sold by weight – although size is not a good indication of quality. Choose roots that are young and tender.

There are two main varieties to choose from: the globe-shaped turnip with creamy white skin and pale white flesh; and the flat-rooted turnip with white and scarlet to purple-tinged skin and pale white flesh.

Preparation and serving: To cook turnips, remove a thin slice from the top and root end and peel thinly. Rinse and cut into large chunks or leave whole. Cook in boiling salted water or stock for 25 to 45 minutes, depending upon size, age and type.

Serve tossed in butter and herbs, in a creamy white sauce or mashed with butter, cream, ground mace and lemon juice. The latter is the traditional way to serve turnips with Scottish haggis – a vegetable dish called 'bashed neeps'.

Nutritional value: Turnips are valuable more for their flavour than nutritional value. They have a very high water content – up to 90% and therefore small amounts of water-soluble vitamins and minerals. Reasonably low in calories, cooked turnips contain only 14 Calories (59 kj) per 100 g/3½ oz.

SWEDE

LONG TURNIPS

ROUND TURNIP

Lamb and Parsnip Broth

25 g/1 oz lard
625 g/1¼ lb lamb, cubed
625 g/1¼ lb parsnips, peeled and
  chopped
600 ml/1 pint meat stock
3 tomatoes, cut into wedges
1 onion, peeled and chopped
1 bay leaf
salt
freshly ground black pepper
125 g/4 oz streaky bacon, chopped
2–3 tablespoons cream
1 sprig of parsley, coarsely chopped

Melt the lard in a large pan. Add the meat and fry, over a high heat, until lightly browned on all sides. Add the parsnips, stock, tomatoes, onion, bay leaf, and salt and pepper to taste. Simmer gently for 45 to 50 minutes.

Ten minutes before the end of the cooking time add the bacon and a little hot water if the consistency of the broth is too thick. Stir in the cream and sprinkle with the parsley. Serve as a main meal, with French bread.
Serves 6

Vegetable Bortsch

500 g/1 lb beetroot
2 tablespoons oil
1 onion, peeled and sliced
1.75 litres/3 pints water
1 large carrot, peeled and chopped
2 sticks celery, chopped
3 teaspoons salt
freshly ground black pepper
250 g/8 oz cabbage, shredded
2 cloves garlic, peeled and chopped
2 tablespoons tomato purée
½ teaspoon sugar
1 tablespoon lemon juice
1 tablespoon chopped parsley
150 ml/¼ pint soured cream

Rinse the beetroot, peel and chop roughly. Heat the oil in a large pan, add the onion and fry until softened, about 5 minutes. Add the water, beetroot, carrot, celery and salt and pepper to taste. Bring to the boil, cover and simmer over a low heat for 30 minutes. Add the cabbage, garlic, tomato purée and sugar and simmer for 20 minutes.

Add the lemon juice and parsley, blending well. Adjust the seasoning. Pour into individual serving bowls and swirl the soured cream over the top. Serve immediately.
Serves 8

French Carrot Broth

20 g/¾ oz butter
150 g/5 oz smoked bacon, diced
625 g/1¼ lb carrots, peeled and sliced
750 ml/1¼ pints water
2 courgettes, thinly sliced
1 × 396 g/14 oz can cannellini beans,
  drained
1 clove garlic, peeled and crushed
salt
freshly ground black pepper
pinch of dried thyme
1 sprig of parsley, chopped

Melt the butter in a pan. Add the bacon and carrots and cook for 4 to 5 minutes. Add the water and simmer gently, over a low heat, for about 15 minutes.

Add the courgettes, beans, garlic, salt and pepper to taste, and the thyme. Cook, over a low heat, for a further 7 to 10 minutes, or until the vegetables are tender. Sprinkle with chopped parsley. Serve with crusty bread as a filling lunch or supper dish.
Serves 4 to 6

Cream of Carrot Soup

25 g/1 oz butter
1 clove garlic, peeled
½ onion, peeled and chopped
400 g/14 oz carrots, peeled and sliced
1 litre/1¾ pints meat stock
1 tablespoon tomato purée
salt
cayenne pepper
120 ml/4 fl oz double cream
2 tablespoons chopped parsley

Melt the butter in a large pan, add the garlic and fry until golden brown. Remove and discard the garlic. Add the onion and carrots. Cook for 2 to 3 minutes, then add the stock. Bring to the boil, lower the heat, cover and simmer for about 25 minutes.

Strain the soup through a sieve into another pan. Place the carrots and onion in an electric blender or food processor and work until smooth. Stir the purée into the strained soup. Add the tomato purée, salt and cayenne pepper to taste, and bring to the boil, stirring.

Meanwhile, lightly whip the cream. Remove the soup from the heat and stir in the cream. Sprinkle with the parsley before serving.
Serves 4

Beetroot Soup

2 beetroot
3 tablespoons oil
1 onion, peeled and sliced into rings
750 ml/1¼ pints meat stock
salt
cayenne pepper
125 g/4 oz leftover roast meat, chopped
50 ml/2 fl oz dry white wine
1 tablespoon chopped parsley
150 ml/¼ pint soured cream

Scrub the beetroot thoroughly and place in a pan. Add enough water to cover, bring to the boil, lower the heat and cook for 1½ hours or until tender. Rinse under cold water, peel and slice.

Heat the oil in a large pan, add the onion rings and beetroot. Cook, over a gentle heat, for 4 to 5 minutes. Add the stock, salt and cayenne pepper to taste, mixing well. Add the meat and cook,

over a very low heat, for 7 minutes.

Stir in the white wine and parsley, blending well. Ladle the soup into individual soup bowls and garnish each with a swirl of soured cream.
Serves 4

ABOVE: *Lamb and parsnip broth; French carrot broth; Vegetable bortsch; Cream of carrot soup*

49

Celeriac and Ham Soup

1 medium celeriac
1 tablespoon lemon juice
15 g/½ oz butter
2 tablespoons oil
1 onion, peeled and chopped
1 litre/1¾ pints meat stock
pinch of cayenne pepper
pinch of grated nutmeg
150 g/5 oz cooked ham, cut into strips
1 egg yolk
150 ml/¼ pint double cream
2 tablespoons chopped parsley

Peel and rinse the celeriac, cut into quarters and coarsely grate. Sprinkle with the lemon juice to prevent discoloration.

Melt the butter and oil in a large pan, add the onion and cook for 4 to 5 minutes. Add the celeriac, stirring constantly. Add the stock, cayenne pepper and nutmeg and simmer, over a low heat, for about 8 minutes. Add the ham and simmer for a further 3 minutes.

Meanwhile, beat the egg yolk with the cream. Remove the soup from the heat and stir in the egg and cream mixture until incorporated.

Transfer the soup to a warmed tureen or ladle into individual soup bowls. Sprinkle with the chopped parsley before serving.
Serves 4

Celeriac and Fruit Salad

2–3 dessert apples
2 bananas
1 small celeriac, peeled and cut into strips
2 tablespoons chopped walnuts
2 tablespoons lemon juice
pinch of salt
pinch of ground allspice
2 tablespoons double cream

Peel, core and slice the apples. Peel the bananas and cut into chunks. Mix the apple with the banana, celeriac and walnuts in a serving bowl.

Mix the lemon juice with the salt and allspice for the dressing, and immediately stir into the salad. Add the cream and toss the ingredients well to mix. Serve immediately.
Serves 4

NOTE: Celeriac and Fruit Salad makes a delicious starter or light summer lunch or supper served with buttered wholemeal bread.

Winter radish salad; Celeriac rémoulade; Celeriac and fruit salad; Radish and Cucumber salad

Winter Radish Salad

1 large winter radish
salt
150 ml/¼ pint soured cream
1 tablespoon snipped chives

Scrub and thinly peel the radish. Grate or cut into very thin slices. Place in a bowl and sprinkle generously with salt. Leave to stand for 10 to 12 minutes.

Rinse thoroughly and place in a serving bowl. Spoon over the soured cream, toss well and sprinkle with the chives. **Serves 4**

Radish and Cucumber Salad

1 winter radish
½ cucumber
salt
1 tablespoon wine vinegar
3 tablespoons oil
1 sprig of dill, finely chopped

Peel and grate the radish. Peel and thinly slice the cucumber. Place in a bowl, sprinkle with a little salt, mix thoroughly and leave to stand for 10 minutes. Rinse and drain thoroughly. Place in a serving bowl.

To make the dressing, beat the wine vinegar with the oil and dill. Pour over the salad and toss well to mix. **Serves 4**

NOTE: Serve as a side salad.

Celeriac Rémoulade

500 g/1 lb celeriac
2 tablespoons Dijon mustard
3 tablespoons mayonnaise
1 teaspoon lemon juice
3 tablespoons soured cream
1 teaspoon chopped parsley

Peel the celeriac and cut into julienne strips. Bring a saucepan of water to the boil, add the celeric strips and blanch for 1 to 2 minutes. Drain thoroughly, then transfer to a serving bowl and allow to cool.

Blend the Dijon mustard with the

mayonnaise, lemon juice and soured cream, for the dressing. Fold into the celeriac, blending well.

Spoon the celeriac salad into a serving dish and sprinkle with the chopped parsley to serve. **Serves 4 to 6**

Potato Salad with Dill Mayonnaise

1 kg/2 lb new potatoes, preferably red
  skinned
salt
3 tablespoons mayonnaise
4 tablespoons double cream
½ Spanish onion, peeled and finely
  chopped
2 sprigs of dill, finely chopped
pinch of cayenne pepper
TO GARNISH:
sprigs of dill or parsley
radish roses

Scrub the potatoes thoroughly and place in a pan. Cover with boiling water, add a pinch of salt and bring back to the boil. Lower the heat and cook for about 20 minutes or until just tender. Drain and leave to cool. Cut the potatoes into halves or quarters, depending upon size.

To make the dressing, beat the mayonnaise with the cream, onion, dill and cayenne pepper. Pour the dressing over the potatoes and toss to mix.

Leave the salad to stand for at least 1 hour to allow the flavours to develop.

Garnish with dill or parsley sprigs and radish roses to serve.
Serves 4

NOTE: Potato Salad with Dill Mayonnaise makes a delicious party, cold buffet or picnic dish.

Slimmer's Radish Sandwiches

4 slices wholemeal bread
20 g/¾ oz low-fat spread
1–2 bunches radishes (depending on size)
salt
125 g/4 oz cottage cheese
1 tablespoon snipped chives
2 tablespoons finely chopped onion

Spread the bread thinly with the low fat spread. Cut the radishes into thick slices, sprinkle with a little salt and leave to stand for about 5 minutes. Rinse and drain thoroughly.

Mix the cottage cheese with salt to taste, the chives and onion and spread the mixture evenly onto the bread. Top each open sandwich with a generous layer of radishes. Serve immediately.
Serves 4

Slimmer's Carrot Salad

325 g/11 oz carrots, peeled and grated
½ Chinese cabbage, shredded
1 × 150 g/5.2 oz carton natural yogurt
1 tablespoon lemon juice
1 teaspoon tomato purée
salt
pinch of sugar (optional)
sprigs of parsley to garnish

Mix the carrots with the Chinese cabbage in a serving bowl.

To make the dressing, beat the yogurt with the lemon juice, tomato purée, salt to taste, and the sugar, if using. Pour over the salad and toss well to coat.

Garnish with parsley before serving.
Serves 4

Radish Salad Platter

1 cabbage lettuce
2 bunches radishes, sliced
125 g/4 oz Camembert cheese, thinly sliced
1 tablespoon snipped chives
1 cucumber, thinly sliced
salt
juice of 1 lemon
½ clove garlic, crushed with salt
freshly ground black pepper
4 tablespoons olive oil
pinch of sugar

Separate the lettuce leaves, place in a sieve, rinse and drain thoroughly. Use the leaves to line a large salad bowl. Mix the radishes with the cheese and chives. Sprinkle the cucumber with salt and leave to stand for about 5 minutes. Rinse and drain thoroughly.

To make the dressing, beat the lemon juice with the garlic, pepper to taste, olive oil and sugar.

Arrange the cucumber in a ring over the lettuce and fill the centre with the radish and cheese mixture. Pour the dressing over the salad to serve.
Serves 4

NOTE: To serve this platter as a side salad, omit the Camembert.

Colourful beetroot salad; Radish salad platter; Slimmer's carrot salad; Potato salad with dill mayonnaise

Colourful Beetroot Salad

625–750 g/1¼–1½ lb beetroot
salt
1 fennel bulb, cut into julienne strips
1 apple, cored and chopped
1 onion, peeled and sliced into rings
1 × 150 g/5.2 oz carton natural yogurt
4 tablespoons double cream
1 teaspoon creamed horseradish
pinch of sugar
1 tablespoon chopped hazelnuts
1–2 hard-boiled eggs, shelled
sprigs of fennel to garnish (optional)

Scrub the beetroot under running water. Place the beetroot in a large saucepan and cover with boiling water. Add a pinch of salt and bring back to the boil. Lower the heat and cook gently for about 1½ hours until tender.

Rinse the beetroot under cold water and leave to cool slightly. Peel, then slice thinly. Place in a large serving bowl. Add the fennel, apple and onion and toss well to mix.

To make the dressing, beat the yogurt with the cream, horseradish, sugar and hazelnuts. Pour over the beetroot salad and toss well to mix.

Cut the hard-boiled egg into quarters and arrange on top of the salad. Garnish with fennel sprigs if liked.
Serves 4

NOTE: This unusual salad makes a delicious accompaniment to cold roast beef.

Ham Steaks with Sweet Potatoes

4 small sweet potatoes
salt
25–40 g/1–1½ oz butter or margarine
4 ham or gammon steaks
1 small onion, peeled and finely chopped
½ teaspoon anchovy paste
50 g/2 oz fresh white breadcrumbs
sprigs of parsley to garnish

Rinse the sweet potatoes and place in a large saucepan. Cover with boiling water, add a pinch of salt and bring back to the boil. Lower the heat and cook gently for about 20 minutes until tender. Rinse under cold water, peel and cut each sweet potato in half.

Spread half the butter or margarine on top of the ham or gammon steaks and cook under a preheated hot grill, for 4 to 5 minutes. Turn the steaks,

baste well and cook for 3 minutes.

Meanwhile, melt the remaining fat in a small pan, add the onion and fry until golden brown. Add the anchovy paste and breadcrumbs, mixing well. Place two sweet potato halves on each steak and cover with the onion mixture. Return the steaks to the grill for about 5 minutes, until golden brown. Serve immediately, garnished with parsley.
Serves 4

Salsify in Ham and Cream Sauce

600 ml/1 pint water
salt
2–3 tablespoons mild wine vinegar
750 g/1½ lb salsify
15 g/½ oz butter
SAUCE:
15 g/½ oz butter
1 tablespoon flour
150 g/5 oz cooked ham, cut into strips
300 ml/½ pint double cream
1 tablespoon chopped parsley

Bring the water to the boil in a pan, add a pinch of salt and the vinegar. Meanwhile, rinse the salsify, peel fairly thickly and cut into equal pieces. Add the salsify to the pan with the butter, lower the heat and cook for about 30 minutes.

Meanwhile, prepare the sauce. Melt the butter in a pan, add the flour and cook for 2 to 3 minutes. Gradually add 300 ml/½ pint of the salsify cooking

liquid, blending well after each addition, to make a smooth sauce. Add the ham and simmer, over a low heat, for 2 minutes. Stir in the cream and parsley.

Drain the salsify thoroughly and place in a warmed serving dish. Pour over the sauce to serve.
Serves 4

NOTE: Serve this lunch or supper dish with boiled rice or new potatoes.

Carrot and Veal Stew Dolce

2 tablespoons oil
750 g/1½ lb stewing veal
1 onion, peeled and chopped
salt
freshly ground black pepper
1 teaspoon ground paprika
325–350 g/11–12 oz carrots, peeled
2 tomatoes, skinned
1 dill cucumber, sliced or chopped
300 ml/½ pint meat stock
1 tablespoon chopped parsley
pinch of cayenne pepper

Heat the oil in a flameproof casserole or heavy-based pan, add the veal and onion and fry until lightly browned. Season with salt and pepper to taste. Add the paprika and cook over a moderate heat, for about 5 minutes, stirring frequently.

Cut the carrots into long thin strips. Cut the tomatoes into wedges. Add the carrots, tomatoes and dill cucumber to the casserole and cook for a further 4 to 5 minutes.

Add the stock and enough hot water to cover the vegetables. Cover and cook over a low heat, for about 1½ to 1¾ hours, stirring occasionally.

Sprinkle with the parsley and cayenne pepper before serving.
Serves 4

NOTE: Carrot and Veal Stew Dolce is delicious served with boiled potatoes or buttered noodles.

Corned Beef Ring with Scorzonera

600 ml/1 pint water
salt
2–3 tablespoons mild wine vinegar
750 g/1½ lb scorzonera
2 × 340 g/12 oz cans corned beef
1 medium bread roll, chopped
1 onion, peeled and finely chopped
2 eggs, beaten
200 ml/⅓ pint milk
2 teaspoons creamed horseradish
1 teaspoon made French mustard
SAUCE:
300 ml/½ pint milk
140 g/4½ oz Cheddar cheese, grated
pinch of grated nutmeg
freshly ground white pepper

Bring the water to the boil in a pan, add a pinch of salt and the vinegar. Meanwhile, rinse the scorzonera, peel fairly thickly and cut into equal pieces. Add to the pan immediately. Bring back to the boil, then lower the heat and cook for about 30 minutes. Drain thoroughly.

Meanwhile, prepare the corned beef ring. Mince or finely chop the corned beef and place in a bowl with the bread, onion, eggs, milk, horseradish and mustard. Mix until smooth, then spoon into a greased 1.2 litre/2 pint ring mould. Cook in a preheated moderate oven (180°C/350°F, Gas Mark 4) for 35 to 40 minutes.

To make the sauce, heat the milk in a pan, add the cheese and stir until completely melted. Season with the nutmeg, salt and pepper to taste. Add the scorzonera.

To serve, turn the corned beef ring out onto a flat dish and fill the centre of the ring with the scorzonera and sauce. Serve immediately.
Serves 6 to 8

Salsify in ham and cream sauce; Carrot and Veal stew dolce; Ham steaks with sweet potatoes

Pike with Beetroot Sauce

1 pike, weighing about 2 kg/4½ lb,
  gutted, scaled and cleaned
juice of 1 lemon
salt
freshly ground black pepper
50 g/2 oz back bacon, derinded
1 bunch herbs (e.g. parsley, chives,
  thyme)
40 g/1½ oz butter
250 g/8 oz cooked beetroot
4 tablespoons dry red wine
1 teaspoon sugar
herbs to garnish

Wash the pike, wipe dry with kitchen paper and sprinkle inside and out with lemon juice. Leave the fish to marinate for about 10 minutes, then season with salt and pepper to taste.

Make deep cuts on each side of the fish with a sharp knife and fill each cut with a slice of bacon. Stuff the fish with the herbs. Place the fish in a large roasting tin and dot with 25 g/1 oz of the butter. Cook in a preheated moderately hot oven (190°C/375°F, Gas Mark 5) for 45 to 50 minutes.

Meanwhile, to make the sauce, purée the beetroot in an electric blender or food processor with the red wine. Transfer to a small pan and heat gently. Stir in the remaining butter, sugar, and salt and pepper to taste.

Arrange the fish on a platter, garnish with herbs and serve with the sauce.
Serves 6 to 8

NOTE: If pike is difficult to obtain from your fishmonger, use another oily fish, such as salmon trout, instead.

Salmon Rolls with Horseradish Cream

120 ml/4 fl oz double cream
2 tablespoons grated horseradish
1 apple, peeled, cored and chopped
150–200 g/5–7 oz smoked salmon,
  sliced
apple slices and celery leaves (optional)

Whip the double cream until it holds its shape, then carefully fold in the horseradish and apple.

Spread each slice of smoked salmon evenly with the cream mixture and roll up neatly. Arrange on a platter and chill

lightly before serving. Garnish with apple slices and celery leaves, if liked.
Serves 4

NOTE: For a less expensive version, replace the salmon with ham.

56

Spanish Vegetable Omelette

8 tablespoons olive oil
4 large potatoes, peeled and chopped or
  sliced
2 onions, peeled and chopped
1 red pepper, cored, seeded and chopped
  or cut into strips
1 green pepper, cored, seeded and
  chopped or cut into strips
2 courgettes, cut into julienne strips
2 small aubergines, finely chopped
2–3 cloves garlic, peeled and crushed or
  finely chopped
350 g/12 oz tomatoes, finely chopped
3 eggs
salt

Heat 5 tablespoons of the oil in a pan, add the potatoes and fry, over a low heat, turning frequently, for about 15 minutes.

Meanwhile, heat the remaining oil in a large non-stick frying pan. Add the onions, peppers, courgettes and aubergines and fry, over a low heat, for about 8 to 10 minutes. Just before the vegetables are cooked, add the garlic, tomatoes and the cooked potatoes.

Beat the eggs with a little salt. Pour the mixture evenly over the vegetables and cook, over a low heat, until the egg has just set.

Turn the omelette out onto a large plate and serve cut into wedges.
Serves 4 to 6

NOTE: This makes a delicious main course served with a salad, or a tasty accompaniment to grilled or roast meat.

A Spanish omelette offers many possibilities for variation. The potato, onion, garlic and peppers are a must (the peppers especially, as these make the omelette juicy and moist), but the remaining vegetables can be replaced with others of your choice. It provides an ideal opportunity to use leftovers.

Celeriac and Tomato with Lemon Sauce

15 g/½ oz butter
1 celeriac, coarsely chopped
375 g/12 oz tomatoes, cut into wedges
salt
freshly ground black pepper
pinch of dried basil
150 ml/¼ pint meat stock
juice of 1 lemon
1 egg yolk
2 tablespoons double cream
sprigs of basil to garnish

Melt the butter in a pan, add the celeriac and cook for 4 to 5 minutes. Add the tomatoes, salt and pepper to taste, and the basil. Stir in the stock and lemon juice and cook, over a low heat, for about 15 minutes.

Beat the egg yolk with the cream. Remove the vegetables from the heat and add the egg and cream mixture, stirring continuously.

Transfer to a warmed serving dish

and garnish with basil sprigs to serve.
Serves 4

NOTE: Celeriac and Tomato with Lemon Sauce is a tasty vegetable dish to serve with fish or grilled steaks.

ABOVE: *Spanish vegetable omelette; Celeriac and tomato with lemon sauce*
LEFT: *Salmon trout with beetroot sauce; Salmon rolls with horseradish cream*

Gratin Dauphinois

*1 kg/2 lb floury potatoes, peeled and
  sliced*
40 g/1½ oz butter
2 cloves garlic, peeled and halved
300 ml/½ pint milk
120 ml/4 fl oz single cream
1 teaspoon salt
freshly ground white pepper
pinch of grated nutmeg
*125 g/4 oz Emmenthal or Gruyère
  cheese, grated*

Lightly grease a shallow casserole dish
and cover the base with potato slices to
a depth of about 2.5 to 4 cm/1 to 1½
inches; the dish will look attractive if
you overlap the potato slices. Melt the
butter in a pan, add the garlic and fry
until golden brown. Remove and discard the garlic and pour the garlic
butter over the potatoes.

Meanwhile, heat the milk and cream
in a pan. Season with the salt, pepper to
taste and nutmeg and pour over the
potatoes. Cover the dish with foil and

cook in a preheated moderate oven
(180°C/350°F, Gas Mark 4) for about
40 minutes.

Remove the foil, sprinkle with the
grated cheese. Increase the oven temperature to hot (200°C/400°F, Gas
Mark 6) and bake for a further 20
minutes until the top is crisp and
golden brown. Serve immediately.
Serves 6

NOTE: Serve as an accompaniment or as
a supper with a crisp salad.

Puréed Carrots

salt
1 kg/2 lb carrots, peeled
pinch of granted nutmeg
40 g/1½ oz butter
150 ml/¼ pint warm milk
1 egg yolk
1 tablespoon tomato purée
freshly ground white pepper
1 tablespoon finely snipped chives

Bring a large pan of water to the boil
and add salt. Meanwhile, cut the
carrots into equal pieces. Place in the
pan with the nutmeg. Bring back to the
boil, lower the heat and cook gently for
20 to 25 minutes. Drain the carrots and
place in an electric blender or food
processor with the butter, milk, egg
yolk, tomato purée, salt and pepper to
taste. Work to a smooth purée.

Stir the carrot purée in a pan over
low heat until heated through and
thickened slightly. Spoon into a warmed serving dish and sprinkle with the
chives. Serve immediately.
Serves 4 to 6

*Jerusalem artichokes in egg sauce; Puréed
carrots; Gratin Dauphinois*

Jerusalem Artichokes in Egg Sauce

1 litre/1¾ pints water
salt
pinch of grated nutmeg
750 g–1 kg/1½–2 lb Jerusalem
    artichokes, peeled and halved
SAUCE:
15 g/½ oz butter
1 tablespoon flour
juice of 1 lemon
150 ml/¼ pint double cream
2 hard-boiled eggs, shelled and chopped
freshly ground white pepper
TO GARNISH:
chopped parsley

Bring the water to the boil in a pan, then add a pinch of salt and the nutmeg. Add the Jerusalem artichokes, bring back to the boil, then lower the heat and cook gently for about 25 minutes. Drain, reserving 150 ml/¼ pint of the cooking liquid.

To make the sauce, melt the butter in a pan, add the flour and cook for 2 to 3 minutes. Whisk in the lemon juice and reserved cooking liquid, to make a smooth sauce.

When the sauce has thickened slightly remove the pan from the heat and carefully stir in the cream and chopped egg. Season the sauce with salt and pepper to taste.

To serve, arrange the Jerusalem artichokes in a warmed serving dish, cover with the sauce and sprinkle with the chopped parsley.
Serves 6

NOTE: Jerusalem Artichokes in Egg Sauce is a tasty vegetable dish to serve with grilled chops.

Sweet Potato and Apple Casserole

8 medium sweet potatoes
4 small apples, cored and sliced into
    rings
2–3 tablespoons caster sugar
2 tablespoons coarsely chopped pecan or
    cashew nuts
25 g/1 oz butter
1 teaspoon salt
pinch of grated nutmeg

Place the sweet potatoes in a pan, cover with boiling water, bring back to the boil, lower the heat and cook for about 15 minutes or until barely tender. Rinse under cold water, peel and cut lengthways into thick slices.

Fill a greased ovenproof dish with alternate layers of sweet potato and apple and sprinkle with the sugar and nuts. Melt the butter in a small pan, season with the salt and nutmeg and pour over the sweet potato and apple mixture. Cook in a preheated moderately hot oven (200°C/400°F, Gas Mark 6) for 20 to 25 minutes. Serve immediately.as a tasty accompaniment to crisp roasted pork.
Serves 4 to 6

Turnip au Gratin

600 ml/1 pint meat stock
dash of vinegar
pinch of sugar
750 g–1 kg/1½–2 lb turnips, peeled and
sliced
15 g/½ oz butter
1 tablespoon flour
4 tablespoons double cream
125 g/4 oz Gruyère cheese, sliced

Bring the stock, vinegar and sugar to the boil in a large pan, add the turnips and return to the boil. Lower the heat and cook gently for 20 minutes.

Meanwhile, melt the butter in a pan, add the flour and cook for 2 to 3 minutes. Gradually whisk in 300 ml/ ½ pint of the turnip cooking liquid, blending well after each addition, to make a smooth sauce. Stir in the cream.

Drain the turnips and transfer to a lightly greased ovenproof dish. Cover with the sauce and top with the cheese. Cook in a preheated hot oven (200°C/ 400°F, Gas Mark 6) for 15 minutes, or until golden. Serve immediately, as an accompaniment to lamb dishes.
Serves 6

Horseradish Relish

4 tablespoons freshly grated horseradish
1 teaspoon French mustard
½ teaspoon caster sugar
salt
freshly ground black pepper
1 tablespoon wine vinegar
150 ml/¼ pint double cream

Mix the horseradish with the mustard, sugar, salt and pepper to taste, and vinegar.

Whip the cream until it stands in soft peaks and fold into the horseradish mixture. Taste and adjust the seasoning and spoon into a dish to serve, or store in an airtight container in the refrigerator until required.
Makes about 200 ml/⅓ pint

NOTE: Horseradish relish is the traditional accompaniment to roast beef. It is also delicious served with cold meats.

Horseradish and Nut Dip

2 tablespoons mayonnaise
300 ml/½ pint soured cream
1½ tablespoons freshly grated
   horseradish
1 tablespoon chopped hazelnuts

Whip the mayonnaise with the soured cream and horseradish until well blended. Fold in the nuts, mixing well. Chill before serving.
Serves 4

NOTE: Horseradish and Nut Dip is a quick sauce to serve with fondue, boiled globe artichokes or cold roast meat.

Horseradish and Apple Sauce

3 cooking apples, peeled, cored and
   quartered
150 ml/¼ pint water
1 tablespoon lemon juice
2 teaspoons sugar
150 ml/¼ pint milk
3 tablespoons freshly grated horseradish
4 tablespoons double cream
salt

Place the apples, water, lemon juice and sugar in a pan. Bring to the boil, then lower the heat and cook for about 10 minutes, until tender. Purée the apple mixture in an electric blender or food processor until smooth.

Return the mixture to the pan, add the milk and bring to the boil, stirring continuously. Cook, stirring, for about 5 minutes.

Fold in the horseradish and cream, season with a little salt and serve immediately.
Serves 4

NOTE: This sauce is delicious served with roast beef or fried fish.

Horseradish and nut dip (also shown served in a globe artichoke); Glazed carrots; Turnip au gratin

Glazed Carrots

salt
625–750 g/1¼–1½ lb carrots
3 tablespoons caster sugar
2 tablespoons water
25 g/1 oz butter
1 tablespoon finely chopped hazelnuts

Bring about 600 ml/1 pint water to the boil in a pan and add salt. Meanwhile, rinse and scrape the carrots. Leave small carrots whole; halve or quarter thick carrots lengthways. Place in the pan, bring back to the boil, then lower the heat and cook for about 5 minutes. Drain thoroughly.

Heat the sugar and water in a pan.

Add the butter and stir to melt. Add the carrots and cook, over a low heat, for 10 minutes, turning the carrots occasionally, until tender. Sprinkle with the hazelnuts before serving.
Serves 4 to 6

NOTE: Glazed Carrots are delicious served with roast meat or fried liver.

Radishes in Cheese Sauce

600 ml/1 pint water
salt
1 tablespoon lemon juice
knob of butter
3 winter radishes, peeled and sliced
SAUCE:
15 g/½ oz butter
2 teaspoons flour
4 tablespoons double cream
50 g/2 oz Parmesan cheese, grated
grated nutmeg
pinch of cayenne pepper

Place the water, with a pinch of salt, lemon juice and butter in a large pan. Bring to the boil, add the radishes, lower the heat and simmer gently for about 20 minutes. Drain, reserving half of the cooking liquid.

To make the sauce, melt the butter in a pan, add the flour and cook for 2 to 3 minutes. Gradually add the reserved radish cooking liquid, blending well after each addition to make a smooth sauce. Add the cream and cheese, stir-ring until the cheese has melted. Add the radishes to the sauce, season with nutmeg, salt and cayenne pepper to taste and serve immediately.

Serves 4 to 6

NOTE: Radishes in Cheese Sauce is delicious served with rissoles or sausages.

American-style Jacket Potatoes

4 large baking potatoes
250 g/8 oz cooked ham, finely chopped
3 tablespoons finely chopped herbs (e.g. chives, parsley, thyme)
salt
freshly ground black pepper
grated nutmeg
4 eggs, separated

Wrap the potatoes individually in foil and bake in a preheated hot oven (220°C/425°F, Gas Mark 7) for about 50 minutes or until cooked. Cut the potatoes in half and scoop out the cooked flesh into a bowl. Add the ham, herbs, salt, pepper, and nutmeg to taste, and the egg yolks. Mix thoroughly.

Whisk the egg whites until stiff and fold into the potato mixture. Spoon the mixture back into the potato skins, place on a baking sheet and return to the oven to cook for about 12 minutes, or until browned.

Serves 4

French Potato and Onion Bake

50 g/2 oz lard
2 Spanish onions, peeled and coarsely chopped or sliced into rings
6 large potatoes, peeled and sliced
salt
freshly ground black pepper

Melt the lard in a frying pan, add the onions and cook for 5 minutes. Fill an ovenproof dish with alternate layers of sliced potato and onion, seasoning each layer with salt and pepper to taste and finishing with a layer of fried onion. Cook in a preheated moderately hot oven (190°C/375°F, Gas Mark 5) for 1 hour or until the potatoes are tender. Serve immediately.

Serves 4 to 6

NOTE: This rustic vegetable dish goes well with baked or grilled fish.

Rösti

1 kg/2 lb potatoes, scrubbed
50 g/2 oz butter
2 tablespoons corn oil
1 teaspoon salt
freshly ground black pepper

Place the potatoes in a pan of cold water and bring to the boil. Cover and simmer for 10 minutes. Drain and leave overnight in the refrigerator.

Peel the potatoes and grate coarsely. Melt half the butter with half the oil in a heavy-based pan, add the potatoes, with salt and pepper to taste. Fry gently for about 10 minutes until the potatoes are golden brown underneath. Loosen the edges with a spatula, invert a plate over the pan, then turn out.

Heat the remaining butter and oil in the pan, add the potatoes, and brown the other side for about 10 minutes, pressing gently to form a cake. Slide onto a warmed serving plate to serve.

Serves 4

NOTE: There are many versions of this tasty Swiss recipe; often onion or bacon is added with the grated potatoes.

Pommes Savoyade

25 g/1 oz butter
750 g/1½ lb potatoes, peeled
2 cloves garlic, peeled and crushed
75 g/3 oz Gruyère cheese, grated
salt
freshly ground black pepper
300 ml/½ pint single cream

Grease a shallow ovenproof dish thickly with the butter. Slice the potatoes thinly and layer in the dish with the garlic, cheese, and salt and pepper to taste. Overlap the top layer of potatoes neatly. Pour over the cream and bake in a preheated moderately hot oven (190°C/375°F Gas Mark 5) for 1 to 1¼ hours until tender. Serve immediately.

Serves 4

Pommes savoyade; Rösti; French potato and onion bake; American-style jacket potatoes

ONION FAMILY

The aromatic members of this group can lift ordinary dishes into the luxury class and turn bland foods into tasty dishes. Such is the indispensable nature of this family which comprises the onion, garlic, leek and shallot.

The prominent member is the onion in all its forms from the pale green to white, slim spring onion, through the firm, round button onion and flattened cousin the shallot, to the large and surprisingly mild Spanish onion. Garlic with its pungent aroma features strongly in several cuisines. Less popular but just as prized by those who grow them, especially the Welsh, is the leek with its long, tightly-packed scroll of papery green leaves.

There are countless dishes based on the onion family. Try classic Vichysoisse, French onion soup and Stuffed baked onions to enjoy the full pungency of these tasty vegetables. Add a hint of them to almost any savoury dish to enhance flavour.

GARLIC

Origin: Garlic (*Allium sativum*) is a member of the Alliaceae family. It has been known and highly valued for at least 5000 years. The ancient Egyptians and the Romans prized it for its health-giving qualities. During the Middle Ages, garlic was used as a remedy for snakebites, rabies, baldness and rashes. In the First World War it was used by the French as an antiseptic.

Availability: Garlic is available all year round, but the supply peaks in March and September. America, Italy and France are the main producers.

Buying: Three major varieties of garlic are cultivated: the Creole or American, the strongest white-skinned variety; the Italian, with its pale pink to mauve skin; and Tahitian, the largest variety.

Garlic is a bulb like the onion, but inside the papery outer skin are small individually wrapped cloves. The best signs for good quality and freshness are plump, juicy cloves and a pale white or translucent mauve skin. The bulbs should not be wrinkled or papery-dry.

Strings of garlic heads are often available, containing up to some 30 bulbs. Only buy one if you use garlic often, and if you have somewhere dry and airy to store it. Commercially crushed or puréed garlic is also available in tubes and jars for convenient use.

Preparation and serving: Garlic may be used as a whole clove, crushed or chopped. A garlic press is a convenient, quick way to crush garlic. Perhaps the best way to retain as much flavour as possible is to peel away the papery skin, place underneath a large, broad knife and hit the blade with your fist. This splits the skin; the garlic can be further chopped or crushed as required. One of the simplest ways to crush garlic is with a fork and $\frac{1}{4}$ teaspoon salt. To avoid a lingering aroma of garlic on the hands, wear rubber gloves or touch only with wet hands.

Used with discretion, garlic will add flavour to almost any savoury dish. For just a hint of garlic, fry halved garlic cloves, in butter or oil, until golden, remove and discard before adding the remaining ingredients. For a mild flavour in salads, simply rub your salad bowl with the cut side of a clove before adding the salad.

To make your own garlic purée in bulk, peel, press or crush one whole bulb of garlic (up to 30 cloves) and place in a screw-top jar. Fill up with sunflower or blended vegetable oil *not* olive oil. Stir once, seal and store in the refrigerator until required. This delicious garlic oil will keep for up to 1 month, and you can remove small amounts daily, as required, to flavour sauces, dressings and other savoury dishes. If you want a strong garlic flavour, scoop out the garlic purée at the bottom of the jar with a teaspoon. Top up the jar with new oil as you remove the flavoured oil and stir again.

There are few savoury dishes that do not gain from the addition of garlic. Soups, stews, casseroles, vegetables dishes, fish, grills and salads are all contenders. Classic dishes based on the extravagant use of garlic include Spanish allioli, a garlic mayonnaise or sauce, bouillabaisse, a French seafood stew, and garlic-studded leg of lamb.

Nutritional value: There are many claims for the nutritional and medicinal values of garlic. It is claimed that garlic helps cure premature ageing, lowers high blood pressure, stimulates the digestion and circulation, prevents stomach ailments and stimulates dull appetites. None have been proved other than its antiseptic qualities.

Garlic contains basically the same nutrients as onions, but since it is consumed in small quantities its major benefit is to add flavour to a dish. A garlic clove contains 3 Calories (13 kj).

LEEKS

Origin: The leek (*Allium porrum*) is a member of the Alliaceae family, like the onion, to which it is related. It has been known since Biblical times in Egypt and the Mediterranean. The Romans were especially fond of leeks, but it was the Phoenician traders who introduced them to Wales, when they came to mine tin. The leek has been the Welsh national emblem since 640 AD, when the Welsh defeated the invading Saxon army partly, according to legend, because of the leeks pinned to their hats, which prevented them from attacking each other by mistake!

Availability: Fresh leeks are available all year, summer leeks from May to August, winter leeks throughout the remainder of the year.

Leeks are grown in almost every country of the world because they are such a hardy vegetable. The United Kingdom grows sufficient for its own consumption.

Buying: Summer and winter leeks differ slightly. The summer leek has a long, white stem, bright green leaves and a mild flavour, whereas the winter leek has a thick, sturdy stem and a stronger, slightly more bitter flavour.

Leeks are generally sold by weight, occasionally in bunches. They can also be found pre-packed into convenient quantities in supermarkets.

Look for well-shaped, medium stems with fresh green tops. Avoid those with obvious signs of age like bruising or decaying patches, or mishandling like ragged edges or split bulbs. Fresh leeks can be stored for several days in the refrigerator if wrapped in a plastic bag or cling film.

Preparation and serving: To clean leeks for cooking, cut away and discard the white root base and fibres, cut off the upper green leaves and any tough outer leaves. If the leeks are to be cooked whole, make a downward slit along the length of the stem, to open out the stem but not to cut it in half, rinse thoroughly under cold running water until all traces of dirt or grit are removed. Chop or slice if required.

LEEK

GARLIC

SHALLOTS

Leeks should be boiled in the minimum amount of boiling salted water. Whole stems take 15 to 20 minutes, chopped leek about 10 minutes. Plain boiled leeks are delicious served as a vegetable accompaniment with melted butter or a cheese or white sauce.

Leeks are excellent in soups, sauces and stews. They are tasty when served as a gratin dish with slices of ham or tongue rolled around them; baked in pastry, as in leek tart; or in salads.

Nutritional value: Leeks are rich in calcium, phosphorus, iron, sodium, potassium and Vitamins B and C. They contain only 31 Calories (128 kj) per 100 g/$3\frac{1}{2}$ oz.

ONIONS

Origin: The onion (*Allium cepa*) is a member of the Alliaceae family. It is thought to have originally come from the Orient. The Egyptians certainly knew them, but it was the ancient Romans who introduced them to the United Kingdom.

The shallot, a delicate sub-species of the onion, was brought back from Asia Minor by the Crusaders and subsequently grown in most Mediterranean countries, but particularly in France.

Availability: Most varieties of onion can be bought all year round, although strong white onions, shallots and pearl onions are generally only available during the summer. Home-produced onions are supplemented by imports from Spain and Italy.

Buying: There are numerous varieties of onion. The most popular in the United Kingdom are the light-skinned 'yellow onion', the kind we tend to buy most for everyday use; the shallot, a small, delicately-flavoured onion; the red onion, with its mild flavour and deep red or purple skin; the Spanish onion, round and very large with a yellowish-brown to copper skin and mild flavour; the pearl onion, small, very white and piquant in flavour, a favourite for pickling; and the spring onion, which is eaten with leaves.

Choose onions that feel firm or dry, with the exception of spring onions. The outer papery skin should look bright and smooth. Avoid any that feel damp at the neck or stem end, have soft or woody centres and certainly those that have begun to sprout.

When buying spring onions, look for bright green, clean tops, of a medium length, and clean white root ends.

With the exception of pearl onions, red onions and spring onions, which should be used quickly after purchase, all other varieties can be stored for months if they are kept cool and dry.

Preparation and serving: All onions, except for spring onions, should have their dry outer skins removed before use. Trim away the stem end with a sharp knife, trim off the roots, but do not remove the root base entirely as this helps to hold the onion intact for slicing and chopping; afterwards discard.

To slice, lay a halved onion cut-side down on a board or surface and make a series of close vertical cuts, starting at the neck end. To chop, lay a halved onion cut-side down on a board or surface and make a series of close cuts as before and then again crossways.

Clean spring onions by washing, then trimming the tops of the stems and trimming away the root. Peel away the thin, outer layer of skin if liked.

If the aroma of onions worries you then always prepare them immersed in water or use rubber gloves. Rinse hands in soapy water after preparation.

All onions can be eaten raw or cooked, but we tend to use them mainly as a pot-herb or flavouring which is invaluable in soups, sauces and stocks. You can however use onions as a vegetable in their own right to add texture and flavour to salads, soups, casseroles, gratins and quiches. Onions are also good as an accompanying vegetable to a main dish, glazed, stewed, braised, stuffed, fried or puréed. Onions also make delicious pickles.

Shallots are ideal for use in delicately-flavoured sauces such as béarnaise. Red onions are delicious in salads, where their colour adds variety. Spanish onions are best for stuffing, and make a good vegetable dish on their own. Pearl onions are the ideal choice for pickling but they can also be used whole in casseroles. Spring onions are suitable for salads and dips.

Nutritional value: Onions contain phosphorus, calcium, a little sodium, Vitamins A and C. They provide 23 Calories (98 kj) per 100 g/$3\frac{1}{2}$ oz.

SPANISH ONION

SPRING ONIONS

RED-SKINNED ONION

YELLOW ONION

French Onion Soup

3 tablespoons olive oil
500 g/1 lb onions, thinly sliced
1 tablespoon plain flour
1.2 litres/2 pints beef stock
1 bouquet garni
salt
freshly ground black pepper
4–5 slices French bread, 1 cm/½ inch
   thick
50 g/2 oz Gruyère cheese, grated

Heat the oil in a large saucepan, add the onions and fry gently, stirring occasionally, for 10 to 15 minutes until golden. Stir in the flour, then gradually add the stock, stirring constantly. Add the bouquet garni and salt and pepper to taste. Cover and simmer for about 30 minutes.

Toast the French bread slices lightly on both sides.

Ladle the soup into individual marmites or flameproof soup bowls and place a piece of toast on each one. Sprinkle with the cheese and place under a preheated hot grill until golden brown and bubbling.
Serves 4 to 5

Vichyssoise

15 g/½ oz butter
625 g/1¼ lb leeks, trimmed, rinsed and
   cut into thick rings
325 g/11 oz floury potatoes, peeled and
   diced
1 ham bone (optional)
1 parsley sprig, chopped
1 litre/1¾ pints chicken stock
300 ml/½ pint milk
pinch of grated nutmeg
pinch of cayenne pepper
salt
150 ml/¼ pint whipping cream
snipped chives to garnish

Melt the butter in a large pan. Add the leeks and cook for about 5 minutes. Add the potatoes, ham bone if using, parsley and stock. Bring to the boil, reduce the heat and simmer for about 30 minutes until the vegetables are tender.

Remove the ham bone with a slotted spoon, if using. Strain the soup into another pan and pass the vegetables through a sieve into the soup. Alternatively, purée the soup in an electric blender or food processor until smooth then return to the pan.

Return to the heat, stir in the milk and bring to the boil. Season with the nutmeg, cayenne pepper and salt to taste. Whip the cream lightly and fold into the soup. Garnish with snipped chives to serve.
Serves 4

NOTE: Vichyssoise is a classic French soup which can be served either hot or chilled.

Garlic and Tomato Soup

6 tablespoons olive oil
4 cloves garlic, peeled and crushed or
   finely chopped
6–8 ripe tomatoes, skinned and chopped
600 ml/1 pint chicken stock
salt
freshly ground black pepper
basil leaves or parsley sprigs to garnish

Heat the oil in a large pan, add the garlic and fry gently until golden. Add the chopped tomatoes and cook gently for about 15 minutes until softened.

Add the stock, bring to the boil, lower the heat and cook for 3 to 4 minutes. Season with salt and pepper to taste.

Ladle the soup into warmed soup plates or bowls and serve immediately, garnished with basil or parsley.
Serves 4

NOTE: Serve this delicious Mediterranean soup with crusty French bread and a glass of full-bodied red wine.

Onion Fritters with Savoury Dip

6 tablespoons plain flour
salt
1 egg, beaten
150 ml/¼ pint beer
oil for deep frying
2 Spanish onions, peeled and thinly
   sliced
SAUCE:
1 × 150 g/5.2 oz carton natural yogurt
1 parsley sprig, chopped
1 teaspoon horseradish cream or relish
pinch of sugar

Sift the flour and salt into a bowl. Make a well in the centre and add the egg. Gradually draw the flour into the egg, adding the beer a little at a time, beating to make a smooth batter. Leave to stand for about 15 minutes.

Meanwhile, prepare the sauce. Place the yogurt in a bowl, add the parsley, horseradish and sugar and beat until thoroughly blended.

Heat the oil in a deep pan or deep fryer until hot, about 190°C/375°F. Working in batches, dip the onion slices into the batter, lower into the oil and fry until crisp and golden brown. Drain the fritters on absorbent kitchen paper and keep warm while cooking the remainder.

Serve the onion fritters immediately, either plain with the sauce handed separately, or with a dot of sauce on each fritter.
Serves 4

NOTE: Onion fritters make an excellent hors d'oeuvre or a substantial snack.

Garlic and tomato soup; French onion soup;
Vichyssoise

Spring Onion and Mushroom Salad

1 bunch spring onions
1 orange
1 red pepper, cored, seeded and cut into
    strips
125 g/4 oz button mushrooms, halved
3 tablespoons dry white wine
1 tablespoon snipped chives
120 ml/4 fl oz soured cream
salt
freshly ground black pepper

Trim the roots from the spring onions and cut both the white and green stems into fine rings. Place in a sieve, rinse and drain thoroughly.

Peel and segment the orange, removing all pith. Mix the spring onions with the orange segments, pepper strips and mushrooms in a serving bowl.

To make the dressing, beat the white wine with the chives, soured cream and salt and pepper to taste. Pour over the salad and toss well to mix.

Leave the salad to stand for about 30 minutes before serving to allow the flavours to develop.
Serves 4

NOTE: Serve in individual dishes with buttered toast as an unusual light starter or side salad.

Red Onion and Salami Salad

4 red onions, peeled
150 g/5 oz German Cervelat
125 g/4 oz Bel Paese, rind removed
1 × 198 g/7 oz can sweetcorn kernels,
    drained
2 tablespoons red wine vinegar
1 clove garlic, peeled and crushed with
    ¼ teaspoon salt
pinch of sugar
freshly ground black pepper
2 teaspoons chopped parsley (optional)
4 tablespoons oil

Chop the red onions or slice them into thin rings. Cut the Cervelat and Bel Paese into strips. Mix the onion with the sweetcorn, Cervelat and Bel Paese in a salad bowl.

To make the dressing, beat the vinegar with the garlic, sugar and pepper to taste, and the parsley if using, then beat in the oil.

Pour the dressing over the salad and toss well to mix. Leave the salad to stand for about 20 minutes before serving to allow the ingredients to absorb the flavour of the dressing.
Serves 4

NOTE: Served with wholemeal rolls or crusty French bread, this salad makes a tasty light lunch or supper dish.

Any other smooth-textured salami can be used in place of Cervelat.

King prawns 'don quixote'; Red onion and salami salad; Spring onion and mushroom salad

King Prawns 'Don Quixote'

16–24 cooked shelled king prawns
2–3 teaspoons lemon juice
12 tablespoons olive oil
4 cloves garlic, peeled and crushed
1 bay leaf
3 peppercorns
pinch of sugar
dash of Tabasco
1 tablespoon chopped parsley

Sprinkle the prawns with the lemon juice.

Heat the oil in a frying pan, add the prawns, garlic, bay leaf, peppercorns and sugar and fry for 4 to 5 minutes, stirring occasionally, until heated through. Remove the bay leaf and peppercorns from the pan, then stir in the Tabasco and parsley. Serve hot.
Serves 4

NOTE: Arrange this hors d'oeuvre in individual dishes and garnish with parsley sprigs if liked. Serve with French bread and a full-bodied white or rosé wine, or Spanish-style with a dry sherry.

Frankish Onion Flan

400 g/14 oz plain flour
40 g/1½ oz fresh yeast
scant 250 ml/8 fl oz lukewarm milk
1 teaspoon sugar
1 egg, beaten
pinch of salt
75 g/3 oz butter or lard
FILLING:
40 g/1½ oz butter
125 g/4 oz streaky bacon, derinded and chopped
875 g/1¾ lb onions, peeled and chopped
1 tablespoon caraway seeds (optional)
1 teaspoon salt
freshly ground white pepper
2 eggs
150 ml/¼ pint soured cream

Sift the flour into a mixing bowl, make a well in the centre and crumble the yeast into the well. Cream the yeast with a little of the milk, the sugar and a little of the flour from the edge of the bowl until smooth. Cover the bowl and leave to stand in a warm place for about 10 minutes.

Mix the yeast mixture with the egg, salt, fat, remaining milk and the remaining flour in the bowl. Beat the dough until it leaves the sides of the bowl clean. Cover and leave to rise in a warm place for 30 minutes, or until doubled in size.

Meanwhile, prepare the filling: Melt the butter in a pan, add the bacon and

fry gently for about 5 minutes. Add the onion and cook without browning, over a low heat, for about 15 minutes. Add the caraway seeds if using, and season with salt and pepper to taste. Beat the eggs with the soured cream and fold into the onion mixture. Allow to cool.

Roll out the risen dough on a lightly floured surface to a round large enough to line the base and sides of a greased 23 cm/9 inch round flan tin. Fill the flan with the onion mixture. Cook in a preheated hot oven (220°C/425°F, Gas Mark 7) for about 35 minutes until golden and firm.

Serve hot or cold.
Serves 4 to 6

Fish Fillets with Onions and Herb Butter

4 haddock or plaice fillets, each
    weighing about 150 g/5 oz
juice of 1 lemon
salt
freshly ground white pepper
pinch of dried rosemary
pinch of ground coriander
1 tablespoon made mustard
4 onions, peeled and sliced
50 g/2 oz butter
1–2 teaspoons chopped parsley
1 teaspoon chopped dill

Sprinkle the fish with the lemon juice and leave to stand for a few minutes. Place each fish fillet on a large piece of greased foil and season both sides with salt and pepper, rosemary and coriander to taste. Spread the top of each fillet thinly with mustard and cover with the onion slices.

Melt the butter in a pan, add the parsley and dill if using, mixing well. Spoon the melted herb butter over the fish fillets. Fold the foil over the fish to enclose completely and pinch the edges to seal.

Cook in a preheated moderately hot oven (200°C/400°F, Gas Mark 6) for about 20 minutes or until tender. Serve immediately.
Serves 4

NOTE: Garnish this light and flavoursome fish dish with lemon slices and dill sprigs if liked. Serve with herb-flavoured potatoes and courgettes.

Cod in Garlic Marinade

4 cod cutlets, each weighing about
    175 g/6 oz
2 teaspoons lemon juice
salt
freshly ground black pepper
3 cloves garlic, peeled and crushed with
    $\frac{1}{4}$ teaspoon salt
4–5 tablespoons oil
25 g/1 oz butter
1 tablespoon chopped parsley

Rinse the cod and pat dry with absorbent kitchen paper. Sprinkle with the lemon juice and leave to stand for about 15 minutes.

Season the fish on both sides with salt and pepper to taste. Mix the garlic with the oil. Dip the fish cutlets into the garlic marinade and then place in an ovenproof dish. Dot with the butter.

Either grill for 3 minutes on each side under a preheated hot grill or cook in a preheated moderately hot oven (200°C/400°F, Gas Mark 6) for 15 to 20 minutes, basting occasionally with the marinade. Sprinkle with the parsley and serve from the cooking dish.
Serves 4

ABOVE: *Fish fillets with onions and herb butter;
Cod in garlic marinade*
RIGHT: *Stuffed spanish onions; Garlic spaghetti
with capers*

Garlic Spaghetti with Capers

275 g/9 oz spaghetti
salt
2 tablespoons olive oil
3 cloves garlic, peeled and lightly
    crushed
25 g/1 oz butter
2–3 tablespoons capers
2 teaspoons chopped basil

Cook the spaghetti in boiling salted water until just tender, according to the packet instructions.

Meanwhile, heat the oil and garlic in a frying pan and fry until the garlic is golden. Add the butter and heat until melted. Remove from the heat and add the capers and salt to taste.

Drain the spaghetti and place in a large warmed serving dish. Stir in the garlic and caper sauce, with the basil. Toss well and serve immediately.
Serves 4

NOTE: Garlic Spaghetti is delicious as a side dish to roast veal or Wiener Schnitzel but it can be served as a main dish if you increase the quantities.

Stuffed Spanish Onions

2 large Spanish onions, peeled and
    halved
salt
25 g/1 oz butter
125 g/4 oz smoked bacon, derinded and
    chopped
3 tomatoes, skinned and chopped
125 g/4 oz button mushrooms, sliced
1 tablespoon chopped parsley
2 tablespoons grated Parmesan cheese
freshly ground black pepper
1–2 teaspoons dried oregano

Scoop a hollow in the centre of each onion half with a teaspoon, reserving the scooped out onion. Place the halves in a pan, cover with water. Add a little salt, bring to the boil and cook for about 15 minutes, until almost tender. Drain well.

Meanwhile, chop the reserved onion. Melt half of the butter in a pan and fry the bacon and onion for 4 to 5 minutes. Add the tomatoes and mushrooms and cook for a further 2 to 3 minutes.

Remove the pan from the heat, stir in the parsley and cheese and season to taste with salt, pepper and oregano.

Fill the onion halves with this mixture and dot with the remaining butter. Place in a greased ovenproof dish. Cook in a preheated hot oven (220°C/425°F, Gas Mark 7) for 12 to 15 minutes.
Serves 4

NOTE: Stuffed Onions are delicious served hot with a salad and toast.

Carp with Leek Butter

1 carp, weighing 1–1.25 kg/2–2½ lb,
  gutted, scaled and cleaned
salt
freshly ground white pepper
65 g/2½ oz butter
2–3 leeks
2 teaspoons mixed chopped fresh herbs
  (chives, parsley, thyme)
pinch of ground allspice

Soak the carp in lightly salted water for 3 to 4 hours. Rinse thoroughly and dry with absorbent kitchen paper. Season inside and out with salt and pepper.

Trim away the root end and green leaves from the leeks and discard. Cut the white leek into thin rings. Rinse and drain thoroughly. Melt half the butter in a frying pan, add the leeks and herbs and cook for 2 to 3 minutes. Season to taste with salt and allspice. Allow to cool slightly.

Stuff the carp with this mixture and place in a greased ovenproof dish. Melt the remaining butter and brush over the fish. Cook in a preheated moderate oven (180°C/350°F, Gas Mark 4) for about 40 minutes, turning the fish over twice during the cooking time. Serve the carp from the baking dish.
Serves 4

NOTE: Serve this dish with buttered potatoes and horseradish cream.

Rump Steak with Onion Purée

4 rump steaks
freshly ground black pepper
paprika
4–5 tablespoons olive oil
salt
50 g/2 oz Emmenthal cheese, grated
ONION PURÉE:
200 g/7 oz shallots or small onions,
  peeled and chopped
120 ml/4 fl oz dry white wine
15 g/½ oz butter
TO GARNISH:
parsley sprigs

First prepare the onion purée: Place the shallots or onions and white wine in a small pan over a low heat for about 10 minutes. Stir in the butter and season with pepper to taste. Pass through a fine sieve or purée in an electric blender or food processor until smooth.

Season the rump steaks on both sides with pepper and paprika to taste. Heat the olive oil in a large frying pan and fry the steaks for 3 minutes each side. Season with a little salt.

Place the steaks on a large piece of

foil and spread each evenly with onion purée. Sprinkle with the cheese and place under a preheated hot grill until the cheese is bubbling, about 3 to 4 minutes. Serve immediately, garnished with parsley.
Serves 4

NOTE: Rump Steak with Onion Purée is delicious served with a Gratin Dauphinois (see page 58) and broccoli, or herb-flavoured long-grain rice and a mixed salad.

Leeks au Gratin

1 kg/2 lb leeks
15 g/½ oz butter
1 clove garlic, peeled and halved
300 ml/½ pint milk
pinch of grated nutmeg
½ teaspoon dried tarragon
salt
freshly ground white pepper
150 ml/¼ pint double cream
125 g/4 oz Emmenthal cheese, grated

Trim away the root end and any thick dark green leaves from the leeks and discard. Cut the leeks into rings about 1–2 cm/½–¾ inch thick. Rinse and drain thoroughly. Place in an ovenproof dish.

Heat the butter and garlic in a small pan and fry until the garlic is golden. Remove the garlic from the pan with a slotted spoon and discard. Pour the butter over the leeks.

Heat the milk with the nutmeg, tarragon and salt and pepper to taste, until almost boiling. Stir in the cream and pour over the leeks. Cover the dish

tightly with greased foil and cook in a preheated moderate oven (180°C/350°F, Gas Mark 4) for 20 minutes.

Remove the foil and sprinkle with the cheese. Increase the oven temperature to hot (200°C/400°F, Gas Mark 6) and bake for a further 15 to 20 minutes until the cheese is golden and bubbling.
Serves 6

NOTE: Leeks au Gratin can be served as a main course with jacket potatoes or as a filling vegetable dish with fish or fried calf's liver.

Pickled Cocktail Onions

750 g/1½ lb cocktail or pickling onions,
  peeled
300 ml/½ pint white wine vinegar
300 ml/½ pint water
2–3 tablespoons sugar
3 bay leaves
10 peppercorns
1 teaspoon mustard seeds
pinch of ground allspice
pinch of dried dill seeds

Place the onions in a tall sterilized heatproof preserving jar. Bring all the remaining ingredients to the boil in a large pan and pour over the onions to cover completely.

Seal the jar with vinegar-proof preserving paper and leave to stand for 4 to 5 days, making sure that the onions are completely covered by the liquid.

Drain the liquid back into a pan, bring to the boil and pour back over the

onions. Allow to cool. To seal the jar tightly, pour in 1 cm/½ inch depth of paraffin wax and leave to set. When the pickle is required, remove the wax.

Serve these cocktail onions with cold meats and cheese platters.
Makes about 750 g/1½ lb

Rump steak with onion purée, served with gratin Dauphinois; Leeks au gratin

BRASSICAS

Consider the button-sized Brussels sprout alongside the Savoy cabbage,
a delicate broccoli stem with a flowery white cauliflower sprig and the
feathery-like curly kale next to the long, straight Chinese cabbage, and
it seems hard to believe that all these Brassicas descended from the basic green
cabbage. So diverse in flavour and appearance, yet closely related, the brassica
family is therefore a challenge to any cook.

Dishes featuring brassicas are just as different in taste, complexity and appearance, as
the basic vegetables themselves. Favourites include Sauerkraut, Brussels sprouts
with chestnuts, Coleslaw, Cauliflower cheese, Red cabbage and apple and
Cauliflower polonaise. Mix and match them with unusual vegetable dishes
like Cauliflower fritters and Chinese cabbage in hot sauce and you'll
have recipes to suit all occasions from the simple to
the sumptuous and grand.

BROCCOLI

Origin: Broccoli (*Brassica oleracea* var. *italica*) is related to the cauliflower. The ancient Romans originally brought it to Europe from Asia Minor in its wild form. Today it is eaten throughout the world.

There are several varieties: white or purple sprouting broccoli, the latter having a distinct purple head with dark green leaves; green broccoli, which has long, green fleshy stalks and compact green florets which form a dense head like a cauliflower; and calabrese, a kind of green sprouting broccoli that produces individual loose spears. All have a delicate, aromatic flavour.

Availability: Sprouting broccoli is in season from late winter to early May while calabrese is in season during the summer months. With imports this means that broccoli is available nearly all year round. It is grown extensively in Italy, France and Spain. Britain boosts its own production with imports mainly from France and Spain.

Buying: Choose broccoli where the spears and heads are firm and bright in colour. Reject any that are limp or showing any signs of age. Most broccoli is sold by weight, but occasionally can be bought per head. Frozen broccoli is also available for convenient use.

Preparation and serving: Always cook broccoli even before use in a salad. Trim away any coarse outer leaves and trim the stems. Place in a sieve, rinse and drain thoroughly. Cook in boiling salted water for 8 to 10 minutes, according to the size of the stems. Drain and serve with melted butter or a hollandaise or cheese sauce.

Broccoli is delicious in salads, soups and as a vegetable accompaniment to most meats, fish and game.

Nutritional value: Broccoli is particularly rich in Vitamin C. It also contains Vitamin A, calcium, iron and potassium. Low in calories, cooked broccoli has only 18 Calories (78 kj) per 100 g/3½ oz.

BRUSSELS SPROUTS

Origin: Brussels sprouts (*Brassica oleracea* var. *gemmifera*) are a member of the Cruciferae family. They supposedly originated first in Belgium, near Brussels, hence their name, and they may have been raised as early as the 17th century.

There are many varieties of Brussels sprouts, even one with red sprouts. All grow on tall, woody stems. The sprouts, which vary in size from one variety to another, cluster thickly on the stems in tight small buds.

CALABRESE

PURPLE SPROUTING BROCCOLI

BRUSSELS SPROUTS

Availability: Brussels sprouts are in season from about September to April. They are grown extensively in Britain, Holland and, of course, Belgium.

Buying: Brussels sprouts are usually sold by weight, although occasionally they can be bought on the stem, holding up to some 50 buds or sprouts.

Choose Brussels sprouts with tight, firm buds, a bright green colour and fresh appearance. Reject any that show any signs of age or have a strong odour.

Preparation and serving: Remove and discard any coarse outer leaves and cut away any excess stalk. Place in a sieve, rinse and drain thoroughly. There is no need to cut a cross in the stalk base before cooking. Cook in boiling salted water for about 8 to 10 minutes. Drain and serve with melted butter or a savoury sauce.

Brussels sprouts also make tasty gratin dishes with ham, cheese or bacon. They are also good made into a soup, or creamed and cooked with nuts.

Nutritional value: Brussels sprouts are an excellent source of Vitamin C. They also supply Vitamin A and calcium. Cooked sprouts contain about 16 Calories (67 kj) per 100 g/3½ oz.

CABBAGE

Origin: The cabbage (*Brassica oleracea* var. *capitata*) is a member of the Cruciferae family. It was known as far back as ancient Roman times, and throughout its long history cabbage has been thought of as food for the poor.

Fermented cabbage, a kind of sauerkraut, was also known in ancient Rome. During the great age of exploration it was an essential sailor's provision, and a remedy for scurvy.

Cabbages are generally classed according to season: spring, summer, autumn and winter, but also according to type: semi-hearted, green-hearted, hard white, and red.

Spring cabbage has smooth dark green leaves that are loose or small-hearted. Green-hearted cabbages may have round or conical hearts; this includes the Savoy, with thick, dark green, crinkly leaves (see page 80). Hard white cabbages include the Dutch and Winter White. Spring greens are young cabbages with no hearts and a delicate flavour. Red cabbage is, as the name suggests, dark red or crimson in colour, and has a dense heart (see page 79). Chinese cabbage is yet another variety (see page 81).

Availability: Cabbage is available all year round according to variety. It is grown in all European countries, including Britain. Large quantities of cabbage are grown in Alsace, where most of the harvest is made into sauerkraut. A great deal of sauerkraut is exported from Alsace and from Italy.

Buying: Choose cabbage with firm heads or leaves, a bright colour and fresh appearance. Avoid any with wilted leaves or puffy appearance. Cabbages are sold whole and by weight depending upon variety. You will need one small white cabbage to serve 4.

Preparation and serving: Prepare by removing the coarse outer leaves, any coarse, thick stems and the central core, if any. Quarter, shred or slice as liked, place in a sieve, rinse and drain. Cook shredded cabbage in a little boiling salted water for 5 to 7 minutes, and wedges or quarters for about 12 minutes.

There are countless ways of serving cabbage: as a plain vegetable accompaniment to roast meats, tossed in a savoury sauce, in soups, in casserole dishes or stuffed. Raw cabbage is also delicious in salads. White cabbage is excellent stuffed, baked or served as a gratin dish.

Sauerkraut is perhaps one of the most famous cabbage dishes, eaten extensively in France, Italy and Germany. In those countries it is available fresh as well as canned. In Britain we generally only see the canned variety. Reheat canned sauerkraut according to the manufacturer's instructions.

Every country seems to boast its own famous or classic cabbage dish: the Alsatians are famous for their choucroûte, a kind of sauerkraut eaten with smoked meat and sausages; the Yugoslavians eat tasty stuffed white cabbage rolls called sarmi; and white cabbage cooked with pork and topped with soured cream is popular in Hungary.

Nutritional value: Cabbage contains plenty of calcium, sodium, iron and phosphorus. It has a good deal of Vitamin C, a little Vitamin B_1 and B_2 and a little Vitamin D. Fresh cabbage contains 20 Calories (85 kj) per 100 g/$3\frac{1}{2}$ oz.

CABBAGE, RED

Origin: Red cabbage (*Brassica oleracea* var. *capitata*) is a member of the Cruciferae family and a result of brassica cross-breeding. True to its name, it is dark red to crimson in colour and has a solid heart of crisp leaves. It is popular in Holland, Denmark, Switzerland and Britain, where it is often pickled.

Availability: Red cabbage is mainly an autumn to winter vegetable in season from September to May. It is grown extensively as a field crop rather than as a garden vegetable in Britain and many other northern European countries.

Buying: Red cabbage is usually sold by weight. Choose heads that are crisp, bright in colour and fresh in appearance. Bottled red cabbage, often pickled, is also available for convenient use.

Preparation and serving: Remove and discard the coarse outer leaves and shred or cut into quarters. Place in a sieve, rinse and drain thoroughly. Cook briefly in a little fat or oil then simmer in stock, apple juice or water flavoured with a little vinegar. Cooking times will vary from 20 to 40 minutes. A bay leaf, a few cloves and a pinch of nutmeg may also be added to give extra flavour.

Red cabbage is delicious with apple slices, pineapple pieces or a few nuts. It is also tasty cooked with ground ginger. It goes particularly well with game, sausages, roast goose or duck. It may also be eaten as a salad vegetable if tossed in a spicy dressing. You will need 1 medium red cabbage to serve 4.

Nutritional value: Red cabbage is rich in calcium, phosphorus and Vitamin C. Low in calories it contains only 20 Calories (86 kj) per 100 g/$3\frac{1}{2}$ oz.

SPRING CABBAGE

RED CABBAGE

WHITE CABBAGE

SAVOY CABBAGE

CAULIFLOWER

CABBAGE, SAVOY

Origin: The Savoy cabbage (*Brassica oleracea* var. *bullata*) is a member of the Cruciferae family. It is a dark green, curly-leafed cabbage, popular throughout northern Europe. It is a very hardy winter vegetable that will withstand many of the severest frosts.

There are a number of varieties, early and late cropping, with differently shaped heads, with either more or less curly leaves, and tighter or looser hearts. Some are dark green, almost blue, while others are lighter. They can weigh from 750 g to 3 kg/1½ to 7 lb.

Availability: Savoy cabbages are in season from September to May. They are grown extensively in Britain and northern Europe.

Buying: Savoy cabbages are usually sold by weight. Choose heads that are solid and compact with crispy green leaves and a fresh appearance.

Preparation and serving: Remove any coarse outer leaves and thick stems. Quarter the cabbage head or shred coarsely. Place in a sieve, rinse and drain thoroughly. This may need several water changes to ensure that all dirt and grit is removed. Savoy cabbage can then be braised, steamed or plain boiled. Braise with bacon, pork dripping or goose fat. If you have a Savoy cabbage with large leaves you can also make delicious stuffed cabbage rolls. Stuff with a savoury meat or cooked rice mixture and braise in stock. Ideal seasonings for Savoy cabbages include grated nutmeg, caraway seeds, cloves and ground coriander.

Nutritional value: Savoy cabbage is useful for its rich supply of Vitamin C and calcium. Low in calories it contains 24 Calories (102 kj) per 100 g/3½ oz.

CAULIFLOWER

Origin: The cauliflower (*Brassica oleracea* var. *botrytis*) is a member of the Cruciferae family. It was first cultivated in the Middle East but known in Europe by the 13th century. It's dense white head gave the plant its Old English name – coleflower or cabbage flower.

Availability: Fresh cauliflower can be bought almost all year round but is best in season during the autumn months, and May and June. Britain boosts its own excellent supply with imports from France.

Buying: Cauliflowers are sold individually or sometimes conveniently prepacked as florets. Frozen cauliflower is also available; frozen as florets.

Look for fresh cauliflowers with compact white heads and green, fresh-looking leaves, if any. Avoid and reject any that have loose or spread out heads – they are a sure sign of overmaturity.

Preparation and serving: Cauliflower is delicious cooked whole. Remove and discard the stalk and outer leaves. Boil in water for 15 to 20 minutes, turning the cauliflower once during the cooking time. To remove the last trace of bitterness, cook the cauliflower in water to which 2 to 3 tablespoons of cream or milk, a knob of butter and a small pinch of sugar have been added.

Cauliflower is often divided into florets for cooking, especially for salads, gratin dishes and soups. Cook in boiling salted water for 8 to 10 minutes. Serve cooked cauliflower with melted butter, a white sauce, as cauliflower cheese or with fried breadcrumbs.

One of the best known cauliflower dishes is Choufleur à la Polonaise, where the cauliflower head is boiled in water and then topped with melted butter, chopped parsley, breadcrumbs and chopped hard-boiled egg.

Cooked cauliflower makes a delicious vegetable accompaniment to almost any meal but it is also a good raw vegetable to serve with dips.

Nutritional value: Cauliflower is not quite so rich in vitamins and minerals as some of its relatives, but it contains valuable amounts of phosphorus, calcium and sodium, and Vitamins A and C. Cauliflower contains only 13 Calories (56 kj) per 100 g/3½ oz.

CHINESE CABBAGE

Origin: Chinese cabbage (*Brassica pekinensis*) is a member of the Cruciferae family. It originated in Eastern Asia many centuries ago.

It is also known as Chinese leaf, Nappa cabbage and celery cabbage, the latter because it looks like a cross between a romaine lettuce and celery. Sometimes it is sold under its oriental names: pe-tsai in Chinese and hakusai in Japanese.

Visually the Chinese cabbage forms an erect, nearly cylindrical head which is white at the base and pale green at the top. The leaves are green and crinkly, like a Savoy cabbage. They are however, tender and very delicate in flavour. They vary in size from 200 g to 1 kg/7 oz to 2 lb.

Availability: Home-grown Chinese cabbage is in season from early autumn to winter, but imported supplies from Israel ensure a supply all year round.

Buying: Chinese cabbage is generally sold by the head or half head but is often also sold by weight. Choose heads that are crisp, bright in colour and fresh in appearance.

Preparation and serving: Chinese cabbage is very easy to prepare. You can divide the head into leaves, or shred them into strips or large pieces as liked. Place them in a sieve, rinse and drain thoroughly. Use in salads or as a cooked vegetable.

The whole head can be boiled and it only takes 8 to 12 minutes, according to size. Boil in salted water or light stock.

In Chinese cuisine, where it features highly, it is used in soups, braised with meat and steamed with fish.

Nutritional value: Chinese cabbage is rich in Vitamin C. It is ideal for slimmers since it only contains 16 Calories (70 kj) per 100 g/3½ oz.

CHINESE CABBAGE

CURLY KALE

KALE

Origin: Kale (*Brassica oleracea* var. *acephala*) is a member of the Cruciferae family. Kale and its relative collard, are closely related members of the cabbage family. They probably originated in the eastern Mediterranean, where they have been cultivated for more than 2000 years. Kale is a popular vegetable in Scotland, northern Germany and Denmark.

There are two basic varieties of kale: the flat-leaf variety; and the curly-leaf variety, which is more popular. Both have aromatic leaves with a bitter-sweet taste.

Availability: Fresh kale is available throughout the winter months, from December to April. It is grown extensively in northern England, Scotland and many parts of northern Europe.

Buying: Kale is generally sold by weight. Choose leaves that are crisp, bright in colour and fresh in appearance. Allow about 1 kg/2 lb kale for 4 people. Frozen kale is also available for convenient use.

Preparation and serving: Experts say that kale should have been subjected to the first frosts of winter before it tastes good. This is because the frost helps to change the starch into sugar.

Kale can be cooked as a vegetable accompaniment or used in a salad. To use in a salad, cut the fresh kale into strips or shred coarsely. Place in a sieve, rinse and drain thoroughly. Toss in a spicy dressing. To serve as a vegetable, remove the thick stalks, shred coarsely and simmer in boiling salted water for 10 minutes. The kale can then be fried with onions and then braised in stock for up to 1 hour, if liked.

Kale is thought of as plain and hearty fare. It can be served in sophisticated cream sauces if liked but it tastes much better and more authentic if served plain with bacon, fatty meats or spicy sausages.

Nutritional value: Kale is considered one of the more nutritious of the brassicas. It has a good supply of Vitamins A and C, calcium, phosphorus and a little protein. It contains only 23 Calories (96 kj) per 100 g/3½ oz.

Cabbage and Smoked Sausage Broth

1 kg/2 lb green cabbage
25 g/1 oz lard
25 g/1 oz streaky bacon, derinded and
    chopped
1 onion, peeled and chopped
600 ml/1 pint meat stock
pinch of freshly ground black pepper
pinch of grated nutmeg
pinch of sugar
1 piece polony, weighing 150–200 g/
    5–7 oz

Remove the thick stems from the cabbage and chop roughly. Place the cabbage in a pan with just enough water to cover. Bring to the boil, then lower the heat and cook for 5 minutes. Drain thoroughly.

Melt the lard in a large pan, add the bacon and cabbage and cook for about 3 minutes. Add the onion, stock, pepper, nutmeg and sugar. Cover and simmer, over a low heat, for about 10 minutes. Add the polony and cook for a further 10 minutes.

To serve, remove the polony with a slotted spoon and slice thickly. Stir into the cabbage broth to serve.
Serves 4 to 6

NOTE: Serve with boiled potatoes.
Polony, also called Bologna sausage, is basically a mixture of cooked smoked pork and beef.

Cauliflower and Ham Soup

1 small or ½ large cauliflower, cut into
    tiny florets
600 ml/1 pint meat stock
300 ml/½ pint milk
pinch of grated nutmeg
salt
15 g/½ oz butter
1 tablespoon plain flour
1 egg yolk
2 tablespoons double cream
125 g/4 oz cooked ham, cut into strips
finely chopped parsley or dill, to
    garnish

Place the cauliflower, stock, milk, nutmeg and a little salt in a pan. Bring to the boil, lower the heat and cook for 15 minutes. Drain, reserving the stock.

Meanwhile, melt the butter in a pan. Add the flour and cook for 2 to 3 minutes. Gradually add the cauliflower stock, blending well. Beat the egg yolk with the cream, remove the pan from the heat and stir the mixture into the soup. Add the cauliflower florets and ham and cook gently for a further 4 to 5 minutes; do not allow to boil. Sprinkle with the parsley or dill before serving. **Serves 4**

Savoy Cabbage Broth

15 g/½ oz lard
25 g/1 oz streaky bacon, chopped
1 small onion, peeled and chopped
750 g/1½ lb Savoy cabbage
750 g/1½ lb potatoes, peeled
150 g/5 oz Cracow or other smoked
    coarse-textured sausage, sliced
600 ml/1 pint meat stock
salt
freshly ground black pepper
1 tablespoon chopped herbs (parsley,
    thyme, sage)

Melt the lard in a large pan, add the bacon and the onion and cook for about 7 to 8 minutes. Meanwhile, shred the cabbage, and chop the potatoes. Add the cabbage and potatoes to the pan with the sausage, stock, salt and pepper to taste. Cover and simmer, over a low heat, for about 30 minutes. Add the herbs at the end of the cooking time, blending well. Serve immediately. **Serves 4 to 6**

Brussels Sprout Soup

20 g/¾ oz butter
25 g/1 oz bacon, derinded and chopped
1 tablespoon flour
750 ml/1¼ pints meat stock
625 g/1¼ lb Brussels sprouts, trimmed
pinch of grated nutmeg
dash of Madeira or dry sherry
salt and freshly ground black pepper

Cauliflower and ham soup; Brussels sprout soup; Savoy cabbage broth

Melt the butter in a pan, add the bacon and fry until crisp. Add the flour and cook for 2 to 3 minutes. Gradually add the stock, blending well after each addition. Add the Brussels sprouts, cover and simmer, over a low heat, for 20 to 25 minutes.

Season and flavour the soup with the nutmeg and Madeira or sherry, stirring well. Season with salt and pepper to taste before serving. **Serves 4 to 6**

Pork and Cabbage Broth

15 g/½ oz lard
1 onion, peeled and chopped
1 carrot, peeled and chopped
625 g/1¼ lb pork, diced
1 small white cabbage, shredded
600 ml/1 pint meat stock
dash of vinegar
1 teaspoon paprika
salt and freshly ground black pepper
1 teaspoon cornflour
120 ml/4 fl oz soured cream

Melt the lard in a large pan. Add the onion, carrot and pork and cook, over a low heat, for about 10 minutes. Add the cabbage and stock, cover and simmer, over a low heat, for about 20 to 30 minutes.

Stir in the vinegar, paprika, and salt and pepper to taste. Blend the cornflour with a little water to make a thin paste; stir into the broth with the soured cream. Simmer for a further 2 minutes, stirring constantly, to allow the broth to thicken.

Spoon into individual warmed soup bowls to serve. **Serves 4 to 6**

NOTE: Serve Pork and Cabbage Broth with brown bread or boiled potatoes. Sprinkle a generous amount of chopped parsley or dill over the soup just before serving.

Cabbage with Soured Cream Dressing

325 g/11 oz green cabbage
2 tablespoons red wine vinegar
4 tablespoons oil
½ small onion, peeled and chopped
1 anchovy fillet, chopped
1 teaspoon lemon juice
1 tablespoon snipped chives
120 ml/4 fl oz soured cream
salt
freshly ground black pepper
TO GARNISH:
hard-boiled egg wedges
few gherkins (optional)
parsley sprigs

Remove the thick stems from the cabbage and cut the leaves into small pieces. Place the leaves in a sieve, rinse and drain thoroughly. Transfer to a serving bowl. Beat the vinegar with the oil, pour over the cabbage and toss to mix. Cover and chill for 1 to 1½ hours.

To make the dressing, mix the onion with the anchovy fillet, lemon juice, chives, soured cream, and salt and pepper to taste.

Pour the dressing over the marinated cabbage and toss well to mix. Arrange the hard-boiled egg and gherkins, if using, on top. Garnish with parsley.
Serves 4 to 6

Chinese Cabbage and Tomato Salad

1 small Chinese cabbage, shredded
275 g/9 oz tomatoes, cut into wedges
2 tablespoons coarsely chopped parsley
juice of 1 lemon
salt
freshly ground black pepper
2–3 tablespoons oil
120 ml/4 fl oz soured cream

Combine the Chinese cabbage, tomatoes and parsley in a serving bowl.

To make the dressing, beat the lemon juice with salt and pepper to taste and the oil. Stir into the soured cream.

Pour the dressing over the salad and toss well to mix. Serve immediately.
Serves 4 to 6

NOTE: Chinese Cabbage and Tomato Salad is delicious with fish or poultry.

Coleslaw

250 g/8 oz firm white cabbage, finely
    shredded
3 sticks celery, sliced
3 red-skinned apples, cored and thinly
    sliced
1 small onion, peeled and finely chopped
50 g/2 oz split almonds, toasted
2 tablespoons chopped dill
150 ml/¼ pint mayonnaise
2 tablespoons single cream
dill sprigs to serve

Place the cabbage, celery, apple, onion, almonds and dill in a mixing bowl. Mix thoroughly. Mix the mayonnaise with the cream and fold into the salad, tossing well. Transfer to a salad bowl and garnish with dill sprigs to serve.
Serves 6 to 8

Coleslaw; Broccoli salad; Cabbage with soured cream dressing; Roman red cabbage salad

Roman Red Cabbage Salad

3 teaspoons lemon juice
2 bananas, peeled and sliced
1 apple, cored and sliced
1 medium red cabbage, shredded
25 g/1 oz walnut halves
2 tablespoons red wine vinegar
1 tablespoon honey
salt
freshly ground black pepper

Sprinkle the lemon juice over the banana and apple slices to prevent discoloration. Mix the cabbage with the banana, apple and walnuts in a serving bowl.

To make the dressing heat the vinegar in a small pan until warm and add the honey, stirring well to dissolve. Season with salt and pepper to taste. Leave until cool.

Pour the dressing over the red cabbage mixture, and toss well. Leave the salad to stand for a few minutes before serving to allow the flavours to develop.
Serves 4 to 6

NOTE: Roman Red Cabbage Salad is excellent with game, duck, pheasant or roast beef.

Broccoli Salad

500 g/1 lb broccoli
600 ml/1 pint meat stock
1 hard-boiled egg, shelled and chopped
3 tablespoons vinaigrette dressing
1 teaspoon lemon juice
salt
freshly ground white pepper

Remove and discard the outer leaves and the stalky ends of the broccoli. Place the broccoli spears in a pan with the stock. Bring to the boil, lower the heat and cook for about 8 to 10 minutes. Drain thoroughly then leave the broccoli to cool slightly.

Separate the broccoli sprigs and place in a salad bowl. Add the chopped egg and toss gently to mix.

To make the dressing, mix the vinaigrette with the lemon juice and season with salt and pepper to taste. Pour over the broccoli mixture and toss well to coat. Serve warm or cold.
Serves 4

Savoy Cabbage Rolls

1 large Savoy cabbage
750 ml/1¼ pints meat stock
40 g/1½ oz butter
1 onion, peeled and finely chopped
500 g/1 lb mixed minced beef and lamb
1 small egg, beaten
salt
freshly ground black pepper
pinch of dried oregano
flour to coat
1 teaspoon cornflour
1 × 64 g/2¼ oz can tomato purée
150 ml/¼ pint soured cream
1 tablespoon chopped parsley

Separate cabbage leaves and remove the thick stems. Bring the stock to the boil, add the cabbage and cook for 5 minutes. Drain, reserving the stock; cool.

Melt 15 g/½ oz butter in a pan, add the onion and minced meat and fry, stirring, for 5 minutes. Mix with the egg, salt and pepper, and the oregano. Divide the filling between the cabbage leaves, placing it in the centre, and roll up. Dip them in flour to coat evenly.

Melt the remaining butter in a flame-proof dish, add the cabbage rolls and cook until lightly browned. Add the stock, cover and cook in a preheated moderate oven (180°C/350°F, Gas Mark 4) for about 45 minutes.

Remove the cabbage rolls with a slotted spoon and place in a warmed serving dish. Blend the cornflour with a little water, to form a thin paste; stir into the stock. Cook for 2 to 3 minutes, stirring constantly. Add the tomato purée and soured cream and whisk the sauce until smooth. Pour over the cabbage rolls and serve sprinkled with chopped parsley.
Serves 6 to 8

Alsace Sauerkraut Platter

2 tablespoons oil
1 small onion, peeled and chopped
750 g/1½ lb sauerkraut
1 bay leaf
2 juniper berries
1 apple, peeled, cored and grated
200 g/7 oz piece smoked streaky bacon
4 pork sausages
2 black puddings
4 small smoked liver sausages

Heat the oil in a large pan. Add the onion and fry for about 5 minutes. Add the sauerkraut, bay leaf, juniper berries, apple and 3 tablespoons water. Add the streaky bacon, cover and cook for 30 to 35 minutes, stirring occasionally.

Meanwhile, grill the pork sausages until crisp and evenly browned. Cook the black puddings and liver sausages in boiling water for 4 to 6 minutes.

Arrange the sauerkraut mixture on a large, flat dish. Slice the bacon and arrange around the sauerkraut with the black pudding and sausages.
Serves 4

RIGHT: *Red cabbage and potato gratin; Sauerkraut and potato bake*
BELOW: *Sauerkraut platter; Savoy cabbage rolls*

Red Cabbage and Potato Gratin

1 kg/2 lb potatoes, peeled, boiled and
  halved
15 g/½ oz butter
50 g/2 oz streaky bacon, derinded and
  chopped
1 small onion, peeled and chopped
325 g/11 oz red cabbage, shredded
salt
pinch of curry powder
pinch of cayenne pepper
pinch of ground paprika

Put the potatoes in a greased oven-proof dish. Melt the butter in a pan, add the bacon and onion and fry until the bacon is crisp. Remove one third of the mixture from the pan and set aside. Add the cabbage to the pan, with salt to taste, the curry powder, cayenne and paprika, stirring well. Cook for 2 to 3 minutes. Spoon over the potatoes and top with the reserved bacon mixture. Brown under a preheated grill.
Serves 4

Sauerkraut and Potato Bake

1 tablespoon oil
200 g/7 oz smoked streaky bacon,
  derinded and chopped
1 × 450 g/1 lb can sauerkraut
salt
freshly ground black pepper
pinch of ground paprika
150 ml/¼ pint water
750 g/1½ lb potatoes, peeled, boiled and
  mashed
1 tablespoon chopped parsley
50 g/2 oz cheese, grated
25 g/1 oz butter

Heat the oil in a pan, add the bacon and fry for 2 to 3 minutes. Remove from the pan, add the sauerkraut and cook for 5 minutes. Season with salt and pepper to taste and the paprika. Add the water and simmer, over a low heat, for 10 minutes, stirring occasionally.

Place a layer of sauerkraut in the base of a greased ovenproof dish. Cover with a layer of bacon and potato. Continue these layers, finishing with potato. Top with parsley, cheese and butter. Cook in a preheated hot oven (200°C/400°F, Gas Mark 6) for 15 minutes.
Serves 4

Cauliflower Casserole

750 ml/1¼ pints meat stock
1 large cauliflower, cut into florets
pinch of grated nutmeg
1 tablespoon chopped herbs (e.g. chives, parsley, thyme)
3 eggs
1 tablespoon creamy milk
1 tablespoon grated Parmesan cheese

Bring the stock to the boil in a large pan, add the cauliflower and nutmeg. Bring back to the boil, lower the heat, cover and cook gently for 10 minutes. Drain and place in a greased casserole dish. Sprinkle with the chopped herbs.

Beat the eggs with the milk and Parmesan cheese and pour over the cauliflower. Cook in a preheated mod-erately hot oven (200°C/400°F, Gas Mark 6) for about 20 minutes or until the egg has set.
Serves 4

NOTE: This casserole makes a light vegetarian supper dish. It can also be made with broccoli spears.

Broccoli in Puff Pastry

350–400 g/12–14 oz broccoli
600 ml/1 pint meat stock
15 g/½ oz butter
125 g/4 oz cooked ham, chopped
salt
freshly ground black pepper
1 × 215 g/7½ oz packet frozen puff pastry, thawed
2 eggs, beaten
1 tablespoon chopped parsley
1 egg yolk

Remove the leaves from the broccoli and trim the spears. Place in a pan with the stock. Bring to the boil, then lower the heat and cook for 8 to 10 minutes.

Meanwhile, melt the butter in a pan and quickly fry the ham. Drain the broccoli thoroughly and chop into small pieces. Season with salt and pep-per to taste and mix with the ham.

Roll out the puff pastry on a lightly floured surface to a 25 cm/10 inch square. Spoon the broccoli and ham mixture into the centre of the pastry square. Carefully pour the beaten eggs over the mixture. Season with salt to taste and sprinkle with the parsley. Brush the pastry edges with a little water. Fold the corners of the pastry to the centre over the filling. Pinch and seal the edges firmly together. Brush with the egg yolk and place on a dampened baking sheet. Cook in a pre-heated hot oven (220°C/425°F, Gas Mark 7) for 25 to 30 minutes.
Serves 6 to 8

NOTE: This broccoli pie can be served hot or cold. Serve as a supper or snack.

Cauliflower Omelettes

½ cauliflower, cut into florets
salt
2 tablespoons double cream
pinch of grated nutmeg
1 egg yolk
1 tablespoon grated Parmesan cheese
pinch of dried basil
6 eggs
oil for frying
75 g/3 oz Emmenthal cheese, grated

Place the cauliflower florets in a pan. Add just enough boiling water to cover, a pinch of salt, the cream and the nutmeg. Bring to the boil, then lower the heat and cook gently for about 20 minutes.

Drain thoroughly and purée in a liquidizer or pass through a fine sieve. Add the egg yolk, Parmesan cheese and basil, mixing well.

Beat the eggs with a little salt. Heat a little oil in an omelette or frying pan. When hot, add one quarter of the egg mixture and cook briskly for 2 to 3 minutes or until set, drawing the cook-ed edges towards the centre during the first minute.

Spread with one quarter of the cauliflower purée, fold over to enclose and sprinkle generously with one quar-ter of the cheese and place under a preheated hot grill until the cheese melts; keep warm. Repeat with the remaining egg and cauliflower mix-tures, making a total of four omelettes.
Serves 4

Red Cabbage with Bacon

1.25 kg/2½ lb red cabbage
1 tablespoon oil
1 onion, peeled and sliced into rings
125 g/4 oz streaky bacon, derinded and chopped
2 cloves
1 bay leaf
1 tablespoon red wine vinegar
300 ml/½ pint water
300 ml/½ pint red wine
1 teaspoon cornflour
salt
freshly ground black pepper

Quarter the cabbage, remove any coarse outer leaves and the thick stalk and shred the leaves.

Heat the oil in a flameproof cas-serole, add the onion and bacon and fry for 4 to 5 minutes. Add the cabbage, cloves, bay leaf and wine vinegar, mix-ing well. Add the water and red wine, cover and cook in a preheated moderate oven (180°C/350°F, Gas Mark 4) for about 1 hour, stirring occasionally.

Remove and discard the bay leaf. Blend the cornflour with a little water and stir into the cabbage mixture. Transfer to the top of the stove and cook, stirring, until thickened. Season with salt and pepper to taste. Serve immediately.
Serves 4

NOTE: This dish is excellent with roast hare or fried sausage.

Cauliflower casserole; Broccoli in puff pastry; Cauliflower omelettes

Sauerkraut Russian-style

2 tablespoons oil
1 onion, peeled and finely chopped
1 bunch herbs (e.g. chives, parsley,
    thyme), chopped
625 g/1¼ lb canned sauerkraut, drained
150 ml/¼ pint meat stock
1 teaspoon cornflour
salt
freshly ground black pepper
pinch of sugar
50 g/2 oz finely chopped cooked bacon
150 ml/¼ pint soured cream

Heat the oil in a large pan, then add the onion and herbs and cook for 5 minutes. Add the sauerkraut, mixing well. Add the stock and cook, over a low heat, for about 15 minutes.

Meanwhile, blend the cornflour with a little water to form a thin paste, stir into the sauerkraut mixture and continue cooking for a few minutes to thicken the liquid. Season with salt and pepper to taste. Add the sugar and bacon, mixing well. Remove from the

heat, fold in the soured cream and serve immediately.
Serves 4

NOTE: Sauerkraut Russian-style is a filling vegetable dish which is excellent served with roast pork.

Italian Cauliflower

1 cauliflower
salt
pinch of grated nutmeg
50 g/2 oz butter
125 g/4 oz smoked ham, chopped or cut
    into strips
1 × 64 g/2¼ oz can tomato purée
1 sprig of parsley, chopped
3 tablespoons cream
freshly ground black pepper
2 tablespoons grated Parmesan cheese

Trim the cauliflower, leaving it whole. Place in a pan, add just enough boiling water to cover, a pinch of salt and the nutmeg. Bring to the boil, lower the heat, cover and cook for 20 minutes.

Meanwhile, melt half the butter in a pan. Add the ham and cook for 2 minutes. Add the tomato purée and parsley, mixing well. Add the cream and salt and pepper to taste.

Drain the cauliflower thoroughly

and place in an ovenproof dish. Cover with the ham sauce and sprinkle with the Parmesan cheese. Dot with the remaining butter and cook in a preheated hot oven (220°C/425°F, Gas Mark 7) for 15 minutes until browned.
Serves 4

NOTE: Italian Cauliflower is excellent with roast or fried meats. Serve with a potato or boiled rice accompaniment.

Broccoli with Egg Cream Sauce

350–400 g/12–14 oz broccoli spears
600 ml/1 pint boiling water
salt
pinch of grated nutmeg
SAUCE:
150 ml/¼ pint double cream
2 egg yolks, beaten
1 sprig of parsley, chopped
freshly ground white pepper

Remove the leaves from the broccoli and trim the spears. Place the broccoli spears in a pan with the water, a pinch of salt and the nutmeg. Bring to the boil, then lower the heat, cover and cook for about 8 to 10 minutes. Drain thoroughly, reserving 150 ml/¼ pint of the cooking liquid.

To make the sauce, place the re-served cooking liquid in a small pan, stir in the cream and bring to just below boiling point. Add the egg yolks, stirring constantly. Add the parsley and salt and pepper to taste.

Pour the egg cream sauce over the broccoli and leave to stand in a warm place for about 5 minutes before serving. **Serves 4**

Chinese Cabbage in Onion Sauce

600 ml/1 pint water
salt
pinch of grated nutmeg
1 small or medium Chinese cabbage,
    trimmed
50 g/2 oz butter
1 small onion, peeled and finely chopped
1 tablespoon flour
300 ml/½ pint milk
1 teaspoon made mustard
freshly ground white pepper
pinch of sugar (optional)
1 tablespoon whole or chopped
    hazelnuts

Bring the water to the boil in a large pan, with the salt and nutmeg added. Add the whole Chinese cabbage, bring back to the boil, then lower the heat and cook, over a low heat, for about 10 minutes.

To make the sauce, melt half the butter in a pan, add the onion and cook until lightly browned. Add the flour and cook for 1 minute. Gradually add the milk, blending well after each addition. Bring to the boil, stirring constantly. Add the mustard and season with salt and pepper to taste, and the sugar, if liked.

Drain the cabbage thoroughly. Place in an ovenproof dish and pour over the sauce. Sprinkle with the hazelnuts, dot with remaining butter and brown under a preheated grill for 3 to 4 minutes. **Serves 4 to 6**

NOTE: This dish is excellent served with grilled chops or veal schnitzel.

Broccoli with egg cream sauce; Italian cauliflower; Chinese cabbage in onion sauce

Piquant Chinese Cabbage

1 small Chinese cabbage
½ cucumber, peeled and chopped
300 ml/½ pint meat stock
1 tablespoon chopped red pepper
15 g/½ oz butter
½ onion, peeled and finely chopped
salt
freshly ground black pepper
pinch of saffron
1 teaspoon cornflour

Quarter the cabbage, remove any coarse outer leaves and thick stalks. Cut the leaves into wide strips.

Place the cabbage and cucumber in a pan with the meat stock. Bring to the boil, then lower the heat and cook, over a low heat, for about 8 minutes. Add the red pepper and cook for a further 2 minutes.

Meanwhile, melt the butter in a pan, add the onion and cook for 3 to 4 minutes. Add to the cabbage mixture with salt and pepper to taste and the

saffron, mixing well. Dissolve the cornflour in a little water, add to the cabbage mixture blending well, and cook, stirring, for about 2 minutes. Serve immediately.
Serves 4

NOTE: Serve Piquant Chinese Cabbage hot with warm French or garlic bread, or for a more substantial meal, with fried meatballs.

Brussels Sprouts with Chestnuts

350 g/12 oz chestnuts
25 g/1 oz butter
150 ml/¼ pint stock
500 g/1 lb Brussels sprouts, trimmed
salt
freshly ground black pepper

Slit the chestnuts with a sharp knife. Place in a pan of cold water, bring to the boil and simmer for 3 minutes. Remove the chestnuts, one at a time, and peel off their outer and inner skins.

Heat the butter in a small pan, add the chestnuts and cook for 5 minutes, stirring occasionally. Add the stock, bring to the boil, cover and simmer for 20 minutes.

Add the Brussels sprouts, adding more liquid if necessary, to just cover the vegetables. Add salt and pepper to taste and cook for a further 10 minutes until the sprouts are just tender. Drain the sprouts and chestnuts, reserving the stock for a soup.

Transfer the Brussels sprouts and chestnuts to a serving dish to serve.
Serves 4

Baked Cauliflower and Vegetables

1 small cauliflower, cut into florets
salt
2 tablespoons creamy milk
275 g/9 oz carrots, roughly chopped
175 g/6 oz frozen peas
2 tablespoons chopped parsley
150 g/5 oz Gouda cheese, cut into strips
25 g/1 oz butter or margarine
freshly ground black pepper

Place the cauliflower florets in a pan. Add enough boiling water to cover, a pinch of salt and the milk. Bring to the boil, then lower the heat and cook for 5 minutes. Add the chopped carrots and cook for 8 to 10 minutes until just tender. Drain thoroughly and mix with the peas in a casserole dish. Sprinkle with the parsley and cheese.

Melt the butter or margarine in a small pan and season with salt and

pepper to taste. Pour over the vegetables. Cook in a preheated hot oven (220°C/425°F, Gas Mark 7) for 12 to 15 minutes, or until brown. Serve immediately.
Serves 4

NOTE: Baked Cauliflower and Vegetables is delicious served with any roast meat, or with grilled or fried fish.

Cauliflower Florets in Batter

1 small cauliflower, cut into florets
600 ml/1 pint milk
pinch of grated nutmeg
oil for deep-frying
BATTER:
4 tablespoons flour
pinch of salt
1 egg
175 ml/6 fl oz beer
TO GARNISH:
1–2 tablespoons chopped parsley
parsley sprigs (optional)

Place the cauliflower in a pan with the milk and nutmeg. Bring to the boil, then lower the heat and cook gently for about 10 minutes until barely tender. Drain thoroughly.

To make the batter, sift the flour and salt into a bowl and gradually add the egg and beer, beating to make a smooth batter.

Heat the oil in a deep-fryer to 190°C/375°F. Dip the cauliflower florets into the batter and fry in the hot oil in batches until golden brown and crisp. Drain on absorbent kitchen paper and keep warm while cooking the remainder. Place the fried cauliflower

florets in a warmed serving dish and sprinkle with the parsley, if liked. Serve immediately.
Serves 4

NOTE: This recipe can also be used for leftover cauliflower. Coat the cold cauliflower in batter and fry as above. Cauliflower Florets in Batter are excellent with fish or meat dishes.

Baked cauliflower and vegetables; Brussels sprouts with chestnuts; Cauliflower florets in batter

Broccoli with Walnut Butter

400 g/14 oz broccoli spears
600 ml/1 pint boiling water
salt
pinch of cayenne pepper
50 g/2 oz butter
2 tablespoons ground walnuts

Using a sharp knife carefully pare away any coarse skin from the broccoli stems. Place in a pan with the water, a pinch of salt and the cayenne pepper. Bring to the boil, then lower the heat and cook for about 8 to 10 minutes.

Meanwhile, make the walnut butter. Melt the butter and cook until golden. Add the ground walnuts and cook for about 30 seconds.

Drain the broccoli thoroughly and place in a serving dish. Spoon the walnut butter over the broccoli spears and serve immediately.
Serves 4

NOTE: This special dish is ideal to serve with fillet steak or a creamed veal dish.

Broccoli with Parisian Butter Sauce

500 g/1 lb broccoli spears
750 ml/1¼ pints boiling water
salt
pinch of grated nutmeg
SAUCE:
75 g/3 oz butter
3 egg yolks
½ teaspoon dried tarragon
freshly ground white pepper
1 teaspoon red wine vinegar
150 ml/¼ pint double cream, lightly
   whipped

Place the broccoli spears in a pan with the water, a pinch of salt and the nutmeg. Bring to the boil, then lower the heat and cook for about 8 to 10 minutes.

Meanwhile, make the sauce. Melt the butter in a pan and leave to cool. Beat the egg yolks in a bowl with the tarragon, salt and pepper to taste, and the vinegar. Place the bowl over a pan of simmering water and whisk until light and frothy. Carefully add the warm (not hot) butter a few drops at a time, whisking continuously. Remove

the sauce from the heat and fold in the whipped cream.

Drain the broccoli thoroughly and place in a warmed serving dish. Top with a little of the butter sauce. Serve the remaining sauce separately.
Serves 4

NOTE: This is a rather expensive dish, but well worth the cost for a delicious dinner-party vegetable to serve with fillet or T-bone steak, roast turkey, entrecôtes, or venison croquettes.

Chinese Cabbage in Hot Sauce

1 medium Chinese cabbage
1 red pepper, cored, seeded and sliced
    into rings
150 ml/¼ pint chicken stock
juice of 1 lemon
SAUCE:
25 g/1 oz butter
1 tablespoon flour
150 ml/¼ pint warmed milk
pinch of grated nutmeg
salt
freshly ground black pepper
dash of chilli or Tabasco sauce

Quarter the cabbage, remove any coarse outer leaves and thick stalks. Cut the leaves into wide strips.

Place the cabbage and red pepper in a pan with the chicken stock and lemon juice. Bring to the boil, lower the heat and simmer for about 10 minutes.

Meanwhile, make the sauce. Melt the butter in a pan and cook until lightly browned. Add the flour and cook for 1 minute. Gradually add the milk, stirring until smooth.

Drain the cabbage mixture, reserving the stock. Add the reserved stock to the sauce, blending well. Season with the nutmeg, salt and pepper to taste, and the chilli or Tabasco sauce. Place the cabbage and pepper mixture in a warmed serving dish and cover with the sauce. Serve immediately.
Serves 4

NOTE This makes a tasty accompaniment to fried fish or liver kebabs.

Farmhouse Braised Cabbage

20 g/¾ oz lard
1 medium white cabbage, coarsely
    chopped
300 ml/½ pint water
dash of wine vinegar
1 teaspoon sugar
1 teaspoon caraway seeds (optional)
salt
freshly ground white pepper
1 onion, peeled and finely chopped
1 apple, peeled, cored and grated

Melt the lard in a pan, add the cabbage and fry, stirring, for 4 to 5 minutes. Add the water, vinegar, sugar, caraway seeds if using, and salt and pepper to taste, mixing well. Simmer over a low heat for about 15 minutes.

Add the onion and apple, mixing well. Cook for a further 12 to 15 minutes. Transfer to a serving dish and serve immediately.
Serves 4

Swiss Cauliflower

1 cauliflower
300 ml/½ pint water
600 ml/1 pint milk
35 g/1¼ oz butter
pinch of freshly ground white pepper
scant 1 teaspoon salt
pinch of grated nutmeg
pinch of sugar
1 sprig of parsley, chopped

Trim the cauliflower leaving it whole. Place in a pan with the water, milk, 7 g (¼ oz) of the butter, pepper, salt, nutmeg and sugar. Bring to the boil, then lower the heat, cover and simmer for 18 to 20 minutes until tender. Drain thoroughly (the stock can be used to make a soup) and place in a serving dish.

Melt the remaining butter in a small pan, add the parsley and mix well. Pour over the cauliflower to serve.
Serves 4

Sauerkraut

3.5 kg/8 lb firm white cabbage, finely
    shredded
175 g/6 oz sea salt
1 tablespoon whole black peppercorns
1 tablespoon juniper berries

Place a layer of cabbage in the base of a large crock and sprinkle with a little salt, a few peppercorns and a few juniper berries. Continue layering in this way until all the ingredients are used.

Press the cabbage down and cover with muslin. Put a plate and a heavy weight on top. Store in a cool place.

Fermentation will start in a few days and the plate will sink under the brine that has formed. Pour off some of this but leave enough to cover the cabbage. It will be ready to eat in about 1 month.
Makes 3.5 kg/8 lb sauerkraut

Swiss cauliflower; Broccoli with Parisian butter sauce; Chinese cabbage in hot sauce

Broccoli in Wine Sauce

350–400 g/12–14 oz broccoli spears
pinch of grated nutmeg
150 ml/¼ pint hot chicken stock
150 ml/¼ pint dry white wine
SAUCE:
15 g/½ oz butter
1 tablespoon flour
salt
freshly ground black pepper
pinch of garlic salt

Place the broccoli spears in a pan with the nutmeg and chicken stock. Bring to the boil, then lower the heat, cover and cook for about 8 to 10 minutes. Add the white wine and leave to stand while making the sauce.

To make the sauce, melt the butter in a pan. Add the flour and cook until golden brown. Drain the broccoli, reserving the cooking liquid. Gradually add the reserved liquid to the flour mixture, blending well to make a smooth sauce. Season with salt and pepper to taste, and the garlic salt. Add the broccoli and mix gently to coat. Serve immediately.
Serves 4

NOTE: This is excellent with roast poultry and veal or fried meat and fish.

White Cabbage Spanish-style

3 tablespoons oil
2 cloves garlic, peeled and crushed with
    ¼ teaspoon salt
275 g/9 oz carrots, peeled
1 small white cabbage, coarsely chopped
300 ml/½ pint water
salt
1 bay leaf
1 small cinnamon stick
300 ml/½ pint white wine
freshly ground black pepper

Heat the oil in a pan, add the garlic and fry for 1 minute. Cut the carrots lengthwise into quarters. Add the cabbage and carrots to the pan and cook for 5 minutes. Add the water, a pinch of salt, the bay leaf and cinnamon stick. Simmer, over a low heat, for about 10 minutes. Add the white wine and cook for a further 10 to 15 minutes. Remove and discard the cinnamon stick and season with salt and pepper to taste. Serve immediately.
Serves 4

NOTE: Serve with roast hare, partridge, fried liver or roast breast of lamb.

RIGHT: *Brussels sprouts in cream sauce; Creamed savoy cabbage*
BELOW: *Broccoli in wine sauce; White cabbage Spanish-style*

Creamed Savoy Cabbage

1 kg/2 lb Savoy cabbage
25 g/1 oz lard
1 onion, peeled and chopped
300 ml/½ pint meat stock
salt
freshly ground black pepper
pinch of grated nutmeg
1 teaspoon caraway seeds (optional)
150 ml/¼ pint soured cream

Remove the thick stems and any damaged leaves from the cabbage and cut into wide strips. Place the cabbage in a sieve, rinse and drain thoroughly.

Melt the lard in a large pan, add the onion and fry for 4 to 5 minutes. Add the cabbage, stock, salt and pepper to taste, nutmeg and caraway seeds, if using. Cover and simmer, over a low heat, for about 20 minutes, stirring occasionally. Drain off any excess liquid.

Mix the soured cream with a little salt to taste. Stir into the cabbage mixture, mixing well. Serve immediately.
Serves 4

NOTE: Creamed Savoy Cabbage is delicious served with roast pork, rissoles or meat loaf.

Brussels Sprouts in Cream Sauce

750 ml/1¼ pints water
salt
pinch of grated nutmeg
750 g–1 kg/1½–2 lb Brussels sprouts, trimmed
SAUCE:
15 g/½ oz butter
1 tablespoon flour
125 ml/4 fl oz dry white wine
1 egg yolk
150 ml/¼ pint double cream
cayenne pepper

Bring the water to the boil in a pan with salt and the nutmeg added. Add the Brussels sprouts. Bring back to the boil, then lower the heat, cover and cook for 10 to 15 minutes. Drain the Brussels sprouts thoroughly, reserving 150 ml/¼ pint of the cooking liquid.

Meanwhile, make the sauce. Melt the butter in a pan, add the flour and cook for 2 to 3 minutes. Gradually add the reserved cooking liquid, stirring to make a smooth sauce. Add the white wine and bring to the boil, stirring. Remove the sauce from the heat, and allow to cool slightly. Beat the egg yolk and cream together. Stir into the sauce and add salt and cayenne to taste.

Place the drained Brussels sprouts in a warmed serving dish and cover with the cream sauce. Serve immediately.
Serves 4

NOTE: This dish is delicious with steaks, cutlets, rissoles or grilled fish.

White Cabbage Palatine

salt
½ white cabbage, shredded
2 tablespoons vinegar
freshly ground black pepper
pinch of sugar
50 g/2 oz smoked streaky bacon,
    derinded and chopped

Bring about 600 ml/1 pint water to the boil, with salt added, in a large pan. Add the cabbage, bring back to the boil, then lower the heat and cook, over a low heat, for about 10 minutes.

To make the marinade, mix the vinegar with salt and pepper to taste, and the sugar. Drain the cabbage thoroughly and while still warm mix with the marinade.

Meanwhile, fry the bacon in its own fat, until crisp. Fold, while still hot, into the cabbage. Serve immediately.
Serves 4

NOTE: White Cabbage Palatine is an ideal accompaniment to crispy roast pork, sucking pig or smoked meats.

Brussels Sprouts au Gratin

750 g/1½ lb Brussels sprouts, trimmed
salt
pinch of grated nutmeg
25 g/1 oz butter
½ onion, peeled and chopped
125 g/4 oz cooked ham, cut into strips
3 tablespoons grated Parmesan cheese

Bring a large pan containing about 600 ml/1 pint water to the boil. Add the Brussels sprouts with a pinch of salt and the nutmeg. Bring back to the boil, then lower the heat, cover and cook, over a low heat, for 10 to 15 minutes. Drain and place in an ovenproof dish.

Melt half of the butter in a small pan, add the onion and fry for 4 to 5 minutes. Add the ham and mix well. Sprinkle the onion and ham mixture over the Brussels sprouts and top with the Parmesan cheese. Dot with the remaining butter. Cook in a preheated moderately hot oven (200°C/400°F, Gas Mark 6) for about 20 minutes, until brown.
Serves 4

NOTE: Brussels Sprouts au Gratin is delicious with many meat, fish and minced meat dishes or fried eggs.

Broccoli in Cheese Sauce

625 g/1¼ lb broccoli spears
pinch of grated nutmeg
300 ml/½ pint meat stock
SAUCE:
15 g/½ oz butter
1 tablespoon flour
4 tablespoons double cream
50 g/2 oz grated Parmesan cheese
salt
cayenne pepper

Place the broccoli spears in a pan with the nutmeg and stock. Bring to the boil, then lower the heat, cover and cook for about 8 to 10 minutes.

Meanwhile, make the sauce. Melt the butter in a pan. Add the flour and cook until golden brown. Drain the broccoli, reserving the cooking liquid. Gradually add the reserved cooking liquid and the cream to the flour mixture, blending well to make a smooth sauce. Add the cheese, mixing well. Season with salt and cayenne pepper to taste. Place the cooked broccoli in a serving dish and cover with the cheese sauce. Serve immediately.
Serves 4

NOTE: Broccoli in Cheese Sauce is excellent with veal and poultry dishes.

Red Cabbage with Apple

1 kg/2 lb red cabbage, shredded
2 tablespoons oil
1 onion, peeled and thinly sliced
2 cooking apples, peeled, cored and
    chopped
3 tablespoons wine vinegar
3 tablespoons water
1 tablespoon soft brown sugar
salt
freshly ground black pepper
1 tablespoon chopped parsley, to
    garnish

Add the cabbage to a large pan of boiling water and blanch for 2 to 3 minutes. Drain thoroughly. Heat the oil in a saucepan, add the onion and cook until softened, about 5 minutes. Add the apple, cover and cook for a further 5 minutes, stirring occasionally. Add the cabbage, vinegar, water, sugar, and salt and pepper to taste, blending well.

Transfer to a casserole dish. Cover and cook in a preheated moderate oven (180°C/350°F, Gas Mark 4) for 1 to 1½ hours until tender. Stir occasionally, adding a little more water if necessary. Turn into a warmed serving dish and sprinkle with parsley to serve.
Serves 4 to 6

NOTE: Red Cabbage with Apple makes a delicious accompaniment to serve with roast pork or baked gammon. Alternatively it may be topped with grilled bacon rashers, sprinkled liberally with grated cheese and browned under the grill for a tasty supper dish.

White cabbage palatine; Red cabbage with apple; Broccoli in cheese sauce; Brussels sprouts au gratin

PODS & SEEDS

Fresh or dried, pods and seeds provide a good, inexpensive source of protein. Highly versatile, they range from the mangetout where both pod and seed are eaten, to the sweetcorn whose kernels are wrapped in a silky husk of fine threads and leaves. In between is a host of varieties including the tender French bean, the broad bean and the endless number of string beans.

Most pods and seeds are at their best during the summer and early autumn and are eaten when young and tender. They can however be easily dried for all year round eating. There are many dried peas and beans to choose from, ranging from the familiar haricot to the more exotic aduki, rose cocoa, black-eye and mung bean.

Pods and seeds can be used to make hearty soups, nourishing casseroles, meal-in-one hot pots, main meal salads and unusual vegetable dishes.

BEANS, BROAD

Origin: The broad bean (*Vicia faba*) is a member of the Leguminosae family. It has a history going back thousands of years – the ancient Romans used to throw a handful of broad beans behind them at midnight to keep away malevolent household spirits!

There are two major classes of broad bean: the 'Longpods', which contain about eight oval-shaped small seeds; and the 'Windsors', which are shorter and usually contain about four larger, round-shaped seeds.

Availability: Fresh homegrown broad beans are in season from May to October.

Buying: Broad beans on sale in Britain are generally fully mature which means the pods are too tough to eat. Occasionally, however, it is possible to buy immature broad beans, no thicker than a finger and about 7.5 cm (3 inches) long, which can be eaten pod and all.

Choose broad beans with a bright green colour, crisp firm pod and fresh appearance. Fresh broad beans are generally sold unshelled by weight. Frozen and canned broad beans are also available for convenient use.

Preparation and serving: Immature young broad beans can be cooked in their pods in boiling salted water for about 10 to 12 minutes, or until tender.

Mature broad beans must first be shelled then cooked in boiling salted water for 10 to 12 minutes, until tender.

Broad beans make a delicious vegetable accompaniment, tossed in butter with a few chopped herbs, or served in a savoury white sauce. They also make a tasty salad or casserole ingredient.

Very mature broad beans find a place in slow-cooking hot pots, or they may be cooked then puréed with butter and salt and pepper to taste.

Nutritional value: Broad beans are rich in calcium, phosphorus, Vitamin C and carbohydrate. They contain 48 Calories (206 kj) per 100 g/$3\frac{1}{2}$ oz.

BEANS, FRENCH OR KIDNEY

Origin: The French bean (*Phaseolus vulgaris*) is a member of the Leguminosae family. It is an exotic plant native to Central and Latin America. There are many types of French bean, but we distinguish three main ones. Dwarf beans are long slender green beans, the finest of which are Princess beans. Climbing beans are grown up poles like runner beans; one of the most striking varieties is the 'purple-podded bean' which is available dried as the kidney bean. The haricot bean is a white or pale green bean, the seeds of which can be dried.

Flageolet beans are a pale green variety of the haricot bean. They have a slightly elongated kidney shape, pale, delicate green colour and mild flavour.

Cannellini beans are a small white variety of the haricot bean; they are popular in Italy.

Availability: Fresh dwarf or French beans are in season in Britain from June to October, although they can be obtained nearly all year round. They are grown throughout the world. Britain boosts its own supply with imports from Spain and Kenya. Dried haricot, kidney and cannellini beans come from South and Central America, North Africa, Italy and the Balkans. Flageolet beans are imported into Britain mainly from France.

Buying: Choose fresh dwarf or French beans that have a pliable velvety feel, not hard or tough. Look for freshness, tenderness and a good green colour. Avoid any that look coarse, wilted or diseased in any way. Use as soon as possible after purchase. They can be kept in the refrigerator for up to 2 days. Dried beans will keep for several years in a tightly covered container.

In Britain we are only likely to find dried, canned or bottled flageolets.

Preparation and serving: Green dwarf and French beans should be topped and tailed and cooked in boiling salted water for 5 to 15 minutes depending upon maturity and variety.

Dried haricot, kidney, cannellini and flageolet beans must be soaked before cooking. Soak 500 g/1 lb beans in 1.5 litres/$2\frac{1}{2}$ pints cold water overnight for best results. Drain and place in a pan of fresh water. (Add a pinch of bicarbonate of soda to speed up the cooking time if liked.) Bring to the boil and cook gently for 1 to $1\frac{1}{2}$ hours, or until tender.

Serve French green beans as a vegetable to accompany main meal dishes, in salads, casseroles and stir-fried dishes. Dried, haricot kidney and cannellini beans are delicious in soups, stews, salads and as an accompaniment.

Flageolet beans can be used in much the same way as haricot or kidney beans but in France they are traditionally served with roast lamb. They are also good in salads or as a plain vegetable accompaniment with a dot of butter and a sprinkling of fresh herbs.

There are many popular dried haricot and kidney bean-based dishes throughout the world: the French classic hearty bean casserole, cassoulet, Mexican chilli con carne, American Boston baked beans and the British canned baked beans.

Nutritional value: Fresh green beans contain a good supply of calcium, phosphorus and Vitamin A, a little Vitamin C, carbohydrate and protein. They provide 7 Calories (32 kj) per 100 g/$3\frac{1}{2}$ oz.

Dried haricot, kidney, cannellini and flageolet beans are invaluable as a good and inexpensive source of protein. They have roughly double the protein of cereals, and more than meat, fish and eggs. They are also rich in carbohydrate, phosphorus and calcium. Raw dried beans contain 271 Calories (1151 kj) per 100 g/$3\frac{1}{2}$ oz.

BEANS, BUTTER OR LIMA

Origin: The butter bean (*Phaseolus lunatus*) is a member of the Leguminosae family. Originating in South America, it is also known as the lima, sieva, Madagascar, curry or pole bean. There are numerous varieties but the yellow-seeded variety is perhaps the most popular.

As the name suggests, lima beans come from Lima in Peru. But long before Columbus made his voyage of discovery, the bean was growing throughout America. Today it is grown in all tropical areas of the world. The species produces two distinct groups, the large, flat butter bean – a favourite in British cooking, and the smaller sieva or lima bean.

Availability: Butter beans are available fresh only in tropical and subtropical countries where they are grown. In Britain we generally only find the dried or canned variety, the beans coming from South and Central America and North Africa.

Buying: Butter beans can be bought dried by weight but need soaking before cooking. Canned and frozen butter or lima beans, ready cooked, are also available for convenient use.

Preparation and serving: Soak dried butter or lima beans in cold water overnight for 6 to 8 hours. Drain and cook in boiling water for about $1\frac{1}{2}$ hours or until tender.

Butter or lima beans make a delicious vegetable accompaniment tossed in a little butter. They also make good salad, stew and casserole ingredients.

Nutritional value: Like other tropical pulses, butter or lima beans are rich in Vitamin A, carbohydrate, protein, calcium and phosphorus. Raw dried butter or lima beans contain 271-Calories (1151 kj) per 100 g/$3\frac{1}{2}$ oz.

BEANS, RUNNER

Origin: The runner bean (*Phaseolus coccineus*) is a member of the Leguminosae family. It is a native of Central and South America and was brought to Europe by Spanish conquistadors in the 16th century. It soon became very popular, down grading the native broad bean, to the status of animal feed.

It is often called the scarlet runner because its flower is often a scarlet red colour, although some varieties have a white, or red and white flower.

Availability: Fresh runner beans are in season from July to October. They are grown extensively in Europe, especially Britain.

Buying: Choose runner beans with a bright green colour, pliable velvety feel, not hard or tough. Avoid any that look coarse or wilted.

Runner beans are sold by weight. Prepared frozen, canned and dried runner beans are also available for convenient use.

Preparation and serving: Top and tail runner beans, remove any stringy edges and slice into diagonal lengths. Cook in boiling salted water for about 5 to 7 minutes. Drain and serve tossed in butter and a few chopped herbs if liked.

Cooked runner beans may also be used in salads, soups and casseroles

Nutritional value: Fresh runner beans contain a good supply of Vitamin C, Vitamin A, carbohydrate and protein. They contain about 7 Calories (32 kj) per 100 g/3½ oz.

BEANS, WAX-POD YELLOW

Origin: Wax-pod yellow beans (*Phaseolus vulgaris*) are members of the Leguminosae family. They include many yellow-podded stringless beans which are grown in tropical and subtropical countries. They are rarely found fresh in Britain but the seeds, the varieties of which are numerous, are readily found in supermarkets and health food stores nationwide. They are also often called snap beans.

Availability: Fresh wax-pod yellow beans rarely reach Britain from their countries of origin: Central and South America, Mexico, North Africa and Italy. Dried beans are imported from America, Africa and Italy.

Buying: There are many varieties of dried wax-pod beans on sale, the most popular of which include: the black bean, which has a shiny black coat and strong flavour; the black-eye bean, which is small, creamy-coloured with a characteristic black eye; the Foule Medame bean, a dull brown bean with a slightly earthy taste; and the Rose Cocoa bean, a longish pink bean with darker flecks and a sweet taste.

Store dried beans in an airtight tin and they will last for a year or so. Cooked dried beans will keep in the refrigerator for up to 4 days.

Preparation and serving: Soak dried beans in cold water for at least 8 hours or overnight. Do not add salt to the soaking water since this tends to toughen the beans. Rinse and place in a pan with fresh water. Bring to the boil and cook gently for 1½ to 2 hours, or until tender. A pinch of bicarbonate of soda can help speed up the cooking.

Use as a vegetable accompaniment to meat, fish and poultry dishes, or cooked in salads, stews and soups. Never eat these kinds of bean raw; they contain a poisonous substance called phasine. Cooking changes this substance and renders it harmless.

Nutritional value: Dried wax-pod beans are valuable as a good and inexpensive source of protein. They have roughly double the protein of cereals and more than fish, meat and eggs. They are valuable too for their carbohydrate, calcium and phosphorus. They add variety and nourishment to any diet at relatively little calorie cost. Dried beans contain 271 Calories (1151 kj) per 100 g/3½ oz. Cooked beans contain 95 Calories (405 kj) per 100 g/3½ oz.

RUNNER BEANS

PURPLE-PODDED KIDNEY BEANS

BROAD BEANS

FRENCH BEANS

BLACK BEANS

HARICOT BEANS

BUTTER BEANS

FLAGEOLETS

KIDNEY BEANS

CANNELLINI BEANS

BLACK-EYED BEANS

CHICK PEAS

Origin: Chick peas (*Cicer arietinum*) are a member of the Leguminosae family. They are known to the Spanish as *garbanzos*, to the French as *pois chiches* and to the Indians as *chana dal*. There are two main varieties: the beige or golden type; and the dark brown variety. They are about the size of a peanut, or a little larger, but more irregular in shape. They have a nutty flavour and slightly crunchy texture.

Wild chick peas grew in Egypt in the time of the Pharaohs, although it is thought that they originated in Western Asia.

Availability: Chick peas are grown extensively in the Mediterranean area, in North Africa and Asia. They are a staple food in the Middle East but they also popular in America, Africa and Australia.

Buying: In Britain we generally only find dried or canned chick peas; the former must be soaked before cooking.

Preparation and serving: If using dried chick peas, soak 500 g/1 lb in 1.5 litres/2½ pints cold water overnight for best results. Drain, place in a pan and cover with fresh water. Bring slowly to the boil then lower the heat and cook, over a gentle heat, for about 1¾ hours.

Chick peas are delicious in soups, salads and casseroles or as a tasty vegetable dish with tomatoes. They are an essential ingredient in couscous, a stew popular in Tunisia, Morocco and Egypt. Chick peas are also ground into a paste and mixed with garlic, oil and lemon juice to make hummus. The Spanish have a popular garlic soup with chick peas and mint while the Portuguese eat chick peas with dried cod and hard-boiled eggs.

Nutritional value: Like dried peas, chick peas have a high carbohydrate and calorific value: 320 Calories (1362 kj) per 100 g/3½ oz.

LENTILS

Origin: The lentil (*Lens esculenta*) is a member of the Leguminosae family and a very ancient cultivated plant. Today lentils are popular throughout the world and feature strongly in Indian, Middle Eastern, German and Spanish cooking. Despite their popularity, they have never made their way into haute cuisine, featuring mainly in peasant type dishes.

There are many different varieties of lentil, usually identified and named after their colour which may be green, reddish-brown, orange, yellow, black or pale brown. They all look like a flattish kind of pea, varying in size from small (sometimes called sugar lentils) to giant (7 to 8 mm/½ to ¾ inch in size). The larger lentils are often more prized than the smaller, although just for their size since there is no discernible difference in flavour.

Availability: Most of the lentils imported into Britain come from outside Europe. The main growing areas and exporters of lentils are Chile, America, Argentina, India, Pakistan and the Near East. Russia grows a great many lentils for home consumption, but no longer exports them.

Buying: Most lentils can be bought from a supermarket or grocers; special varieties can be found in most wholefood shops. Larger lentils, for the reasons already mentioned, cost more than smaller lentils. If stored in a cool, dry place, lentils will keep in good condition for at least a year.

Preparation and serving: Lentils are the only pulse which may not require soaking before being cooked. Wash the lentils thoroughly before cooking. Place them in a pan, cover with cold water, bring to the boil, then lower the heat and cook gently for about 1½–2 hours, according to size or age. Add salt just before the end of the cooking time.

Lentils are used in making casseroles, soups, stews, vegetable-type rissoles and salads. They also make a piquant vegetable accompaniment to a main meal dish.

The French like their lentils cooked in red wine with onions and bacon; the Spanish eat lentils with garlic and raw onion; they are served with dripping and soured cream in Russia; and the people of India and Pakistan eat them highly seasoned with curry powder, nutmeg and ginger. In their native Orient, lentils are served as a salad, with a dressing of lemon juice, olive oil and garlic.

Nutritional value: Lentils are richer in protein than any other pulse with the exception of the soya bean. They are also rich in carbohydrate, calcium, phosphorus, Vitamin A and iron. Raw lentils contain 304 Calories (1293 kj) per 100 g/3½ oz.

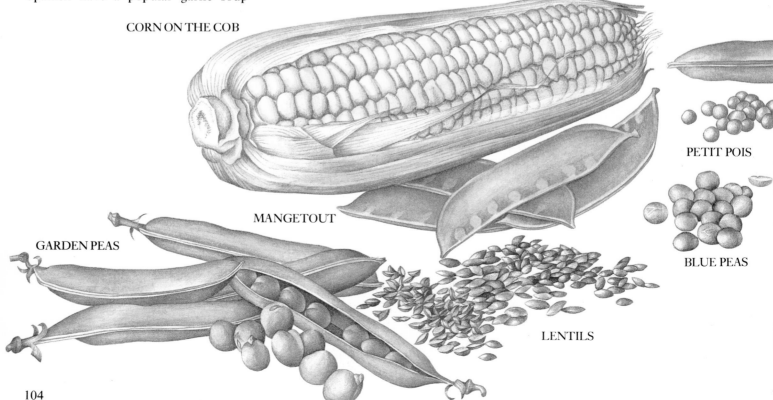

CORN ON THE COB

PETIT POIS

MANGETOUT

GARDEN PEAS

BLUE PEAS

LENTILS

PEAS

Origin: The pea (*Pisum sativum*) is the best known member of the Leguminosae family. It originally came from the Near East, and was introduced into Europe in the early Middle Ages. Pease porridge soon became the winter staple food all over northern Europe and remained so until the 17th century. It was one of the few vegetables that could be dried for use during the winter months. It wasn't until new varieties with better flavour were developed that people started eating peas fresh.

There are a great many different varieties of garden peas grown in Britain. There are three main types: the round-seeded, with tough pods and round, smooth seeds, which when mature are ideal for drying; the wrinkle-seeded or marrowfat, with tough pods and seeds that are wrinkled when mature but unsuitable for drying; and the sugar pea or mangetout, with tender young pods and seeds, which is eaten whole. All types freeze well.

All fresh peas are really immature seeds, and the less mature they are, the better they taste.

Dried peas include whole marrowfat 'blue' peas, and the skinless yellow or green split peas which cook to a purée.

Availability: Fresh peas are in season from June to mid-August. Dried and frozen peas are available all year round. Britain is one of the major growers and exporters of garden peas.

Buying: Fresh peas vary a great deal in quality, flavour and size. Small young peas bought early in the season are most certainly likely to be tender; later

MARROWFAT PEAS

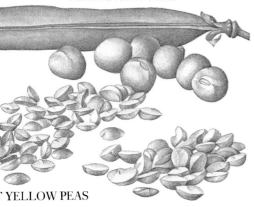

YELLOW PEAS

SPLIT GREEN PEAS

CHICK PEAS

in the season they are likely to be larger and more floury.

Garden peas and mangetout are sold loose by weight. Look for small, shiny green pods that are almost velvety to the touch. Avoid those pods that look filled to bursting point – they will generally be old, tough and mealy. Reject any pods that are faded, discoloured or damaged.

Dried and frozen peas can be bought by weight. Canned peas are also available for convenient use. Extra small peas, called petits pois, can be bought canned or frozen.

Preparation and serving: Shell the peas and cook in boiling salted water for 8 to 15 minutes, according to size and age. Add a pinch of sugar, a small knob of butter, a few herbs or other seasonings if liked. In Britain, mint is the classic herb to use with peas.

Peas can be served plain, with a herb butter, in a sauce or with other vegetables, such as asparagus, carrots, tomatoes or lettuce.

Cook frozen peas according to the manufacturer's instructions. There is no need to defrost them first. Canned peas simply need reheating. Dried peas need to be soaked in cold water to cover overnight. Drain, place in a pan, cover with cold water, bring to the boil, then lower the heat and cook gently for 2 to 3 hours. Cook with smoked meats, sausage or bacon if liked. It is also possible to buy packets of freeze-dried peas which generally do not need soaking prior to cooking, and cook in just 25 to 30 minutes.

Dried peas make excellent hearty soups and casseroles as well as being a tasty vegetable to accompany main meal dishes.

There are many classic or popular pea-based dishes throughout the world: the Italians serve peas with rice in risi e bisi, the French have a speciality called Peas Parmentier, peas in a savoury béchamel sauce; there is a favourite Sardinian national dish called corda, which consists of strips of cuttlefish in a garlic sauce with peas and tomatoes; and the Chinese stir-fry mangetout in many of their classic dishes.

Nutritional value: Peas are a very nutritious vegetable. Young green peas contain good supplies of protein, carbohydrate and Vitamins B and E. Dried peas are also rich in phosphorus, calcium, sodium and Vitamin A. Fresh young green peas contain 67 Calories (283 kj) per 100 g/3½ oz, while raw dried peas contain 286 Calories (1215 kj) per 100 g/3½ oz. Split peas have the most calories with 320 Calories (1362 kj) per 100 g/3½ oz.

SWEETCORN

Origin: Sweetcorn (*Zea mays*) is a member of the Gramineae family. It is also known as maize, corn on the cob and Indian corn.

It is native to Central and Southern America. Archaeological excavations of the Aztec settlements in New Mexico and Mesa Verde, Colorado, have shown that the Pueblo Indians were growing maize for grain and as a vegetable about 1100 AD. However, it did not reach Europe until the discovery of the New World, and then, initially, it was only imported. The Italians began to grow it in the middle of the 17th century. Maize soon became popular and the famous Italian polenta is a kind of porridge made of cornmeal.

Maize forms part of the staple diet in Mexico, Central America and many South American countries, where cornmeal is used for baking.

Sweetcorn first made its way into some European countries in the form of cornflour, used for thickening liquids, corn oil or in pickles. In Britain, maize was initially grown as chicken feed. Today, we can grow our own delicious cobs, since varieties have been developed to suit our climate.

Availability: Fresh sweetcorn is in season during the summer and early autumn months. Britain boosts its own supply with imports from America, especially Florida, and Italy.

The kernels are also available canned or frozen for convenient use.

Buying: Fresh sweetcorn is sold by the cob. Sweetcorn kernels are generally only available canned or frozen.

Choose corn with creamy yellow, plump kernels, fresh green husks and silky white threads.

Preparation and serving: Strip the outer husks from the cob in a downward direction, pull off the silky threads and trim the hard stalk close to the cob. Cook in boiling salted water for about 8 minutes. Drain and serve with melted butter or a sauce.

You can strip the kernels from the cob by using a fork. Cook as above and serve as a plain vegetable with butter or with a creamy sauce.

There are many ways of serving corn: sliced cobs may be threaded onto kebabs with other vegetables, meat, fish or poultry ingredients; sweetcorn kernels can be added to salads, soups, casseroles, relishes and fritters; while whole cobs are tasty barbecued.

Nutritional value: Corn is a good source of Vitamin A. Sweetcorn kernels contain 76 Calories (325 kj) per 100 g/3½ oz, while an average corn on the cob contains 84 Calories (362 kj).

Bean and Lamb Broth

750 g/1½ lb neck of lamb, chopped
1 litre/1¾ pints meat stock
750 g/1½ lb green beans
4 potatoes, peeled and diced
freshly ground black pepper
dried oregano
15 g/½ oz butter
2 cloves garlic, peeled
1 teaspoon plain flour
1 × 64 g/2¼ oz can tomato purée
pinch of sugar
salt (optional)

Place the lamb in a large pan, pour over the stock and bring to the boil. Reduce the heat and cook gently for about 30 minutes.

Top and tail the leaves and add to the pan with the potatoes, and pepper and oregano to taste. Cover and simmer for a further 30 minutes. Skim off any fat.

Meanwhile, heat the butter in a frying pan and fry the garlic until golden brown. Remove with a slotted spoon and discard. Sprinkle the flour into the garlic butter and cook for 1 minute. Whisk in the tomato purée and sugar. Stir into the bean and lamb broth, mixing well. Season to taste with salt and serve hot.

Serves 6 to 8

ABOVE: *Runner Bean Soup with Mint; Sweet and Sour Lentil Soup with Bacon; Pea and Ham Soup*

Tunisian Chick Pea Soup

500 g/1lb chick peas, soaked overnight
   in cold water
1 litre/1¾ pints water
salt
6 tablespoons olive oil
1 tablespoon caraway seeds
3 cloves garlic, peeled and crushed with
   salt
1 tablespoon tahini paste
juice of 1 lemon

Drain the chick peas and place in a pan with the water, salt to taste, the oil and caraway seeds. Bring slowly to the boil, then lower the heat and cook gently for about 1¼ hours.

Add the garlic and tahini paste, blending well. Simmer for a further 25 to 30 minutes. Stir in the lemon juice and serve hot.
Serves 4 to 6

Runner Bean Soup with Mint

750 g/1½ lb runner beans, topped and
   tailed
1 marrow bone
3 tablespoons oil
1 tablespoon flour
1 litre/1¾ pints meat stock
1 clove garlic, peeled and crushed with
   salt
1 stem of savory
1 bay leaf
150 g/5 oz Cracow or other smoked
   sausage, sliced
2–3 sprigs of fresh mint, chopped
salt
freshly ground black pepper
mint sprigs to garnish

Remove any strings from the beans and cut them into equal lengths.

Remove the marrow from the bone and chop into small pieces. Heat the oil in a large pan. Add the marrow and fry for 2 to 3 minutes. Add the flour and cook for 1 minute. Gradually whisk in the stock and bring to the boil, stirring. Add the beans, garlic, savory and bay leaf. Cover and simmer over a low heat for about 10 to 15 minutes.

Add the sausage and mint and simmer for a further 5 minutes. Season to taste with salt and pepper. Serve garnished with mint sprigs.
Serves 4 to 6

Sweet and Sour Lentil Soup with Bacon

500 g/1 lb lentils
750 ml/1¼ pints meat stock
40 g/1½ oz butter
salt
cayenne pepper
pinch of grated nutmeg
3 tablespoons red wine vinegar
1 teaspoon sugar
125 g/4 oz streaky bacon, derinded,
   chopped and fried until crisp
2 tablespoons chopped parsley to
   garnish

Place the lentils in a pan, cover with cold water, bring to the boil and cook for 1½ hours or until tender. Drain off the water, pour in the stock and bring slowly to the boil. Add the butter and stir until melted. Add the salt and cayenne pepper to taste, the nutmeg, vinegar and sugar. Lower the heat and cook gently for about 10 minutes.

Stir the bacon into the soup. Sprinkle with the parsley and serve immediately.
Serves 4 to 6

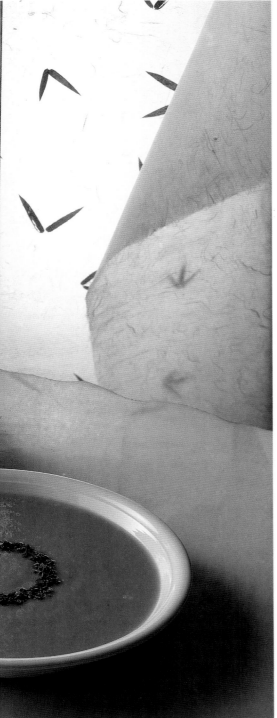

Pea and Ham Soup

1 tablespoon oil
50 g/2 oz smoked streaky bacon,
   derinded and chopped
1 onion, chopped
1 carrot, chopped
250 g/8 oz dried peas, soaked overnight
   in cold water and drained
1.2 litres/2 pints water, or ham stock
   (see note)
salt
freshly ground black pepper
1 tablespoon chopped parsley to garnish

Heat the oil in a large heavy-based pan, add the bacon and onion and sauté until turning golden. Add the carrot and fry for a further 5 to 10 minutes. Add the peas, water or stock, and salt and pepper to taste. Cover and simmer gently for 2 to 3 hours until the peas are soft.

Cool slightly then place half the soup in an electric blender or food processor and work to a smooth purée. Repeat with the remainder. Return to the pan

and reheat, adding a little more water or stock if the soup is too thick. Remove from the heat, adjust the seasoning, pour into a warmed tureen and sprinkle with the chopped parsley.
Serves 4

NOTE: If you have any ham stock, use this in place of the water providing it is not too salty.

107

Cream of Sweetcorn Soup

2 × 325 g/11 oz can sweetcorn kernels
15 g/½ oz butter or 1 tablespoon oil
1 small leek, sliced into rings
1 small carrot, peeled and sliced
600 ml/1 pint meat stock
2 egg yolks
4–5 teaspoons double cream
salt
freshly ground black pepper
pinch of curry powder
1 tablespoon chopped parsley to garnish

Drain the liquid from the sweetcorn into a bowl and reserve. Heat the butter or oil in a pan. Add the sweetcorn, leek and carrot and cook for 4 to 5 minutes. Stir in the stock and the reserved liquid from the sweetcorn. Simmer over a low heat for about 20 minutes.

Meanwhile, beat the egg yolks with the cream. Remove the soup from the heat and allow to cool slightly. Mix 2 to 3 tablespoons of the soup with the egg and cream mixture. Stir this mixture into the soup until incorporated. Season with salt, pepper and curry powder to taste. Sprinkle with the chopped parsley before serving.
Serves 4

Country Pea Broth

25 g/1 oz lard
1 clove garlic, peeled and halved
½ onion, peeled and chopped
500 g/1 lb yellow or green dried peas, soaked overnight in cold water
2 carrots, peeled and sliced
3 potatoes, peeled and diced
1 smoked pig's trotter or 175 g/6 oz smoked bacon, in one piece
1 litre/1¾ pints meat stock
freshly ground black pepper
dried thyme
1 sprig of parsley, chopped, to garnish

Melt the lard in a large pan. Add the garlic and fry until golden brown. Remove the garlic with a slotted spoon and discard. Add the onion to the flavoured fat and cook until transparent, about 5 minutes. Add the drained peas, carrots, potatoes and pig's trotter or bacon. Cover with the stock, bring to the boil, then lower the heat and cook gently for about 1¾ hours.

Remove the pig's trotter or bacon from the pan with a slotted spoon. Remove the meat from the bone and cut into slices or cubes. Place in a warmed serving bowl or tureen. Season the broth with pepper and thyme to taste. Pour the broth over the meat and sprinkle with parsley to serve.
Serves 4 to 6

NOTE: This nourishing soup is substantial enough to be served as a meal in itself. Serve it with plenty of crusty French bread.

Bavarian Lentil Broth

500 g/1 lb lentils
1 litre/1¾ pints meat stock
1 smoked pig's trotter or 175 g/6 oz smoked bacon, in one piece
1 small bunch mixed herbs (e.g. chives, parsley and thyme), chopped
1 small onion, peeled and chopped
1 tablespoon chopped chervil
salt
freshly ground black pepper
1 teaspoon ground paprika

Place the lentils, stock, pig's trotter or bacon, herbs and onion in a pan. Bring slowly to the boil, then lower the heat and cook gently for about 2 hours, stirring occasionally.

Remove the pig's trotter or bacon from the pan with a slotted spoon. Remove the meat from the bone, chop into small pieces and transfer to a warmed soup tureen. Flavour the broth with the chervil, salt and pepper to taste and paprika. Pour the hot broth over the meat and serve immediately.
Serves 4 to 6

NOTE: You can add chopped potato and carrot to this broth, if liked, or give it a sweet and sour flavour by adding vinegar and sugar to taste.

French Bean Salad with Vinaigrette Dressing

500 g/1 lb wax or French green beans, topped and tailed
salt
1 savory sprig, chopped
1 onion, peeled and finely chopped
1 teaspoon finely chopped dill
2 teaspoons snipped chives
½ clove garlic, peeled and crushed with salt
1 tablespoon wine vinegar
3 tablespoons white wine
1 teaspoon lemon juice
4 tablespoons olive oil
freshly ground black pepper
pinch of sugar

Bring 600 ml/1 pint water to the boil in a large pan, add the beans with a little salt and the savory. Bring back to the boil, lower the heat and cook gently for 10 to 12 minutes. Drain and cool.

To make the dressing, mix the onion with the dill, chives and garlic in a bowl. Add the vinegar, wine, lemon juice and oil, blending well. Season to taste with salt, pepper and the sugar.

Place the beans in a serving bowl and pour over the dressing. Leave to stand for about 1 hour for the flavours to develop. Toss again before serving.
Serves 4 to 6

NOTE: French Bean Salad with Vinaigrette Dressing is excellent served as an accompaniment to poached or grilled fish, or cold meat platters.

French Bean Salad with Vinaigrette Dressing; Chick Pea Salad

Chick Pea Salad

275 g/9 oz chick peas, soaked overnight
    in cold water
150 g/5 oz cooked smoked haddock or
    mackerel
3–4 tomatoes, cut into wedges
2 small onions, peeled and sliced into
    fine rings
4–6 stoned black olives
1 tablespoon chopped parsley
3 tablespoons Italian dressing
2 tablespoons orange juice
1 teaspoon chopped mint

Drain the chick peas and place in a pan with just enough cold water to cover. Bring to the boil, then lower the heat and cook gently for about 1½ hours. Drain in a sieve and place in a serving bowl. Remove any skin and bones from the fish and flake. Add to the chick peas with the tomatoes, onion rings, olives and parsley, mixing well.

To make the dressing, beat the Italian dressing with the orange juice and mint. Pour over the salad and toss to mix. Leave to stand for at least 20 minutes to allow the flavours to develop. Toss again before serving.
Serves 4

NOTE: Served with French bread and red wine, this salad makes an excellent supper or summer lunch dish.

Greek Bean Salad

275 g/9 oz dried black-eye or white
  haricot beans, soaked overnight in
  cold water
1 litre/1¾ pints water
salt
cayenne pepper
4 tomatoes, diced
2 large onions, peeled and chopped
125 g/4 oz feta cheese, cubed
2 cloves garlic, peeled and crushed with
  salt
2 tablespoons wine vinegar
4 tablespoons olive oil
½ teaspoon chopped oregano leaves

Drain the beans and place in a pan with the water. Bring slowly to the boil, then lower the heat and cook gently for about 1 hour. Season to taste with salt and cayenne pepper and cook for a further 10 to 20 minutes, until just tender. Drain in a sieve and leave to cool.

Place the beans in a large serving bowl and mix with the tomatoes, onion and cheese.

To make the dressing, beat the garlic with the vinegar, olive oil and oregano. Pour over the salad and toss to mix.

Leave to stand for 10 to 15 minutes to allow the flavours to develop. Toss again before serving.
Serves 4

NOTE: This salad can be served as part of a cold buffet for parties or picnics or, with brown bread and butter, as a lunch. If fresh oregano is unobtainable, use chopped parsley instead.

Colourful Bean Salad; Viennese Lentil Salad; Greek Bean Salad; Sweetcorn Salad

Sweetcorn Salad

1 × 198 g/7 oz can sweetcorn kernels,
  drained
4 tablespoons sliced, stoned green olives
1 tablespoon chopped, canned pimiento
25 g/1 oz cheese or cooked meat, diced
  or cut into strips
3 tablespoons olive oil
1 tablespoon lemon juice
1 clove garlic, peeled and crushed
salt
pinch of cayenne pepper

Mix the sweetcorn with the olives, pimiento, and cheese or cold meat in a salad bowl.

To make the dressing, beat the olive oil with the lemon juice, garlic, salt to taste and cayenne pepper until combined. Pour over the salad and toss to mix. Cover and chill in the refrigerator for 10 minutes to allow the flavours to develop. Toss again before serving.
Serves 4

Viennese Lentil Salad

350 g/12 oz green lentils
salt
freshly ground black pepper
1 clove garlic, peeled and crushed with
  salt
2 small onions, peeled and finely
  chopped
4 tablespoons French dressing
200 g/7 oz cooked ham, cut into fine
  strips

Place the lentils in a pan, cover with cold water, bring to the boil and cook for 1½ hours until tender. Drain, rinse under cold water and place in a serving bowl. Season to taste with salt and pepper. Stir in the garlic and onion.

Pour the dressing over the lentil mixture and toss thoroughly. Sprinkle the strips of ham over, or stir into the salad, as liked. Serve immediately.
Serves 4

Colourful Bean Salad

500 g/1 lb green beans, topped and
  tailed
salt
pinch of grated nutmeg
625 g/1¼ lb new potatoes, scrubbed and
  boiled in their skins
3–4 tomatoes, chopped or cut into
  wedges
1 onion, peeled and chopped
1 small bunch herbs, (e.g. chives,
  parsley, thyme), chopped
2 tablespoons mayonnaise
6 tablespoons double or soured cream
freshly ground black pepper

Bring 600 ml/1 pint water to the boil in a large pan, add the beans with a little salt and the nutmeg. Bring back to the boil, then lower the heat and cook gently for 10 to 12 minutes until just tender. Drain, rinse under cold water and transfer to a serving bowl. Add the potatoes and tomatoes and toss well. Scatter the onion and herbs on top.

To make the dressing, blend the mayonnaise with the cream and salt and pepper to taste. Pour over the bean salad and toss well to mix.
Serves 4 to 6

Pea and Chicken Casserole

4 chicken legs
salt
freshly ground black pepper
ground paprika
2–3 tablespoons oil
500 g/1 lb shelled peas, fresh or frozen
600 ml/1 pint meat stock
15 g/½ oz butter or margarine
scant 1 tablespoon flour
150 ml/¼ pint double cream
1 egg, separated
pinch of grated nutmeg
2 tablespoons chopped parsley
500 g/1 lb cooked long-grain rice

Season the chicken legs with salt, pepper and paprika to taste. Heat the oil in a frying pan, add the chicken legs and fry until crisp and golden brown all over. Transfer to a casserole dish.

Place the peas in a pan with the stock. Bring to the boil, then lower the heat and cook gently for about 15 minutes for fresh peas, 2 minutes for frozen ones, until almost tender. Drain, reserving half the stock.

Melt the butter or margarine in a pan. Add the flour and cook for 2 to 3 minutes, stirring constantly. Gradually add the reserved stock, blending well. Mix the cream with the egg yolk and stir into the sauce. Remove the pan immediately from the heat and season with the nutmeg. Whisk the egg white until it stands in stiff peaks. Fold into the sauce with the chopped parsley.

Add the peas and rice to the chicken, mixing well. Spoon over the frothy sauce. Cook in a preheated hot oven (220°C/425°F, Gas Mark 7) for about 15 minutes, until golden brown. Serve immediately.
Serves 4

Farmhouse Sweetcorn Stew

15 g/½ oz lard
400–500 g/14 oz–1 lb stewing beef, cubed
2 large onions, peeled and chopped
1 carrot, peeled and chopped
600 ml/1 pint meat stock
salt
freshly ground black pepper
1 teaspoon ground paprika
1 × 325 g/11½ oz can sweetcorn
1 × 64 g/2½ oz can tomato purée
150 ml/¼ pint soured cream

Melt the lard in a flameproof casserole, add the beef and brown on all sides. Add the onion and carrot and cook for about 5 minutes. Gradually add the stock, blending well. Season with salt and pepper to taste and the paprika. Cover and cook in a preheated moderate oven (160°C/325°F, Gas Mark 3) for 1 to 1¼ hours until tender.

Add the sweetcorn with the can juice, mixing well. Cover and cook for a further 30 minutes, stirring occasion-ally. Add the tomato purée, blending well. Reheat gently on top of the cooker but do not allow to boil. Add the soured cream and serve immediately.
Serves 4

NOTE: If you like a stew with a hot flavour, add 1 to 2 finely sliced chilli peppers to the mixture during the last 10 minutes of the cooking time.

Barbecue Beans with Chicken

4 chicken legs
salt
2 teaspoons ground paprika
1 tablespoon plain flour
4 tablespoons olive oil
1 × 439 g/15½ oz can red kidney beans
40 g/1½ oz butter
1 small onion, peeled and chopped
1 tablespoon caster sugar
1 tablespoon vinegar
½ teaspoon chilli powder
3 tablespoons tomato ketchup
75 ml/3 fl oz natural yogurt
parsley sprigs to garnish

Wash and dry the chicken legs, season with salt and half of the paprika and coat with the flour. Heat the oil in a frying pan and fry the chicken until golden brown and crisp all over. Trans-fer to a medium casserole dish. Drain the kidney beans and add to the casserole.

Melt the butter in a small pan, add the onion and cook for 5 minutes. Add the sugar and stir until dissolved. Add the vinegar, chilli powder and remain-ing paprika. Mix the tomato ketchup with the yogurt and add to the pan, stirring well to combine. Bring to the boil, then pour the sauce over the chicken and beans. Cook in a preheated moderately hot oven (200°C/400°F, Gas Mark 6) for about 20 minutes. Serve garnished with parsley.
Serves 4

Barbecue Beans with Chicken; Farmhouse Sweetcorn Stew; Sweetcorn and Tomato Bake

Quick Farmhouse Casserole

15 g/½ oz lard
1 onion, peeled and chopped
1 clove garlic, crushed
1 × 439 g/15½ oz can cannellini beans
1 × 439 g/15½ oz can red kidney beans
1 teaspoon chilli powder
1 teaspoon ground paprika
2 small smoked sausages
pinch of dried ground oregano
2 × 418 g/14¾ oz cans stewing beef
salt
freshly ground black pepper
1–2 tablespoons chopped parsley

Melt the lard in a flameproof casserole or deep heavy-based pan. Add the onion and garlic and cook gently for 5 minutes. Add the cannellini beans with their liquid and the kidney beans with their liquid. Stir in the chilli powder and paprika.

Cut each sausage into 3 slices, lay on top of the mixture and sprinkle with the oregano. Cover and cook over a low heat for 10 minutes.

Meanwhile, chop the stewing beef into bite-sized pieces, then add to the pan and stir well to mix. Cook for a further 5 to 10 minutes, until the meat is thoroughly heated through. Season with salt and pepper to taste and sprinkle with chopped parsley to taste before serving.
Serves 6 to 8

NOTE: This recipe is also an ideal way of using up cooked leftover meat to make a quick, nourishing meal.

Sweetcorn and Tomato Bake

3 tablespoons oil
1 clove garlic, peeled
275 g/9 oz tomatoes, cut into wedges
1 green pepper, cored, seeded and
    chopped
1 × 326 g/11½ oz can sweetcorn
salt
freshly ground black pepper
pinch of grated nutmeg
2 tablespoons unsalted peanuts, chopped
4–5 tablespoons double cream
1 egg yolk
2 egg whites

Heat the oil in a pan, add the garlic and fry until golden brown. Remove with a slotted spoon and discard. Add the tomatoes and green pepper and cook for 5 minutes. Add the sweetcorn with the can juice, salt and pepper to taste and the nutmeg. Cook, over a low heat, for about 8 minutes. Transfer to a medium ovenproof dish or a 1.2 litre/2 pint soufflé dish and stir in the peanuts.

Mix the cream with the egg yolk and stir into the vegetable mixture, blend-ing well. Whisk the egg whites until they stand in stiff peaks, then fold into the vegetable mixture with a metal spoon. Cook in a preheated hot oven (220°C/425°F, Gas Mark 7) for 25 to 30 minutes.
Serves 4

NOTE: This savoury bake is delicious and very filling. It can be served as a meal in itself with French bread. If you are serving it as an accompaniment, keep the meat portions fairly small.

Flageolets in Cayenne Butter Sauce

1 × 555 g/1 lb 2 oz can flageolet
   beans
15 g/½ oz butter
1 clove garlic, peeled and crushed
pinch of cayenne pepper
1–2 tablespoons finely chopped parsley,
   to garnish

Place the beans and their can juice in a pan. Bring slowly to the boil, then lower the heat and stir in the butter and garlic, blending well. Season with cayenne pepper to taste and sprinkle with parsley before serving.
Serves 8

Ratatouille with Cannellini Beans and Sausage

2 aubergines
salt
15 g/½ oz lard
50 g/2 oz smoked bacon, derinded and
   chopped
1–2 onions, peeled and sliced into rings
2–3 courgettes, sliced
4 tomatoes, cut into wedges
freshly ground black pepper
1 tablespoon dried Herbes de Provence
   (or mixture of dried rosemary, thyme
   and oregano)
1 litre/1¾ pints chicken stock
1 × 396 g/14 oz can cannellini beans,
   drained
275 g/9 oz garlic sausage, sliced
50 g/2 oz ham, finely chopped

Chop the aubergines into bite-sized pieces. Place in a sieve, sprinkle with salt and leave to drain for 30 minutes. Rinse and drain thoroughly. Pat dry with kitchen paper.

Melt the lard in a large pan. Add the bacon and fry until crisp. Add the aubergine, onions and courgettes and cook for 4 to 5 minutes. Add the tomatoes, salt and pepper to taste, and the herbs. Pour in the chicken stock, stir in the beans and cook gently for about 20 minutes.

Add the garlic sausage and ham and cook for a further 5 minutes until heated through. Serve immediately.
Serves 4

Broad Beans with Smoked Bacon

1 tablespoon oil
1 onion, peeled and chopped
325 g/11 oz smoked bacon, chopped
400 g/14 oz shelled broad beans
300 ml/½ pint meat stock
salt
ground paprika
1 teaspoon cornflour
1–2 tablespoons chopped parsley, to
    garnish

Heat the oil in a pan, add the onion and fry for about 5 minutes until golden. Add the smoked bacon, broad beans, stock, salt and paprika to taste. Cover and cook gently for about 15 minutes until the beans are tender.

Mix the cornflour with a little water to make a thin paste. Stir into the liquid in the pan, blending well. Bring to the boil, stirring continuously, and cook for 2 minutes until thickened.

Transfer to a warmed serving dish, sprinkle with chopped parsley to taste and serve immediately.
Serves 4

NOTE: Broad Beans with Smoked Bacon is delicious served with boiled potatoes or crusty brown bread.

Pease Pudding

500 g/1 lb dried split peas, soaked in
    cold water for 2 hours
25 g/1 oz butter
1 egg
1 tablespoon chopped mint
salt
freshly ground black pepper

ABOVE: *Flageolets in Cayenne Butter Sauce;
Broad Beans with Smoked Bacon*
LEFT: *Ratatouille with Cannellini Beans and
Sausage*

Drain the peas and cover with cold water, bring to the boil, skim and simmer for 1 hour. Drain, cool slightly, then place in an electric blender or food processor and work until smooth.

Add the butter, egg, mint, and seasoning to taste, and blend for a further 30 seconds.

Turn into a greased 1.5 litre/2½ pint ovenproof dish and bake in a preheated moderately hot oven (190°C/375°F, Gas Mark 5) for 30 to 35 minutes.
Serves 4 to 6

NOTE: Pease Pudding makes a delicious accompaniment to roast pork.

Instead of baking, Pease Pudding may be steamed or boiled. To steam, spoon into a 1.5 litre/2½ pint pudding basin. Cover with foil, making a pleat in the centre. Place the basin in a steamer over a saucepan, half-filled with simmering water, or on an upturned saucer in a saucepan and fill with boiling water to come two-thirds up the side of the basin. Cover with a lid and steam for 45 to 50 minutes.

To boil, turn the mixture into the centre of a 40 cm/16 inch square cotton cloth, tie tightly and place in a pan of simmering water. Cover and cook for 1 hour until tender.

Corn on the Cob Kebabs

2 large fresh corn on the cobs
pinch of salt
8 small tomatoes
125 g/4 oz smoked bacon, derinded and
    cubed
1 onion, peeled and sliced into thick
    rings
4–5 tablespoons oil
freshly ground black pepper
1 teaspoon ground paprika
pinch of garlic salt

Remove the husks and silky threads from the corn on the cobs. Bring a large pan of water to the boil, add the corn on the cobs and salt, lower the heat and cook gently for 8 to 10 minutes, or until tender. Drain thoroughly and cut into slices about 1½ cm/¾ inch thick.

Thread the corn on the cob slices, tomatoes, bacon and onion onto 4 wooden skewers, alternating the ingredients. Mix the oil with the pepper to taste, paprika and garlic salt. Brush the kebabs with the seasoned oil. Cook under a preheated hot grill for about 10 minutes until golden brown, turning and brushing regularly with the oil mixture. Serve immediately.
Serves 4

NOTE: Corn on the Cob Kebabs are delicious served with a risotto or creamy mashed potato.

Peas à la Française

500 g/1 lb shelled fresh peas
1 bunch spring onions, trimmed and
    chopped
50 g/2 oz butter
1 teaspoon sugar
salt
freshly ground black pepper
60 ml/2 fl oz water
1 crisp head of lettuce

Place the peas in a heavy-based pan with the spring onions, half of the butter, the sugar, salt and pepper to taste, and the water. Bring to the boil, lower the heat, cover and simmer for 10 minutes.

Remove the outer leaves of the lettuce and discard. Cut the heart into quarters and add to the pan. Cover the pan and simmer for a further 3 to 5 minutes, shaking the pan occasionally to turn over the contents.

Remove from the heat, add the remaining butter and toss well. Transfer to a warmed serving dish and serve immediately.
Serves 4

Mexican Sweetcorn

25 g/1 oz butter
1 × 326 g/11½ oz can sweetcorn,
    drained
½ chilli pepper, seeded and sliced
1 red pepper, cored, seeded and chopped
2 cloves garlic, peeled and crushed
½ tablespoon lemon juice
salt

Melt half of the butter in a pan. Drain the sweetcorn and add to the pan with the chilli, red pepper and garlic. Mix thoroughly and cook over a low heat for 4 to 5 minutes. Add the lemon juice, salt to taste, and the remaining butter, mixing well. Serve immediately.
Serves 4

NOTE: Mexican Sweetcorn is a hot vegetable dish, excellent with grills like porterhouse steak. By adding cooked long-grain rice and slices of garlic sausage you can turn this vegetable dish into a Mexican casserole, suitable to serve as a main meal dish.

Peas in Butter and Parmesan

750 g/1½ lb shelled fresh peas
300 ml/½ pint chicken stock
25 g/1 oz butter
1 clove garlic, peeled
25 g/1 oz bacon, derinded and chopped
4–5 tablespoons double cream
2 eggs
50 g/2 oz Parmesan cheese, grated
2 tablespoons chopped parsley

Place the peas and chicken stock in a pan. Bring to the boil, then lower the heat and cook gently for about 15 to 20 minutes.

Meanwhile, melt the butter in a small pan, add the garlic and fry until golden brown. Remove and discard the garlic. Add the bacon to the garlic butter and fry until lightly browned.

Add the cream and bring to the boil. Keep hot over a gentle heat.

Meanwhile, beat the eggs with the Parmesan cheese and parsley. Drain the peas thoroughly and mix with the egg mixture. Pour the hot cream and bacon sauce over the peas and stir well to mix. Serve immediately.
Serves 6 to 8

Peas in Mint Sauce

500 g/1 lb shelled fresh peas
2 tomatoes, peeled and chopped
150 ml/¼ pint meat stock
15 g/½ oz butter
1 mint sprig, chopped
4 tablespoons double cream
salt
freshly ground black pepper

Place the peas and tomatoes in a pan with the stock. Bring to the boil, then lower the heat and cook gently for about 15 to 20 minutes. Add the butter. Stir the mint into the cream with a little of the pea cooking liquid. Remove the pan from the heat and stir the mint mixture into the peas. Season with salt and pepper to taste. Transfer to a warmed serving dish and serve immediately.
Serves 4 to 6

LEFT: *Peas in Butter and Parmesan; Peas à la Française; Mexican Sweetcorn*

Beans in Wine and Cream Sauce

750 g/1½ lb green beans, topped, tailed
   and sliced
salt
1 savory sprig (optional)
pinch of grated nutmeg
15 g/½ oz butter
1 tablespoon flour
120 ml/4 fl oz dry white wine
4 tablespoons double cream
50 g/2 oz cooked ham, chopped
cayenne pepper

Place the beans in a pan with just enough salted water to cover. Add the savory if using, and the nutmeg, bring to the boil, then lower the heat and cook gently for 8 to 10 minutes. Drain and reserve half of the cooking liquid from the beans. Discard the savory.

Melt the butter in a pan. Add the flour and cook for 4 to 5 minutes until light brown. Gradually add the reserved cooking liquid and the white wine, stirring well to combine. Bring to the boil, stirring constantly. Remove the pan from the heat and stir in the cream and ham. Season with salt and cayenne pepper to taste.

Add the beans to the sauce and toss well to serve. Alternatively the sauce may be handed separately.
Serves 6

NOTE: Serve with steak or roast lamb.

Sweetcorn and Aubergines

275 g/9 oz aubergines
juice of 1 lemon
salt
4 tablespoons olive oil
1 × 326 g/11½ oz can sweetcorn
1 green pepper, cored, seeded and sliced
   into strips
freshly ground black pepper
pinch of cayenne pepper
15 g/½ oz butter
1 tablespoon chopped parsley, to
   garnish

Slice the aubergines and cut any large slices in half. Place in a sieve, sprinkle with the lemon juice and salt, cover and leave to drain for about 15 minutes. Rinse thoroughly and pat dry with kitchen paper.

Heat the oil in a pan. Add the aubergines and fry until golden on both sides. Add the sweetcorn with its can juice and the green pepper. Cook, over a low heat, for about 10 minutes. Season with salt and pepper to taste, and the cayenne pepper. Stir in the butter and sprinkle with the chopped parsley. Serve immediately.
Serves 4 to 6

NOTE: Sweetcorn and Aubergines is delicious served with omelettes, scrambled egg or spicy sausages.

Haricot Beans Burgundy Style; Beans in Wine and Cream Sauce, Mangetout in Garlic Butter

Haricot Beans Burgundy-style

500 g/1 lb haricot beans, soaked
    overnight in cold water
600 ml/1 pint water
½ sprig of rosemary
2 shallots, peeled and finely sliced
1 bay leaf
1 × 64 g/2¼ oz can tomato purée
1 tablespoon oil
125 g/4 oz bacon, derinded and
    chopped
150 ml/¼ pint dry red wine
salt and freshly ground black pepper
1 tablespoon chopped herbs

Drain the haricot beans and place them in a pan with the water. Add the rosemary, bring slowly to the boil, then lower the heat, cover and cook gently for about 30 minutes.

Add the shallots, bay leaf and tomato purée and stir well. Cover and simmer over a low heat, for a further 20 to 30 minutes. Discard the rosemary sprig.

Meanwhile heat the oil in a large pan. Add the bacon and fry until crisp and brown. Add the red wine and the beans with their cooking liquid. Season with salt and pepper to taste and cook for a further 5 minutes. Discard the bay leaf. Sprinkle with the herbs before serving.
Serves 6

NOTE: Serve this filling bean dish with smoked meat or leg of lamb.

Mangetout in Garlic Butter

750 g/1½ lb mangetout, topped and
    tailed
pinch of salt
1 tablespoon oil
25 g/1 oz butter
1 clove garlic, peeled and chopped
1 tablespoon chopped parsley, to
    garnish

Place the mangetout in a pan with just enough water to cover. Add the salt and the oil. Bring to the boil, then lower the heat and cook gently for about 5 to 10 minutes, depending on the ripeness and freshness of the mangetout (very young pods will need only about 2 minutes).

Meanwhile, melt the butter in a pan, add the garlic and fry for 2 minutes.

Drain the mangetout thoroughly and place in a warmed serving dish. Pour over the hot garlic butter. Sprinkle with parsley before serving.
Serves 4

NOTE: Mangetout in Garlic Butter is a delicious vegetable dish to serve with eggs or poultry.

French Beans with Bacon

750 g/1½ lb French beans, topped and tailed
salt
1 savory sprig (optional)
25 g/1 oz butter
40 g/1½ oz bacon, derinded and chopped
1 parsley sprig, chopped
freshly ground black pepper

Place the beans in a pan with just enough salted water to cover. Add the savory if using, and bring to the boil, then lower the heat and cook gently for 10 to 12 minutes. Remove and discard the savory if used.

Melt the butter in a pan, add the bacon and fry gently until crisp. Add the parsley and pepper to taste.

Drain the French beans and place in a serving bowl. Pour over the bacon and butter. Toss well to mix. Serve immediately.
Serves 6

NOTE: French Beans with Bacon is delicious served as a vegetable accompaniment to rissoles or grilled chops.

Mangetout with Piquant Dressing

750 g/1½ lb mangetout, topped and tailed
salt
3 tablespoons vinegar
3 tablespoons water
4 tablespoons sesame or olive oil
1 teaspoon French mustard
1 tablespoon chive or other herb mustard
1 tablespoon soy sauce
1 sprig of parsley, chopped
pinch of freshly ground black pepper

Place the mangetout in a pan with just enough water to cover. Add a pinch of salt and bring to the boil, then lower the heat and cook gently for 5 to 10 minutes, depending on the ripeness and freshness of the mangetout (very young pods will need only about 2 minutes).

To make the dressing, beat together the vinegar, water, oil, mustards, soy sauce, parsley, and salt and pepper to taste until blended.

Drain the mangetout thoroughly and transfer them to a serving bowl. Pour the dressing over the mangetout while they are still warm. Leave to marinate for at least 5 minutes before serving. Allow to stand for about 45 minutes if serving cold.
Serves 6

NOTE: This dish is equally delicious served hot as a vegetable dish, or cold as part of a buffet.

Italian-style Peas

4 tablespoons olive oil
1 clove garlic, peeled and halved
50 g/2 oz gammon, sliced into fine
  strips
400 g/14 oz shelled fresh or frozen peas
275 g/9 oz tomatoes, peeled and
  chopped
salt
freshly ground black pepper
TO GARNISH:
1 basil sprig, chopped
1 tablespoon chopped parsley

Heat the oil in a pan. Add the garlic and fry until golden brown. Remove and discard the garlic. Add the gammon, peas and tomatoes to the pan, mixing well. Season with salt and pepper to taste and cook, over a low heat, for about 10 to 15 minutes, adding a little water if necessary. Sprinkle with the basil and parsley before serving.
Serves 4

NOTE: Serve with veal or poultry.

Haricot Beans in Pepper Cream Sauce

1 × 396 g/14 oz can haricot beans
1 red pepper, cored, seeded and cut into
  strips
1 teaspoon ground paprika
pinch of chilli powder
15 g/½ oz butter
2 teaspoons plain flour
150 ml/¼ pint double cream
2 tablespoons fresh or canned green
  peppercorns
1 parsley sprig, chopped
salt
cayenne pepper

*Italian-style Peas; Grilled Corn on the Cob;
Mangetout with Piquant Dressing*

Place the beans with their can juice in a pan. Add the pepper, paprika and chilli powder. Bring slowly to the boil.

Meanwhile, melt the butter in a pan. Add the flour and cook for 1 minute. Gradually add a little of the bean liquid and the cream, blending well after each addition. Add the peppercorns and parsley and cook over a gentle heat for 2 to 3 minutes. Pour the pepper sauce over the beans, season with salt and cayenne to taste, mixing well. Bring to the boil, stirring constantly. Serve hot.
Serves 4

NOTE: This quick bean dish is excellent with sausages.

Grilled Corn on the Cob

4 fresh corn on the cobs
pinch of salt
pinch of cayenne pepper
freshly ground white pepper
125 g/4 oz butter

Remove the husks and silky threads from the corn on the cobs. Bring a large pan of water to the boil, add the corn on the cobs, salt and cayenne, lower the heat and cook for about 8 to 10 minutes, or until tender. Drain the cobs thoroughly and season to taste with salt and pepper.

Meanwhile, melt the butter in a pan. Place the corn on the cobs on a grill rack over a drip tray. Brush with some of the melted butter. Cook, under a preheated hot grill until golden brown on every side, turning and brushing regularly with more melted butter.

To serve, arrange the corn on the cobs on a warmed serving dish and pour over the butter from the drip tray. Serve immediately.
Serves 4

NOTE: Corn on the cob makes a mouth-watering barbecue or starter dish. Served with French bread and a fresh salad, it also makes a delicious light summer supper dish.

Grilled Flageolet Beans and Bone Marrow

1 × 555 g/1 lb 2 oz can flageolet beans
salt
freshly ground black pepper
2 tablespoons chopped parsley
2 marrow bones
2 rashers bacon, derinded

Place the flageolet beans and their can juice in a pan. Bring slowly to the boil, then lower the heat and cook gently for 2 minutes. Season with salt and pepper to taste and stir in the parsley. Transfer to a flameproof serving dish.

Remove the marrow from the bones with a pointed knife and cut into fine slices. Arrange the slices of marrow and bacon over the beans. Cook under a preheated hot grill for 5 to 8 minutes. Serve immediately.
Serves 8

NOTE: This is delicious served with steak, veal, turkey or fish dishes.

FRUITING VEGETABLES

Richly colourful and exotic in nature, the fruiting vegetable family ranges from the simple and mildly-flavoured cucumber to the sweetly aromatic pepper in its spectrum of colours. Mixed and matched with members of their own family, like the aubergine, tomato or courgette, they make a vegetable combination that is hard to beat in flavour and colour.

Squashes, also fruiting vegetables, range in size from the fingerlength courgette to the marrow and balloon-sized pumpkin. They all have a rather elusive, almost sweet flavour and high water content. They can be boiled, braised, sautéed, puréed or cooked and preserved in an infinite number of ways with extremely tasty results.

Raw, cooked or preserved, fruiting vegetables offer a rich versatility of dishes. Stuff them with meat or cheese mixtures, serve them with a rich creamy sauce or sauté them in a garlic, herb or spice-flavoured oil and they become a hearty main meal or delicious accompaniment.

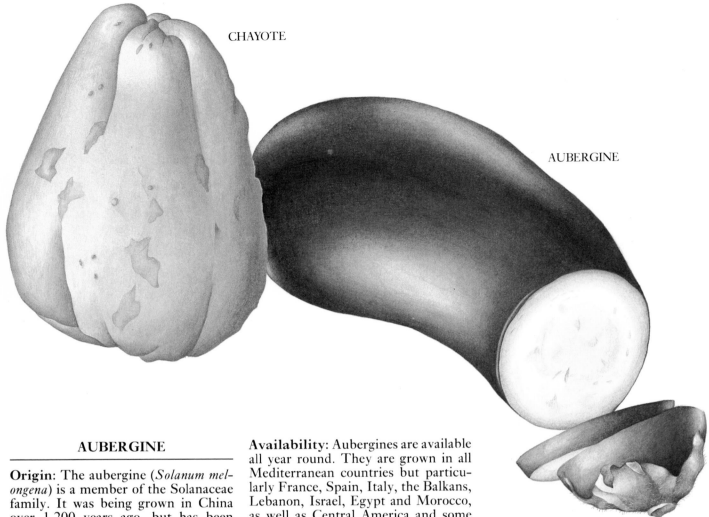

CHAYOTE

AUBERGINE

AUBERGINE

Origin: The aubergine (*Solanum melongena*) is a member of the Solanaceae family. It was being grown in China over 1,200 years ago, but has been known for even longer in its native East Indies. There the aubergine fruits first grew to the size and shape of eggs, hence their unusual alternative name of eggplant. The aubergine did not arrive in Europe until the 17th century but it quickly became a popular vegetable.

The aubergine may now be considered to all intent, and purpose, a typical Mediterranean vegetable – there is no southern European or North African country where it is not known and highly popular.

In appearance aubergines are firm, elongated fruits, sometimes curved, which vary considerably in size. Their smooth, shiny skins vary from a purple red colour to an almost black purple. The inner flesh is white with tiny soft seeds, which are eaten with the vegetable. There is a small, hard calyx at the stalk end.

The aubergine does not have a very pronounced flavour of its own; it relies upon the addition of lemon juice, garlic, herbs and other flavourings to enhance its flavour. Aubergine combines particularly well with tomatoes, courgettes and sweet peppers.

Availability: Aubergines are available all year round. They are grown in all Mediterranean countries but particularly France, Spain, Italy, the Balkans, Lebanon, Israel, Egypt and Morocco, as well as Central America and some African countries. The main imports reaching Britain come from Italy, Spain, Israel, Morocco and France.

Buying: Aubergines are sold by weight. You will need about 125 g/ 4 oz per serving. Choose fruits with firm, shiny and plump skins without blemishes. The calyx should be fresh and bright green. Avoid any that look shrivelled or bruised – signs of bruising or decay will show up as dark brown spots on the surface of the fruit.

Preparation and serving: Remove the calyx and rinse the vegetable before preparation. For most dishes the fruit is sliced thinly. Aubergines contain the substance solanin, which gives the flesh a slightly bitter taste when it is not quite ripe. To remove this, sprinkle the cut flesh with salt and lemon juice and leave to stand for about 30 minutes to draw out the bitter juices. Rinse and dry before use.

Sliced aubergines may then be lightly fried – but take care for they will absorb a great deal of oil during this process. Alternatively they may be braised, steamed or baked. Perhaps the most popular and classic dish using aubergines prepared in this way is the tasty vegetable dish ratatouille – where aubergines are cooked with peppers, tomatoes and sometimes courgettes.

Another popular way of serving aubergines is stuffed and baked. Halve the aubergine lengthwise and remove the flesh with a sharp spoon. Cut into small pieces and degorge as before. Mix with a variety of stuffing ingredients, such as tomatoes, cheese, breadcrumbs, bacon and herbs. Return to the shell and bake until crisp and golden, about 45 minutes.

Aubergines are also used in the classic meat dish, moussaka where they are layered with a savoury meat mixture and potatoes, and topped with a cheese or white sauce.

Nutritional value: Aubergines are valuable for their vitamins B_1, B_2 and C. They also provide a little iron and calcium, and some carbohydrate. Low in calories they contain only 14 Calories (59 kj) per 100 g/$3\frac{1}{2}$ oz.

CHAYOTE

Origin: The chayote (*Sechium edule*) is a member of the Cucurbitaceae family, and is therefore a squash or gourd. It originated in South America. It is now grown in many tropical countries but is particularly popular in South and Central America. It takes its most popular name chayote from the Aztec word chayoti, but is also known as choko, chaco and xuxu.

The chayote is one of the more exotic kinds of squash. Its green or sometimes yellowish green fruits look rather like irregular-shaped pears. It has a ridged, rough skin, which may be spiny, covering a flesh that is white and slightly sticky. It has a soft, flat seed in its centre which is usually removed for cooking.

The chayote flavour is somewhere between that of cucumber, pumpkin and courgette and slightly sweetish. The size and weights of the fruit vary between 7.5 to 15 cm/3 to 6 inches long and 250 to 400 g/8 to 14 oz.

Availability: Chayotes are in season from December to March. They are grown in South America, especially Brazil, Central America, the West Indies, Mexico, eastern Asia and North Africa. Main imports come to Britain from Mexico and Brazil.

Buying: Chayotes are sold individually. Choose fruits that are firm, fresh looking and of good appearance. Avoid any with shrivelled or bruised skins.

Preparation and serving: Chayotes cannot be eaten raw. Peel under running water, halve and remove the seed. Slice or cut into smaller pieces and cook in boiling salted water for 45 to 50 minutes until tender. Drain and serve with melted butter. Chayote can also be served in a savoury sauce, baked in a gratin, made into a soup or used as part of a salad. Cooked with sugar and spices it will also make a delicious dessert on its own or an ingredient to add to a fruit salad.

Nutritional value: Chayotes are valuable for their good supply of Vitamin C. They also have a little protein. Low in calories they contain only 30 Calories (125 kj) per 100 g/3½ oz.

CHILLIS

Origin: The chilli (*Capsicum annuum*) is a member of the Solanaceae family. It is a small hot pepper, native to South America. It was brought to Europe by the Spanish.

In appearance chillis resemble finger-length miniature sweet peppers; they may be green, yellow, orange or red in colour. Many varieties are wider towards the stalk end, some are narrow all along their length. Chillis contain a great many small white seeds which are very hot indeed. The flavour is like that of a sweet pepper but a great deal hotter and stronger.

Availability: Chillis are in season during the summer and autumn and occasionally may be found at other times of the year. They are grown in all hot countries of the world, but are extensively grown in India and South America. Most of the chillis imported into Britain come from Italy, Morocco and the Balkans.

Buying: Fresh chillis are sold by weight. Only buy a small quantity since they will go a long way. Most supermarkets pre-pack the peppers in small 125 g/4 oz packs for convenient use.

Choose fruits that are firm, well-formed and of fresh appearance. The colour of the fruits is no guide to just how hot they will be.

Chillis are available in other convenient forms: dried chillis may be sold whole or ground into a powder for use in casseroles, curries and other spicy concoctions like chilli con carne; cayenne pepper is also a ground mild chilli powder; and crushed fresh chillis may be purchased as chilli pastes and sauces, one of the hottest being known as Tabasco sauce.

Preparation and serving: If you wish to use chillis to simply heat up a dish, all you need to do is to chop the flesh into small pieces or strips, discarding the stalk and seeds as you do so. However, if you intend to use chilli peppers to impart a strong flavour then slice open the chilli, remove the seeds, cover with boiling water and leave to stand overnight. The chillis can then be chopped, sliced or ground to a purée for use.

Nutritional value: Since only small quantities of chillis are used in any dish they are eaten mainly for their flavour rather than nutritional value. Low in calories they contain only 15 Calories (65 kj) per 100 g/3½ oz.

COURGETTES

Origin: The courgette (*Cucurbita pepo*) is a member of the Cucurbitaceae family. It is really an immature or baby vegetable marrow. The courgette is also known as zucchini, its Italian name.

Courgettes originated in the warm zones of America, particularly South America, and in Africa. They were brought to Europe about 400 years ago and were first grown in Italy.

In appearance they are light to dark green in colour, usually with a light-coloured speckling on their skins. Long and slender they usually measure 10 to 15 cm/4 to 6 inches long and are slightly reminiscent of cucumbers. Their flavour is very delicate and almost elusive – it only becomes stronger when cooked with other flavourings, such as

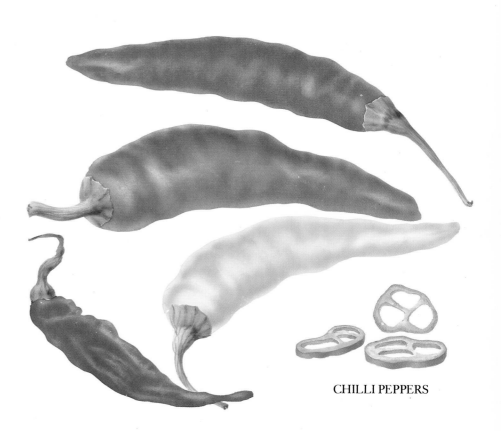

CHILLI PEPPERS

herbs, garlic and spices. However this means that courgettes are ideal to serve with almost any fish, meat, poultry or game dish.

Availability: Courgettes are available all year round. Homegrown courgettes can be found during the summer and early autumn. Courgettes are grown in almost all sunny countries, but especially in North Africa, the East and Italy. Most of those imported into Britain arrive from Italy.

Buying: Courgettes are sold by weight. Choose fruits that are of an even size, fresh appearance and good green colour. Avoid any that are withered or soft to the touch – they will generally be old and of poor flavour.

Preparation and serving: Courgettes have a soft, edible skin that is usually eaten with the inner flesh. To prepare, simply rinse the courgettes and remove the stem end. Cook whole, sliced or cubed, in boiling salted water for about 10 to 15 minutes, according to size and maturity. Drain and toss in butter, with a few chopped herbs or with seasonings if liked.

Courgettes can also be fried in a little butter or sautéed in a garlic-flavoured oil. Alternatively, stuff and bake them in the same way as aubergines, for a tasty supper dish.

Nutritional value: Courgettes are valuable for their Vitamin C. They contain a great deal of water and are consequently low in calories, with only 7 Calories (32 kj) per 100 g/$3\frac{1}{2}$ oz.

CUCUMBER

Origin: The cucumber (*Cucumis sativus*) is a member of the Cucurbitaceae family. It originally came from South-East Asia, and was being grown there some 4,000 years ago. It soon reached Egypt, ancient Greece and Rome, where it became very popular as both a vegetable and a medicinal plant. The cucumber did not become popular in the rest of Europe until the 16th century.

In more northern European countries it is largely grown in glasshouses, since it is extremely sensitive to frost, although the small ridge cucumbers will grow well out of doors in the British climate.

In appearance the cucumber is a long, smooth-skinned fruiting vegetable, ridged and dark green in colour. There are, however, many different varieties of cucumber and the related gherkin to choose from – coming in many different sizes and shapes. Some varieties find particular use in salads, others for cooking and others are most suitable for pickling.

Some of the shorter varieties have a white striped and tougher skin, while other larger varieties look more like marrows and can weigh up to 4 kg/9 lb.

Availability: Fresh cucumbers for salad and cooking purposes are available all year round. The main harvesting season for outdoor cucumbers in Europe is from August to late September. Those sold during the spring, autumn and winter months are almost exclusively grown under glass. Cucumbers suitable for pickling are in season twice a year, in spring and autumn.

Cucumbers are grown in almost every country in the world. Hungary is a country which traditionally grows a great deal. Most of the imports coming to Britain arrive from Holland, Italy and Belgium.

Buying: Cucumbers for salad use are bought whole, in halves or even quarters. Small cucumbers for pickling are generally sold by weight. Look for fruits that are firm and fresh in appearance. Reject any that look limp or tired.

Preparation and serving: There is generally no need to peel cucumbers before using in a salad or cooked dish. Simply rinse and dry before slicing or chopping.

Cook sliced, chopped or strips of cucumber in boiling salted water for about 10 minutes, or steam and top with butter to serve. Alternatively dot with butter and bake for about 30 minutes until tender.

Cucumber makes a delicious salad vegetable, an attractive garnish, and an unusual vegetable dish as well as a tasty relish, pickle or base for a soup.

Nutritional value: Cucumbers are valuable for their supply of Vitamin A, phosphorus, iron and calcium. Very low in calories they are ideal for slimmers, containing only 10 Calories (43 kj) per 100 g/$3\frac{1}{2}$ oz.

MARROW

Origin: The vegetable marrow (*Cucurbita pepo*) is a member of the Cucurbitaceae family. It originated in Central and South America and was probably introduced into this country during the Middle Ages.

Marrows are long, oval-shaped, edible gourds with ridged green skins; some are distinctively striped green and white. For many years they have been popular with the home vegetable gardener, although their flavour is

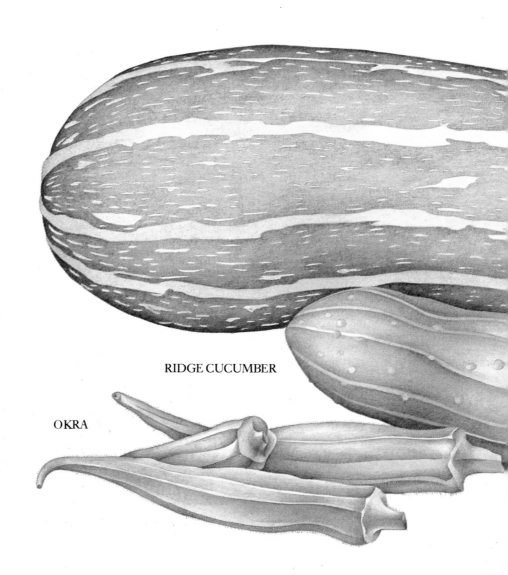

RIDGE CUCUMBER

OKRA

rather bland. Courgettes, which are marrows picked when very young, have a much more delicate flavour.

Availability: Marrows are in season from July to October. Most of those on sale here are produced in this country.

Buying: Marrows are usually sold whole, priced by weight. Choose fruits that are firm and fresh in appearance. For tenderness and flavour, select or pick marrows from the garden when they are no more than 30 cm/12 inches.

Preparation and serving: Young marrows are delicious stuffed and baked; enrich them with stronger tasting vegetables, such as onions, garlic and tomatoes. Larger marrows have tougher skins which must be peeled away before use. After peeling, halve the marrow lengthwise, scrape out all seeds and stringy fibres and cut each half into 3 or 4 pieces. Cook gently in butter or the minimum amount of water for about 10 minutes until just tender. Serve tossed in butter or with a tomato, cheese or herb-flavoured white sauce. Marrows will also make a delicious gratin or soup.

Nutritional value: Marrows have a very high water content and therefore provide water-soluble vitamins B and C, and minerals. They only contain 7 Calories (32 kj) per 100 g/3½ oz.

OKRA

Origin: Okra (*Hibiscus esculentus*) is a member of the Malvaceae family. It is also known as gumbo and lady's fingers. Okra is one of the oldest vegetables in the world, coming originally from Africa, or more precisely Abyssinia. It was grown by the Bantu tribes in Africa, and the plants were brought to the Caribbean islands by Negro slaves. From the Caribbean it spread to America, where it became known as gumbo. Today, it is part of everyday cooking in the Balkans, the East and South America. It is very popular in America, and in its native Africa, where the main growing areas lie.

The young green okra pods can vary between pale and bright green. They grow to a finger-length size, hence the American name of lady's fingers. The pods are slender, six-sided, and sometimes covered with a very slightly hairy down. Inside, they are white with small soft seeds, that give off a sticky juice during cooking. Their flavour is neutral to slightly bitter, and very mild.

Availability: Fresh okra is available in the United Kingdom, imported mainly from Kenya. It is in season from summer to early autumn, but is often available at other times of the year, at a

price. Canned okra is imported into this country from the Balkans and America.

Buying: Okra is sold by weight. Choose pods that are firm, bright green or fresh in appearance.

Preparation and serving: Cut off the tips and stalk ends of the okra to use. Halve any long or very broad pods and cut into pieces if liked. Place in a sieve, rinse and drain thoroughly.

To cook, boil the okra in salted water for about 5 minutes, until tender, then follow the specific recipe instructions. For casseroles and soups, cut the pods into small pieces; they will give off a great deal of their sticky juices, which helps to thicken or bind the dish.

Canned okra must be rinsed before use then reheated according to the manufacturer's instructions.

Okra is delicious with almost all kinds of meat, with offal and fish. It is widely used in the southern States of America in soups and rice dishes. It appears in Indian cuisine as bhindi, and as bamia in the Middle East, cooked in a lamb stew. Okra is especially delicious in curries, soups, stews and fried as fritters.

Nutritional value: Okra is a rich source of several vitamins and minerals, especially calcium. It contains only 17 Calories (71 kj) per 100 g/3½ oz.

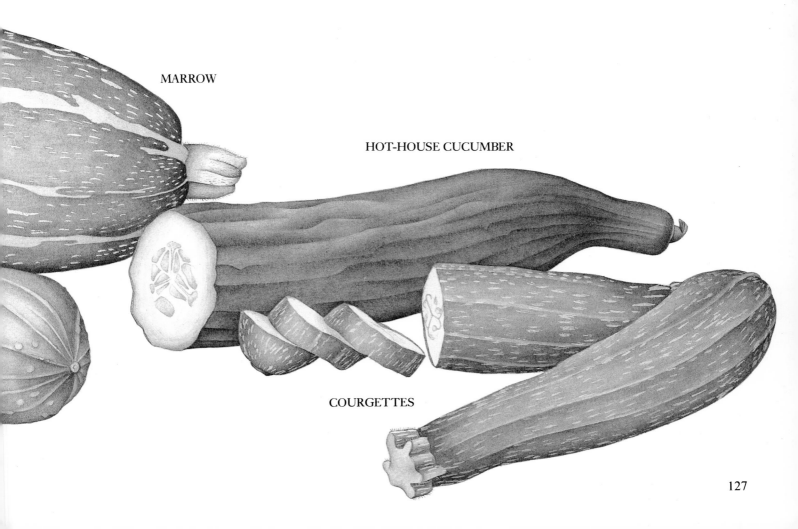

MARROW

HOT-HOUSE CUCUMBER

COURGETTES

SWEET PEPPERS

Origin: The sweet pepper (*Capsicum annuum*) is a member of the Solanaceae family, and is related to the hotter chilli pepper (see page 125). It is a native of Central America. It was discovered there by Columbus and taken to Spain, but did not reach Hungary, which is the main area of cultivation, until the 16th century.

Sweet peppers come in many sizes and colours. Green peppers are the unripened fruit and therefore the least sweet. Most peppers grown in this country are picked at this stage because they are otherwise slow to ripen.

As sweet peppers ripen, they turn yellow, through orange, to red. They can however only do this on the plant — once picked they will hardly ripen any further. Red peppers are the mildest ones. White and black sweet pepper varieties are now also available.

Availability: Peppers are available all year round. They are grown in Hungary, Spain, Bulgaria, Italy, Czechoslovakia, North Africa, Central and South America and Israel. Imports reaching Britain from these countries arrive during the summer and autumn. Peppers on sale in Britain during the winter come from Israel.

Canned sweet peppers, or pimientos, are conveniently available.

Buying: Sweet peppers should always be firm, smooth and shiny in appearance. Look for well-formed fruits that are unblemished.

Preparation and serving: Peppers are delicious both cooked and raw. Use them raw in salads, sandwiches and marinated dishes. Cooked they make a delicious vegetable accompaniment to roast meats and, cooked with aubergines, courgettes and tomatoes, they are a tasty supper or starter dish. Whole peppers can be stuffed with savoury meat and rice mixtures and baked in the oven.

To prepare a sweet pepper, unless serving whole, halve lengthwise and remove the central core, white pith and seeds. Rinse and chop or slice thinly.

To prepare a pepper for stuffing, cut around the core with a sharp knife and remove, then scrape out the pith and seeds. Rinse thoroughly.

To peel sweet peppers, place under a preheated hot grill and turn frequently until the skin is charred and blistered all over. The skins can then be easily removed under cold running water.

Nutritional value: Peppers are very rich in Vitamin C, B_1, B_2 and D. Low in calories they are a useful in slimming diets. They contain only 15 Calories (65 kj) per 100 g/$3\frac{1}{2}$ oz.

PUMPKIN

Origin: Pumpkin (*Cucurbita maxima*) is a member of the Cucurbitaceae family, and as such is one of the numerous species of the pumpkin and squash family, which includes giant pumpkins, smaller pumpkins, gourds, squashes, custard marrows, custard squash and vegetable marrows.

Pumpkin is native to Central America, Mexico and the West Indies. It was being used as a vegetable fruit as far back as the times of the ancient Egyptians and Greeks, and was popular in

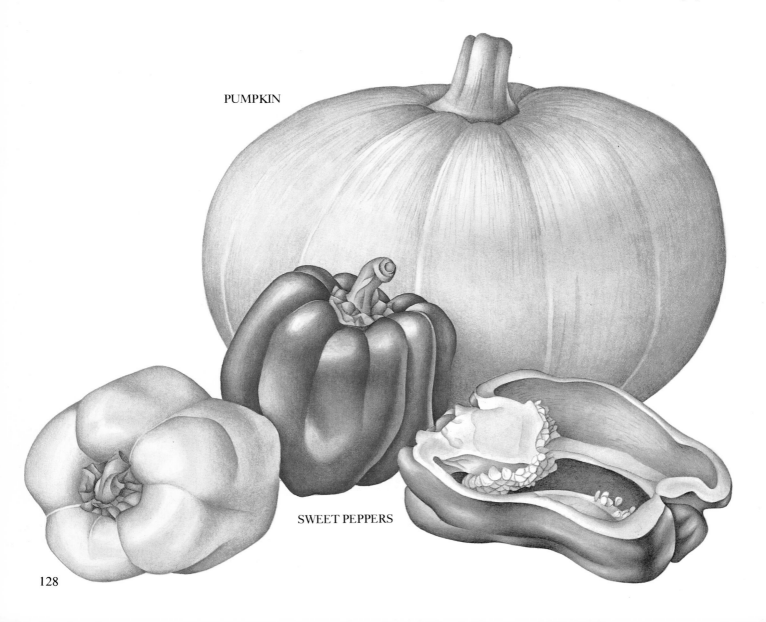

PUMPKIN

SWEET PEPPERS

BEEFSTEAK TOMATO

ENGLISH TOMATOES

PLUM TOMATO

CHERRY TOMATOES

Europe in the Middle Ages.

Nowadays pumpkins are associated with Hallowe'en in Britain, but they are rarely eaten as a vegetable. Pumpkins vary a great deal in their size and can weigh up to 50 kg/110 lb.

Availability: Pumpkins are in season during September and October but can generally be found until the end of November. They are grown throughout the world, but particularly in Russia, Romania, Central America and the USA. Imported pumpkin comes to Britain from America and the Balkans.

Buying: Whole small pumpkins are generally sold individually but priced according to weight. Larger pumpkins are halved or sold in slices or pieces and priced according to weight.

Canned pumpkin is also available and sometimes it is possible to find frozen pumpkin prepared in a savoury sauce.

Preparation and serving: Rinse pumpkin well, peel and remove any seeds. Cut into cubes and cook in boiling salted water until tender, 15 to 30 minutes, depending upon size and type. Drain thoroughly and serve tossed in butter and chopped herbs, or with a savoury sauce.

Pumpkin is also delicious baked and then puréed, or stuffed and baked.

It can also be pickled, made into tasty soups, or used to make the traditional American pumpkin pie which is served on Thanksgiving Day.

Nutritional value: Pumpkin contains a good supply of Vitamins A and C. Low in calories it has only 15 Calories (65 kj) per 100 g/3½ oz.

TOMATOES

Origin: The tomato (*Lycopersicum esculentum*) is a member of the Solanaceae family. It is native to South America, to be more precise to Peru and Mexico. Tomatoes were first brought to Europe by Cortez in the 15th century, after his conquest of Mexico. The first European tomatoes were not much bigger than little mirabelle plums, and looked rather like the 'cherry' tomatoes on sale today. Tomatoes were originally grown in gardens for their decorative effect – it was not until the 18th century that they were grown for their value as a food. The Italians were particularly successful at cultivating them.

There are many varieties of tomato in cultivation today. The uniform round, smooth tomatoes are the most popular kind grown in Britain. They are very juicy and full of seeds, mild in flavour and suitable for use in making salads soups, for grilling and for cooking. The much larger irregular-shaped tomatoes are very popular in the Mediterranean countries. These fleshy tomatoes can be used raw or cooked. It is the 'beef' or beefsteak variety which is more frequently on sale in this country than the marmande variety. Finally there are 'plum' tomatoes, mainly imported from Italy and seldom found elsewhere in their fresh state. They are dark red, elongated in shape and sweet to taste. Plum tomatoes are often sold as canned peeled tomatoes, or puréed and packaged as juice, tomato ketchup and tomato sauce.

Availability: Tomatoes are available all year round. Britain enjoys its own homegrown tomatoes from June to October. Imports reach Britain during the rest of the year from Italy, Holland and the Canary Islands.

Buying: Look for firm, fresh tomatoes with a bright colour and fresh green tops. Tomatoes that are soft can still be used for cooking purposes and for making soups, sauces and juices. Tomatoes are sold by weight, or sometimes per tomato.

Preparation and serving: Tomatoes require little preparation before serving raw or cooked. Simply remove the green top and peel if liked. This can quickly be done by plunging in boiling water for about 30 seconds. Remove and peel away the skin. The seeds can be removed if liked but they are quite edible.

Serve tomatoes sliced, chopped or whole as liked. Cook them gently in a little butter for a delicious vegetable to accompany most meat, fish and poultry dishes.

Tomatoes can be used raw in salads, used as a colourful garnish, stuffed and baked as a vegetable dish, baked as a gratin or served plain as a fruit.

Tomatoes also make delicious soups, sauces and drinks when combined with other savoury vegetables like onions, peppers and mushrooms.

Nutritional value: Tomatoes are very rich in Vitamins C and A. They also contain significant quantities of other trace minerals that are important in the diet. Low in calories they contain only 14 Calories (59 kj) per 100 g/3½ oz.

Italian Tomato Soup

4 tablespoons olive oil
2 cloves garlic, peeled and halved
1 onion, peeled and chopped
750 g/1½ lb tomatoes, skinned and
  chopped
1 litre/1¾ pints meat stock
2 tablespoons long-grain rice
1 basil sprig, chopped
salt and freshly ground black pepper
basil leaves to garnish

Heat the oil in a large pan, add the garlic and fry until golden brown. Remove and discard the garlic. Add the onion and tomatoes to the garlic-flavoured oil and fry for 2 to 3 minutes, stirring frequently.

Add the stock, rice and chopped basil and simmer, over a low heat, for about 20 minutes. Season with salt and pepper to taste.

Transfer to a warmed soup tureen and garnish with basil leaves to serve.
Serves 4 to 6

NOTE: Italian Tomato Soup is delicious served with freshly grated Parmesan cheese and French or garlic bread.

Cucumber Soup with Shrimps

1 large or 2 small cucumbers
15 g/½ oz butter
1 clove garlic, peeled
½ onion, peeled and chopped
1 teaspoon plain flour
1 litre/1¾ pints chicken stock
1 dill sprig, chopped
50 ml/2 fl oz dry white wine
125 g/4 oz peeled shrimps
salt
freshly ground black pepper
pinch of sugar

Peel and halve the cucumber lengthwise, scoop out the seeds and discard. Chop the cucumber flesh into small pieces.

Melt the butter in a pan, add the garlic and fry until golden brown. Remove and discard the garlic. Add the onion and cucumber to the pan and cook for 2 to 3 minutes.

Add the flour to the pan, blending well, and cook for 2 minutes, stirring constantly. Add the stock gradually and half of the dill and cook, over a low heat, for about 25 minutes.

Remove half of the cucumber from the soup with a slotted spoon and purée in an electric blender or food processor until smooth. Return the purée to the soup and stir well to blend. Add the wine and shrimps and cook gently for about 5 minutes. Season with salt and pepper to taste and the sugar.

Transfer to warmed individual soup bowls and sprinkle with the remaining dill to serve.
Serves 4 to 6

English Marrow Soup

750 g/1½ lb marrow, peeled and
  chopped
salt
600 ml/1 pint meat or chicken stock
150 ml/¼ pint milk
1 tablespoon brandy
freshly ground black pepper
pinch of ground ginger
pinch of grated nutmeg
150 ml/¼ pint cream
15 g/½ oz butter
watercress sprigs to garnish

Place the marrow in a pan. Add just enough boiling water to cover, and a pinch of salt. Bring back to the boil, then lower the heat and cook gently for about 30 minutes. Drain thoroughly and purée in an electric blender or food processor until smooth.

Return the purée to the pan, add the stock and milk and bring to the boil, stirring constantly. Remove the soup from the heat and add the brandy, pepper to taste, ginger, nutmeg, cream and butter, stirring well to blend.

Ladle the soup into warmed soup bowls and garnish with the watercress sprigs to serve.
Serves 4 to 6

NOTE: English Marrow Soup can be served as a starter or, with crusty bread and cheese, as a light main meal.

Ratatouille

6 tablespoons olive oil
1 Spanish onion, peeled and coarsely
  chopped
2 large aubergines, sliced
3 courgettes, sliced
1 red pepper, cored, seeded and cut into
  strips
1 green pepper, cored, seeded and cut
  into strips
4–5 tomatoes, skinned and quartered
2 cloves garlic, peeled and crushed
1 bouquet garni
salt
freshly ground black pepper
basil leaves to garnish

Heat the oil in a large pan, add the onion, aubergines and courgettes and fry gently until golden brown. Add the peppers, tomatoes, garlic and bouquet garni. Season with salt and pepper to taste, cover and simmer, over a low heat, for 20 to 30 minutes, stirring occasionally.

Discard the bouquet garni. Serve the ratatouille hot or cold, garnished with basil leaves.
Serves 4 to 6

NOTE: Ratatouille is delicious served hot with French bread and a full-bodied red wine. For a more substantial meal, serve with small grilled lamb chops or fried eggs.

In some parts of France ratatouille is made with pumpkin instead of courgettes, or fennel instead of peppers.

*Italian Tomato Soup; Cucumber Soup with
Shrimps; Gazpacho*

Gazpacho

500 g/1 lb tomatoes, skinned, seeded
 and chopped
2 cloves garlic, chopped
2 tablespoons tomato purée
3 tablespoons olive oil
2 tablespoons wine vinegar
600 ml/1 pint water
½ teaspoon sugar
salt
freshly ground black pepper
1 cucumber, halved
1 small onion, chopped
1 small green pepper, diced
croûtons

Place the tomatoes in an electric blender or food processor with the garlic, tomato purée, olive oil, wine vinegar, water and sugar. Add salt and pepper to taste. Skin and roughly chop one cucumber half and add to the blender. Blend on maximum for 30 seconds or until smooth.

Pour the gazpacho into a soup tureen and chill in the refrigerator for at least 2 hours.

Dice the remaining cucumber and place in a small serving bowl. Place the chopped onion, diced green pepper and croûtons in other small bowls. Serve the chilled gazpacho with the vegetable accompaniments.

Serves 6

NOTE: Gazpacho is the famous chilled Spanish soup, which is popular throughout Europe. Ingredients can be varied to taste. When tomatoes are at their best and full of flavour, the tomato purée may not be necessary.

Tomatoes Stuffed with Shrimps

8 medium tomatoes
3 hard-boiled eggs, shelled and chopped
125 g/4 oz shrimps
1 tablespoon mayonnaise
1 tablespoon chopped dill
150 ml/¼ pint soured cream
salt
freshly ground black pepper
dill sprigs to garnish

Rinse the tomatoes, wipe dry and cut a lid from the top of each; reserve. Remove the seeds with a small spoon and discard. Turn each tomato upside-down and leave to drain for about 5 minutes.

Meanwhile, mix the chopped egg with the shrimps, mayonnaise, dill and soured cream, blending well. Season

the insides of the tomatoes with salt and pepper to taste and fill with the egg and shrimp mixture. Replace the tomato caps and garnish with small dill sprigs to serve.

Serves 4

Peperonata

3 tablespoons olive oil
25 g/1 oz butter
1 onion, sliced
2 red peppers, cored, seeded and sliced
2 yellow peppers, cored, seeded and
    sliced
2 cloves garlic, crushed
500 g/1 lb tomatoes, peeled, seeded and
    quartered
salt
freshly ground black pepper

Heat the oil and butter in a large pan and fry the onion until softened. Add the peppers and garlic, cover and cook for 10 to 15 minutes over a low heat, stirring occasionally.

Add the tomatoes, and salt and pepper to taste. Cover and cook for 10 to 15 minutes, stirring occasionally.
Serves 8

NOTE: Serve hot or cold as a delicious first course, or side salad.

Marinated Courgettes

3 tablespoons olive oil
500 g/1 lb courgettes, thickly sliced
2 cloves garlic, peeled and crushed
salt
freshly ground black pepper
pinch of sugar
1 sprig of parsley, chopped
pinch of dried oregano
juice of 1 lemon
tomato wedges to garnish

Heat the oil in a pan, add the courgettes and fry until light golden. Add the garlic, salt and pepper to taste and sugar, mixing well. Cook for a further 4 to 5 minutes.

Sprinkle with the herbs and lemon juice and leave to cool in the juices. Toss the courgettes before serving, garnished with tomato wedges.
Serves 4 to 6

NOTE: Marinated Courgettes is an Italian speciality, an essential part of any hors d'oeuvre table.

Fried Aubergine Hors d'Oeuvre

2–3 aubergines (depending on size), cut
    into thick slices
juice of 1 lemon
salt
freshly ground black pepper
2 cloves garlic, peeled and crushed
2–3 tablespoons plain flour
olive oil for shallow frying
TO GARNISH:
2–3 tomatoes, sliced
basil leaves

Marinated Courgettes; Tomatoes Stuffed with Shrimps; Peperonata

Place the aubergine slices in a colander. Sprinkle with the lemon juice and salt and leave them to stand for about 15 minutes. Rinse and wipe dry, then season with the pepper and garlic. Dip in the flour to coat evenly.

Heat the oil in a pan and fry the aubergine slices in batches until golden brown on both sides. Drain on kitchen paper. Arrange on a warmed serving dish and keep warm while cooking the remainder.

Garnish the aubergines with the tomato slices and basil leaves to serve.
Serves 4

Stuffed Green Peppers

4 small green peppers
6 tomatoes, skinned and chopped
1 tablespoon chopped dill or basil
salt
freshly ground black pepper
4 eggs
ground paprika

Cut a large lid from the top of each green pepper, remove the seeds and pith, rinse and leave to drain.

Season the tomatoes with the dill or basil and salt and pepper to taste. Stuff the peppers with the tomato mixture.

Crack a raw egg into each pepper, over the tomato mixture, and sprinkle with salt and paprika to taste. Place in an ovenproof dish and cook in a pre-heated hot oven (220°C/425°F, Gas Mark 7) for 10 to 15 minutes. Serve immediately.
Serves 4

NOTE: Stuffed Green Peppers make an unusual hors d'oeuvre or a light summer supper dish.

Aubergine Salad

1 large or 2 small aubergines
600 ml/1 pint light stock
juice of 1 lemon
1 clove garlic, peeled and crushed
1–2 anchovy fillets, finely chopped
4 tablespoons olive oil
1 tablespoon red wine vinegar
salt
freshly ground black pepper
300 g/10 oz tomatoes, cut into wedges
½ green pepper, cored, seeded and cut
   into thin strips
1 small salami, thinly sliced
basil leaves to garnish

Remove the stalks from the aubergines and cut the flesh into thick slices. Halve or quarter any very large slices. Place the stock and lemon juice in a pan. Bring to the boil, add the aubergines, then lower the heat and cook gently for about 8 minutes. Drain and leave to cool. Place in a serving bowl.

To make the dressing, beat the garlic with the anchovies, oil, vinegar, and salt and pepper to taste. Pour over the aubergines and leave to marinate in the refrigerator for about 15 minutes.

Add the tomatoes, pepper and salami and toss well to mix. Leave to stand for a further 15 minutes to allow the flavours to develop. Garnish with the basil leaves before serving.
Serves 4

NOTE: Serve Aubergine Salad as part of a cold buffet spread or light hors d'oeuvre.

Country-style Tomato Platter

750 g/1½ lb beef tomatoes, cut into
   thick slices
salt
freshly ground black pepper
1 onion, peeled and chopped
300 ml/½ pint soured cream
1 basil sprig, chopped
basil leaves to garnish

Arrange the tomato slices on a flat serving dish and season with salt and pepper to taste. Scatter the onion evenly over the tomatoes. Mix the soured cream with the basil, blending well. Using a teaspoon, place a dot of cream on each tomato slice. Garnish with basil leaves before serving.
Serves 4 to 6

Okra Salad with Vinaigrette Dressing

350–400 g/12–14 oz okra
juice of ½ lemon
salt
DRESSING:
2 tablespoons salad oil
1 clove garlic, peeled and crushed or
   chopped
1 onion, peeled and finely chopped
2 teaspoons lemon juice
6 tablespoons dry white wine
freshly ground black pepper
½ teaspoon French mustard

Bring 300 ml/½ pint water to the boil in a pan. Add the okra, lemon juice and salt, then bring back to the boil, lower the heat and cook for about 10 minutes. Drain and leave to cool.

To make the dressing, beat the oil with the garlic, onion, lemon juice, white wine, salt and pepper to taste and the mustard.

Cut each okra in half and place in a salad bowl. Pour over the vinaigrette dressing and toss well to mix. Cover and chill in the refrigerator for about 5 to 10 minutes, to allow the flavours to develop. Toss again before serving.
Serves 4

Pepper and Tomato Salad

2 red peppers, cored and seeded
6 tomatoes, skinned, seeded and each
   cut into 8 wedges
75 g/3 oz black olives, stoned
4 tablespoons olive oil
1 tablespoon lemon juice
1 clove garlic, peeled and crushed
salt
freshly ground black pepper
1 tablespoon chopped basil

Cut the peppers into strips and place in a salad bowl with the tomato wedges and olives. Mix all the remaining ingredients together to make the dressing. Pour over the vegetables and toss thoroughly to serve.
Serves 4 to 6

NOTE: This is a delicious summer salad to serve with cold meats. It can also be served as part of an hors d'oeuvre.

Colourful Sweet Pepper Salad

2 green peppers
2 red peppers
1 bunch spring onions
12–16 black olives
MARINADE:
3 tablespoons red wine vinegar
4 tablespoons oil
salt
freshly ground black pepper
pinch of sugar
1 tablespoon chopped parsley

Halve the peppers, remove the stems, seeds and pith. Rinse, drain and cut into strips. Place the peppers in a salad bowl. Trim and rinse the spring onions and cut into fine rings. Add to the peppers with the olives.

To make the marinade, beat the vinegar with the oil, salt and pepper to taste, sugar and parsley. Pour over the salad and toss well to mix.

Leave the salad to marinate for about 20 minutes, to allow the flavours to develop. Toss again before serving. **Serves 4**

NOTE: Serve this salad as an hors d'oeuvre or as a refreshing accompaniment to grilled or fried meat.

In the summer and autumn when a good variety of peppers are in season, you can make this salad even more colourful by replacing one of the red peppers with a yellow pepper.

Colourful Sweet Pepper Salad; Country Style Tomato Platter; Okra Salad with Vinaigrette Dressing

Fish Fillet with Puréed Peppers

750 g/1½ lb fish fillet (e.g. cod or
  plaice)
2 tablespoons lemon juice
salt
freshly ground white pepper
40 g/1½ oz butter
4 red peppers, cored, seeded and
  quartered
1 clove garlic, peeled and chopped
½ onion, peeled and chopped
1 sprig of parsley, chopped

Divide the fish into four equal portions, sprinkle with the lemon juice and leave to stand for about 5 minutes. Season both sides with salt and pepper to taste. Melt 25 g/1 oz of the butter in a frying pan. Add the fish and fry quickly on both sides until lightly browned. Transfer to an ovenproof dish.

Meanwhile, purée the peppers in an electric blender with the garlic and onion. Add the parsley and season with salt to taste. Spread evenly over the fish fillets. Dot with the remaining butter. Cook in a preheated hot oven (200°C/400°F, Gas Mark 6) for about 15 minutes. Serve immediately.
Serves 4

NOTE: Serve this tasty main course with plain boiled rice or buttered new potatoes and a fresh green salad.

Salade Niçoise

1 head of lettuce, washed and dried
2 hard-boiled eggs, shelled and cut into
  quarters
4 tomatoes, cut into quarters
1 × 50 g/1¾ oz can anchovy fillets,
  drained
1 × 198 g/7 oz can tuna fish, drained
1 red pepper, cored, seeded and thinly
  sliced
12 black olives
4 tablespoons olive oil
1 tablespoon wine vinegar
1 clove garlic, peeled and crushed
½ teaspoon Dijon mustard
salt
freshly ground black pepper

Line a salad bowl with the lettuce leaves. Layer the eggs, tomatoes and anchovy fillets on top. Break the tuna fish into large pieces and place on top. Sprinkle with the pepper and olives.

To make the dressing, place the olive oil, vinegar, garlic, mustard and salt and pepper in a screw-topped jar and shake thoroughly to combine. Pour the dressing over the salad and toss just before serving.
Serves 4 to 6

NOTE: This classic French salad is frequently served as a light lunch with crusty bread throughout France.

Piquant Cucumber and Potato Salad

750 g/1½ lb waxy potatoes
1 large cucumber, finely sliced
salt
125 g/4 oz cooked ham, cut into strips
300 ml/½ pint soured cream
1 teaspoon chive or other herb-
  flavoured mustard
freshly ground white pepper
½ onion, peeled and chopped
1 tablespoon chopped dill or chives

Rinse the potatoes, place in a pan and add just enough boiling water to cover. Bring back to the boil, lower the heat and cook for 15 to 20 minutes. Drain, rinse under cold water and, when cool enough to handle, peel away the skins.

Sprinkle the cucumber with salt and leave to drain for about 5 minutes. Rinse and dry thoroughly.

Slice the potatoes and place in a bowl with the cucumber and ham.

To make the dressing, beat the cream with the mustard, salt and pepper to taste, onion and chopped herbs, blending well. Fold the dressing into the salad, mixing well.
Serves 4

NOTE: This juicy salad is excellent with Wiener Schnitzel or fried fish.

Courgette and Radicchio Salad

6 tablespoons French dressing
1 clove garlic, peeled and crushed
250 g/8 oz courgettes, thinly sliced
1 head of radicchio
50 g/2 oz black olives, halved and
  stoned
1 tablespoon pine nuts
salt
freshly ground black pepper

Place the French dressing and garlic in a salad bowl. Add the sliced courgettes and toss well. Leave to stand for 30 minutes to allow the courgettes to absorb the flavour of the dressing.

Tear the radicchio leaves into manageable pieces and add to the courgettes and dressing with the black olives and pine nuts. Season with salt and pepper to taste. Toss the salad thoroughly before serving.
Serves 6

NOTE: This delicious crisp salad can be served with cold meats or fish, or as a side salad with grilled meats.

*Salade Niçoise; Courgette and Radicchio
Salad; Piquant Cucumber and Potato Salad*

South American Chayote Casserole

2 chayotes
juice of 1 lemon
salt
500 g/1 lb cooked long-grain rice
200 g/7 oz garlic sausage, skinned and
    sliced
2–3 tablespoons fresh white
    breadcrumbs, moistened in a little
    milk
125 g/4 oz Emmenthal cheese, grated
15 g/½ oz butter
BÉCHAMEL SAUCE:
25 g/1 oz butter or margarine
2 tablespoons flour
300 ml/½ pint milk, warmed
freshly ground black pepper

Peel the chayotes under running water, then halve and cut into fairly large pieces. Bring 600 ml/1 pint water to the boil with the lemon juice and a pinch of salt added. Put the chayotes in the pan, bring back to the boil, lower the heat and cook gently for about 40 minutes until tender.

Meanwhile, prepare the béchamel sauce. Melt the butter or margarine in a pan, add the flour and cook for 2 to 3 minutes. Gradually whisk in the milk. Bring to the boil, stirring constantly. Lower the heat and simmer gently for about 10 minutes, then season with salt and pepper to taste.

Drain the chayotes thoroughly. Arrange in alternate layers with the rice and sausage in an ovenproof dish, spooning a little béchamel sauce over each layer. Top with the breadcrumbs and cheese and dot with the butter. Cook in a preheated hot oven (220°C/425°F, Gas Mark 7) for about 15 minutes, or until the top is golden brown and crisp.
Serves 4

NOTE: Serve South American Chayote Casserole in the cooking dish, with a seasonal salad and chilled beer.

Courgette Kebabs

2 courgettes, thickly sliced
200 g/7 oz small button mushrooms
juice of 1 lemon
125 g/4 oz streaky bacon, derinded,
    halved and rolled
200 g/7 oz turkey liver, cubed
freshly ground black pepper
ground paprika
chopped basil
olive oil
salt

Sprinkle the courgettes and mushrooms with the lemon juice. Thread the courgettes, mushrooms, bacon rolls and turkey liver alternately on 4 long wooden skewers. Season with pepper, paprika and basil and brush with oil.

Cook, under a preheated hot grill, for about 10 minutes, turning occasionally until brown and crisp. Season lightly with salt and serve immediately.
Serves 4

NOTE: Serve Courgette Kebabs with wholemeal toast and a spicy tomato relish or home-made tomato sauce.

RIGHT: *Hungarian Peppers with Veal and Chicken; Sweet Peppers Stuffed with Beef or Lamb*
BELOW: *Courgette Kebabs*

Hungarian Peppers with Veal and Chicken

25g/1 oz lard
350 g/12 oz veal, chopped
400 g/14 oz boned chicken, chopped
3–4 green peppers, cored, seeded and chopped
2 onions, peeled and chopped
300 ml/½ pint meat stock
salt and freshly ground black pepper
ground paprika
150 ml/¼ pint soured cream
chopped parsley to garnish (optional)

Melt the lard in a flameproof casserole or heavy-based pan. Add the veal and chicken and cook, stirring, over a high heat until lightly browned.

Add the chopped peppers and onions and cook for 2 to 3 minutes. Pour in the stock and season with salt, pepper and paprika to taste. Cover and simmer over a low heat for about 40 minutes or until the meat is tender, stirring occasionally.

Stir in the soured cream and serve immediately, garnished with chopped parsley if preferred.
Serves 4

NOTE: Hungarian Peppers with Veal and Chicken are delicious served with plain boiled long-grain rice or new potatoes and sautéed courgettes.

Sweet Peppers Stuffed with Beef or Lamb

4 large or 8 small green or red peppers
50 g/2 oz streaky bacon, derinded and chopped
1 onion, peeled and chopped
400 g/14 oz minced beef or lamb
2 eggs, beaten
2 tablespoons chopped parsley
325 g/11 oz cooked long-grain rice
salt
freshly ground black pepper
1 teaspoon ground oregano
pinch of grated nutmeg
600 ml/1 pint meat stock
1 tablespoon tomato purée
1 teaspoon cornflour
150 ml/¼ pint double or soured cream

Cut the tops from the sweet peppers and set aside for lids. Scoop out the seeds and pith from the peppers. Rinse and drain thoroughly.

Fry the bacon in a small pan until the fat runs. Add the onion and cook gently for 5 minutes. Add the minced meat and fry, stirring, until browned.

Place the meat mixture in a bowl and add the eggs, parsley, rice, salt and pepper to taste, oregano and nutmeg. Mix thoroughly. Stuff the peppers with this mixture and replace the lids.

Pour the stock into a large ovenproof dish and stand the peppers in the stock. Cook in a preheated moderately hot oven (190°C/375°F, Gas Mark 5) for 40 to 45 minutes, basting the peppers with the stock occasionally.

Remove the peppers with a slotted spoon and place on a warmed serving dish; keep warm. Pour the stock into a pan. Mix the tomato purée with the cornflour to form a smooth paste, then gradually stir into the stock, blending well. Bring to the boil, stirring continuously, and cook for 2 minutes. Remove from the heat and stir in the cream.

Serve hot, accompanied by the cream sauce, as a main course.
Serves 4

Greek Moussaka

2 large aubergines, thinly sliced
salt
olive oil for shallow frying
5–6 potatoes, peeled and thinly sliced
375 g/13 oz cooked lamb or beef,
  minced
freshly ground black pepper
ground paprika
15 g/½ oz butter
2 teaspoons plain flour
300 ml/½ pint meat stock
2 eggs
5 tablespoons milk
1 teaspoon dried oregano

Sprinkle the aubergine slices with salt and leave to drain for 15 minutes. Rinse and dry with kitchen paper.

Meanwhile, heat 2 to 3 tablespoons oil in a frying pan. Add the potatoes and fry until golden on both sides. Remove from the pan and set aside. Add the aubergine slices to the pan in batches and fry quickly on both sides until golden, adding more oil as necessary. Remove and set aside. Mix the meat with salt, pepper and paprika to taste in a bowl.

Melt the butter in a pan, add the flour and cook for 2 to 3 minutes. Whisk in the stock and bring to the boil, stirring.

Arrange alternate layers of potato, meat and aubergine in a greased ovenproof dish, sprinkling the vegetables with a little salt, and finishing with a layer of potato. Top with the sauce.

Beat the eggs with the milk and oregano and pour over the moussaka. Cook in a preheated moderately hot oven (190°C/375°F, Gas Mark 5) for 30 to 40 minutes until puffed and golden brown. Serve from the dish.
Serves 4

Stuffed Courgettes

2–3 large courgettes
salt
2 tablespoons olive oil
1 small onion, peeled and chopped
2 tomatoes, skinned and chopped
400 g/14 oz cooked beef, minced
1 egg, beaten
freshly ground black pepper
ground paprika
grated nutmeg
1 teaspoon dried oregano
300 ml/½ pint meat stock
125 g/4 oz cheese, grated
150 ml/¼ pint double cream

Place the courgettes in a pan, add just enough boiling water to cover and a pinch of salt. Bring back to the boil, lower the heat and cook for 5 to 7 minutes. Drain, halve lengthwise and scoop out the flesh with a spoon, reserving the shells. Chop the flesh coarsely and place in a bowl.

Meanwhile, heat the oil in a pan, add the onion and tomatoes and fry for about 8 minutes or until soft. Remove from the heat and stir in the minced meat. Add the egg, salt, pepper, paprika and nutmeg to taste, and the

oregano. Mix thoroughly.

Stuff the courgettes with this mixture and place in an ovenproof dish with the stock. Cook in a preheated moderately hot oven (200°C/400°F, Gas Mark 6) for 15 minutes.

Sprinkle the courgettes with the grated cheese and cook for a further 10 minutes.

Pour the stock into a pan and mix with cream. Heat gently until the sauce thickens. Serve the courgettes, accompanied by the cream sauce.
Serves 4

Stuffed Cucumbers with Tomato Sauce

2 cucumbers
400 g/14 oz pork sausagemeat
1 egg, beaten
2 tablespoons fresh white breadcrumbs
1 sprig of parsley, chopped
2–3 tablespoons tomato ketchup
¼ teaspoon dried marjoram
salt and freshly ground white pepper
600 ml/1 pint meat stock
2 × 64 g/2¼ oz cans tomato purée
4 tablespoons double cream

Rinse the cucumbers and peel thinly if the skin is tough. Cut the cucumbers in half, then halve again lengthways and scrape out the seeds with a spoon.

Mix the sausagemeat with the egg, breadcrumbs, herbs, tomato ketchup, marjoram and salt and pepper to taste. Stuff the cucumber halves with this mixture. Place in an ovenproof dish with the stock. Cook in a preheated moderately hot oven (200°C/400°F,

Gas Mark 6) for 30 to 40 minutes.

Pour the stock into a pan, stir in the tomato purée and bring to the boil. Remove from the heat and stir in the cream.

Serve the stuffed cucumbers with the tomato sauce.
Serves 4

NOTE: Serve with creamed potatoes or plain boiled rice.

Aubergines with Veal

3 tablespoons oil
350 g/12 oz veal, cut into large cubes
2 medium aubergines, chopped
2 tomatoes, skinned and quartered
1 onion, peeled and cut into rings
1 clove garlic, peeled and crushed
1 sprig of parsley or basil, chopped
juice of ½ lemon
salt and freshly ground black pepper
ground paprika
150 ml/¼ pint soured cream

Heat the oil in a flameproof casserole, add the veal and brown on all sides. Add the aubergines, tomatoes and onion and cook for 5 to 8 minutes. Add the garlic, herbs and lemon juice and season with salt and pepper to taste, and the paprika.

Cover and simmer, over a low heat, for about 40 minutes, adding 2 to 3 tablespoons hot water if the mixture becomes too dry.

Stir in the soured cream. Serve immediately, with buttered noodles or plain boiled rice.
Serves 4

Stuffed Cucumbers with Tomato Sauce; Greek Moussaka; Stuffed Courgettes

Aubergines au Gratin

2 large aubergines, cut into large cubes
salt
3 tomatoes, sliced
1 courgette, sliced
1 bunch of mixed herbs (e.g. parsley,
    basil, rosemary), chopped
150 ml/¼ pint double cream
2 eggs, beaten
freshly ground black pepper
15 g/½ oz butter
1 clove garlic, peeled and halved
2 tablespoons dry white breadcrumbs

Sprinkle the aubergines with salt and leave to drain for about 15 minutes. Rinse and wipe dry with kitchen paper. Arrange alternate layers of aubergine, tomato and courgette in a greased ovenproof dish. Sprinkle with the chopped herbs.

Mix the cream with the eggs, salt and pepper to taste and pour over the vegetable mixture.

Melt the butter in a small pan, add the garlic and fry until golden brown.

Remove and discard the garlic. Add the breadcrumbs to the garlic-flavoured butter and cook for 1 to 2 minutes. Sprinkle over the vegetables in the dish. Cook in a preheated hot oven (220°C/425°F, Gas Mark 7) for 12 to 15 minutes, or until golden brown. Serve immediately.
Serves 4

NOTE: This dish is delicious served with French bread and a red wine.

Aubergines Stuffed with Chicken

2 aubergines
600 ml/1 pint meat stock
30 g/1¼ oz butter
1 onion, peeled and chopped
50 g/2 oz streaky bacon, derinded and
    chopped
275 g/9 oz cooked chicken, chopped
salt
freshly ground white pepper
4 slices Gouda cheese
1 teaspoon cornflour (optional)
2–3 tablespoons dry white wine
    (optional)

Remove the stalks from the aubergines, cut in half lengthwise, scoop out the flesh and set aside. Pour the stock into a flameproof casserole and arrange the aubergine shells in the dish. Bring to the boil, lower the heat and cook gently for about 10 minutes. Drain, reserving the stock.

Meanwhile, finely chop the reserved aubergine flesh. Melt the butter in a small pan, add the onion and cook for 5 minutes. Add the bacon, chicken and chopped aubergine. Season with salt and pepper to taste and cook for 4 to 5 minutes. Stuff the aubergine halves with the chicken mixture and cover each half with a slice of Gouda cheese.

Place the stuffed aubergines in the flameproof dish with the reserved stock. Cook in a pre-heated hot oven (220°C/425°F, Gas Mark 7) for about 10 minutes until the cheese is melted and bubbling.

Transfer the stuffed aubergines to a serving dish. If a thicker sauce is required, blend the cornflour with the white wine, stir into the stock and cook, stirring, for 2 minutes.

Serve the aubergines with the sauce.
Serves 4

NOTE: Stuffed Aubergines are delicious served with rice and a dry white wine.

Pissaladière

250 g/8 oz plain flour
½ teaspoon salt
7 g/¼ oz fresh yeast
4–5 tablespoons warm water
1 egg, beaten
1 tablespoon vegetable oil
TOPPING:
4 tablespoons olive oil
500 g/1 lb onions, peeled and sliced
4 large tomatoes, skinned and sliced
2 cloves garlic, peeled and crushed
salt
freshly ground black pepper
1 × 50 g/1¾ oz can anchovy fillets,
  drained and halved lengthways
12–14 black olives, halved and stoned

Sift the flour and salt into a bowl. Cream the yeast with a little of the water and leave for about 15 minutes, until frothy. Add the yeast liquid to the flour with the egg, vegetable oil and remaining water; mix to a soft dough.

Turn onto a lightly floured surface and knead for 8 to 10 minutes until smooth and elastic. Place in a clean bowl, cover with a damp cloth, and leave to rise, in a warm place, for about 2 hours, or until doubled in size.

Turn onto a lightly floured surface, knead for a few minutes, and shape into a 28 cm/11 inch round. Place on a greased pizza pan or baking sheet, knock up the edges and shape as desired.

Heat the olive oil in a pan, add the onions and cook gently for about 5 minutes, or until softened. Add the tomatoes, garlic and salt and pepper to taste. Cook gently, for 5 minutes. Spoon onto the prepared dough and spread to the edges. Arrange the anchovies in a lattice pattern on top, and arrange an olive in each diamond.

Leave to rise for 5 to 10 minutes in a warm place, then bake in a preheated moderately hot oven (200°C/400°F, Gas Mark 6) for 15 to 20 minutes. Serve hot, cut into wedges.
Serves 4

Courgette Bake

25 g/1 oz butter
400 g/14 oz courgettes, sliced
30 g/1¼ oz streaky bacon, derinded and
  chopped
125 g/4 oz cooked ham, cut into strips
125 g/4 oz Emmenthal cheese, cut into
  strips
2 eggs
4 tablespoons milk or cream
salt
freshly ground black pepper
ground paprika
1 tablespoon chopped parsley

Melt the butter in a frying pan, add the courgettes and fry for 4 to 5 minutes until golden brown. Remove the courgettes with a slotted spoon and place in a 15 cm/6 inch soufflé dish. Add the bacon to the pan juices and fry until crisp. Mix together the ham, cheese and fried bacon and spoon over the courgettes.

Beat the eggs with the milk or cream, salt, pepper and paprika to taste. Add the parsley and pour over the courgettes. Cook in a preheated hot oven (220°C/425°F, Gas Mark 7) for about 20 minutes until the egg is crisp and golden brown. Serve immediately.
Serves 4

NOTE: If you double the quantities, this can be served as a meal in itself, which needs to be cooked for about 35 to 40 minutes.

Aubergines au Gratin; Courgette Bake; Pissaladière

Aubergines Calabrian-style

2 medium aubergines
3 tablespoons olive oil
75 g/3 oz fresh white bread crusts,
    chopped
6–8 black olives, halved and stoned
2 anchovy fillets, chopped
1 onion, peeled and chopped
1 tablespoon capers
2 tomatoes, skinned and chopped
125 g/4 oz Edam or Emmenthal cheese,
    derinded and cut into strips

Halve the aubergines, scoop out the
flesh with a spoon and chop into small
pieces. Heat the oil in a pan and add the
bread crusts. Remove from the heat
and leave to stand for 5 to 10 minutes.

Add the chopped aubergine, olives,
anchovies, onion, capers and tomatoes,
mixing well. Stuff the aubergine shells
with this mixture and place in a greased
ovenproof dish. Top with the strips of
cheese. Cook in a preheated moderately

hot oven (190°C/375°F, Gas Mark 5)
for about 30 minutes, or until the
aubergines are tender and the cheese
has melted. Serve immediately.
Serves 4

NOTE: Serve Aubergines Calabrian-
style with a seasonal salad and, of
course, an Italian red wine.

Spaghetti with Pepper Sauce

400–500 g/14 oz–1 lb spaghetti
salt
15 g/½ oz butter
SAUCE:
4 tablespoons olive oil
2 red peppers, cored, seeded and cut
    into strips
1 × 227 g/8 oz can peeled tomatoes
6–8 black olives, stoned
1 anchovy fillet, finely chopped
1 sprig of parsley, chopped
1 clove garlic, peeled and crushed
1 green chilli pepper, seeded and cut
    into fine rings
pinch of sugar

Cook the spaghetti in boiling salted water for 12 minutes or according to packet instructions. Drain thoroughly.

Meanwhile, make the sauce. Heat the oil in a pan, add the red peppers and cook for 5 minutes. Add the tomatoes with their juice, olives, anchovy, parsley and garlic, mixing well. Simmer gently for 8 to 10 minutes. Add the chilli and salt and sugar to taste.

Toss the spaghetti in the butter and place in a warmed serving dish. Pour the sauce over the spaghetti and toss before serving.
Serves 4

Fried Pepper with Egg

4 tablespoons oil
1 onion, peeled and sliced into rings
3 green peppers, cored, seeded and
    chopped or cut into strips
4 tomatoes, skinned and chopped
1 × 198 g/7 oz can sweetcorn, drained
125 g/4 oz cooked ham, chopped
salt
cayenne pepper
3–4 tablespoons double cream
4 hard-boiled eggs, shelled and chopped
parsley sprigs to garnish

Heat the oil in a pan. Add the onion and cook for 5 minutes. Add the peppers and tomatoes and cook over a low heat, for 5 to 7 minutes.

Stir in the sweetcorn and ham. Season with salt and cayenne pepper to taste. Fold in the cream and eggs, mixing well. Stir over a low heat until heated through. Transfer to a warmed serving dish, garnish with parsley sprigs and serve immediately.
Serves 4

Ham and Cheese Stuffed Tomatoes

8 large tomatoes
salt
freshly ground black pepper
125 g/4 oz Gouda cheese, cubed
125 g/4 oz cooked ham, chopped
1 onion, peeled and chopped
1 tablespoon chopped parsley
15 g/½ oz butter

Courgette Omelette; Ham and Cheese Stuffed Tomatoes; Spaghetti with Pepper Sauce

Cut a lid from each tomato, scoop out the seeds with a spoon and discard. Season the inside of each tomato with salt and pepper to taste. Mix the cheese with the ham, onion and parsley. Stuff the tomatoes with this mixture.

Place the tomatoes in a greased oven-proof dish, dot with butter and replace lids. Cook in a preheated moderately hot oven (200°C/400°F, Gas Mark 6) for about 15 minutes. Serve hot.
Serves 4

Courgette Omelette

2 medium courgettes, sliced
juice of ½ lemon
1 tablespoon oil
1 onion, peeled and finely chopped
50 g/2 oz bacon, derinded and chopped
salt and freshly ground black pepper
ground paprika
4 eggs
2 tablespoons double cream
1 tablespoon grated Parmesan cheese
1 tablespoon chopped parsley

Sprinkle the courgettes with the lemon juice and leave to stand for about 5 minutes. Dry on kitchen paper.

Meanwhile, heat the oil in a frying pan or omelette pan, add the onion and bacon and cook until lightly browned. Add the courgettes and fry for 5 minutes, stirring occasionally. Season with salt, pepper and paprika to taste.

Beat the eggs with the cream, Parmesan cheese and parsley.

Remove half the courgette mixture with a slotted spoon and set aside. Pour half of the egg mixture into the pan. Cook over a low heat until the egg has set. Remove and transfer to a warmed serving plate; keep warm. Repeat with the remaining mixture to make a second omelette. Serve immediately.
Serves 2

NOTE: Serve with a tomato salad.

Marrow Stuffed with Ham and Mushrooms

1 marrow, weighing 1 kg/2 lb
1 tablespoon oil
1 onion, peeled and chopped
125 g/4 oz mushrooms, chopped
125 g/4 oz cooked ham, diced
25 g/1 oz fresh white breadcrumbs
1 tablespoon chopped parsley
1 tablespoon chopped basil
salt
freshly ground black pepper

Cut the marrow crosswise into 5 cm/ 2 inch rings, discarding the seeds. Put the marrow rings in a lightly greased baking dish.

Heat the oil in a pan. Add the onion and fry gently for 3 minutes, stirring occasionally. Add the mushrooms and fry for a further 3 minutes. Remove from the heat, add the remaining ingredients and mix well.

Spoon the stuffing mixture into the centre of the marrow rings, then cover the dish with foil. Bake in a preheated moderate oven (180°C/350°F, Gas Mark 4) for 20 to 30 minutes until the marrow is just tender. Serve hot.
Serves 4

Marrow in Dill Butter

1 kg/2 lb marrow
65 g/2½ oz butter
2 onions, peeled and finely chopped
1 sprig of dill, chopped
salt
freshly ground black pepper

Peel the marrow, remove the seeds and cut into cubes. Melt the butter in a large pan, add the onion and cook for 5 minutes. Add the marrow, stirring well. Cook over a low heat for 10 to 15 minutes, until tender. Serve hot, sprinkled with the dill and salt and pepper to taste.
Serves 4

NOTE: Marrow in Dill Butter is delicious served hot with spare ribs.

Aubergines Bonne Femme

3 medium aubergines
5 tablespoons olive oil
1 large onion, peeled and coarsely
    chopped
2 cloves garlic, peeled and halved
275 g/9 oz tomatoes, roughly
    chopped
salt
freshly ground black pepper
1 teaspoon chopped fresh oregano
1 sprig of parsley, chopped
50 g/2 oz Parmesan cheese, grated
15 g/½ oz butter

Cut the aubergines into quarters lengthwise, then cut into 2 cm/¾ inch slices. Heat the oil in a pan, add the aubergines, onion and garlic and fry for 7 to 8 minutes. Remove and discard the garlic.

Add the tomatoes to the pan and season with salt and pepper to taste, oregano and parsley. Transfer the mixture to a shallow ovenproof dish. Sprinkle with the Parmesan cheese and dot with the butter. Cook in a preheated moderately hot oven (200°C/ 400°F, Gas Mark 6) for about 20 minutes. Serve immediately.
Serves 4 to 6

NOTE: This delicious aubergine dish is excellent with fried meats. Serve with French bread and a French red wine.

Marrow in Dill Butter; Braised Pumpkin; Aubergines Bonne Femme

Braised Pumpkin

750 g–1 kg/1½–2 lb pumpkin
juice of 1 lemon
2 tablespoons oil
50 g/2 oz streaky bacon, derinded and
  chopped
pinch of celery salt
pinch of dried oregano
pinch of sugar (optional)
150 ml/¼ pint meat stock
1 sprig of dill, chopped
150 ml/¼ pint soured cream
freshly ground black pepper

Peel the pumpkin, remove the seeds and cut into cubes. Sprinkle with lemon juice and leave to stand for 5 minutes.

Heat the oil in a large pan, add the bacon and fry until crisp. Add the pumpkin and cook for 3 to 5 minutes. Add the celery salt, oregano and the sugar, if using, mixing well. Add the stock. Cover and simmer over a low heat for 15 to 20 minutes, or until the pumpkin is tender.

Add the dill, soured cream and pepper to taste. Toss well and serve immediately.
Serves 4

NOTE: Braised Pumpkin is a delicately flavoured dish that is delicious with fried chicken drumsticks.

Red Pepper Rice

1 litre/1¾ pints meat stock
750 g/1½ lb long-grain rice
salt
1 onion, peeled and chopped
3–4 red peppers, cored, seeded and
  chopped
15 g/½ oz butter
1 teaspoon ground paprika

Place the stock in a pan, bring to the boil, add the rice and a little salt. Lower the heat and cook gently for about 20 minutes until tender.

Meanwhile, purée the onion and red peppers in an electric blender or food processor until smooth. Drain the rice if necessary. Return to the pan and stir in the onion and pepper purée, butter

and paprika, blending well.

Spoon into oiled individual moulds or a large ring mould and turn out onto a flat dish. Serve immediately.
Serves 6 to 8

NOTE: Red Pepper Rice is a delicious vegetable dish to serve with goulash or a chicken fricassée.

Parmesan Tomatoes

8 large tomatoes
salt
freshly ground black pepper
40 g/1½ oz Parmesan cheese, grated
1 tablespoon chopped fresh basil
15 g/½ oz butter

Cut a fairly deep cross in the top of each tomato, open out and sprinkle with salt and pepper to taste. Fill the open tomatoes with the cheese and basil.

Place on a grill tray covered with aluminium foil and dot with the butter. Cook, under a preheated hot grill, for 4 to 5 minutes. Alternatively, place in an

ovenproof dish and cook in a preheated moderately hot oven (200°C/400°F, Gas Mark 6) for 15 minutes or until the cheese is golden brown.
Serves 4

NOTE: Serve with grilled meat or as part of a vegetable platter.

Arabian Aubergines

2 medium aubergines, sliced
salt
juice of 2 lemons
40 g/1½ oz butter
2 cloves garlic, peeled and halved
2 Spanish onions, peeled and chopped
1 tablespoon chopped parsley
pinch of cayenne pepper
pinch of ground cinnamon
2 tablespoons olive oil

Sprinkle the sliced aubergines with a little salt and the lemon juice and leave to stand for about 15 minutes. Drain and wipe dry with kitchen paper.

Melt the butter in a small pan, add the garlic and fry until golden brown. Remove and discard the garlic.

Dip the aubergine slices in the hot garlic butter to coat. Arrange half the aubergine slices in an ovenproof dish.

Sprinkle with half of the onion. Top with the remaining aubergine slices and sprinkle with the remaining ingredients. Cover with aluminium foil and cook in a preheated moderately hot oven (190°C/375°F, Gas Mark 5) for 20 minutes. Remove the foil and cook for a further 15 minutes, or until the aubergines are tender. Serve hot.
Serves 4

Provençal Tomatoes

300 ml/½ pint lukewarm milk
2 bread rolls, crusts removed, chopped
4 beef tomatoes, thickly sliced
2 tablespoons olive oil
3 cloves garlic, peeled and thinly sliced
2 tablespoons chopped herbs (e.g. basil and oregano)
salt
freshly ground black pepper

Pour the milk over the bread in a bowl, leave to stand for 5 minutes and then squeeze to remove any excess liquid. Arrange the tomatoes in an ovenproof dish and cover evenly with the bread.

Heat the oil in a small pan, add the garlic and fry until golden brown. Add the herbs and spoon evenly over the tomatoes and bread mixture. Season with salt and pepper to taste.

Cook in a preheated moderately hot oven (190°C/375°F, Gas Mark 5) for 20 to 25 minutes, until golden brown. Serve hot.
Serves 4

NOTE: Provençal Tomatoes is a tasty vegetable dish to serve with grilled meat or fish.

Creole Okra Rice

2 tablespoons oil
500 g/1 lb long-grain rice
600 ml/1 pint meat stock
½ teaspoon salt
2 chillis, seeded and cut into fine strips
1 red pepper, cored, seeded and chopped
marrow from 1 veal bone, (optional)
275 g/9 oz okra, trimmed

Heat the oil in a pan, add the rice and fry for 2 minutes. Add the stock, salt, chillis and red pepper, stirring well. Cover and cook for 5 minutes.

Chop the marrow if using, and add to the pan with the okra. Cover and continue to cook, over a low heat, until the rice has absorbed all of the stock

and is tender but still firm, about 12 to 15 minutes. Serve hot.
Serves 4

NOTE: Creole Okra Rice is tasty served with meat kebabs or fried liver.

Chayote in Tomato Sauce

2 chayotes
600 ml/1 pint meat stock
15 g/½ oz butter
1 tablespoon plain flour
2 tablespoons tomato purée
150 ml/¼ pint double cream
pinch of cayenne pepper
salt

Peel the chayotes under running water, remove the seeds and cut into halves or quarters. Place in a pan with the stock. Bring to the boil, lower the heat and cook gently for 45 to 50 minutes. Drain, reserving half of the stock.

Melt the butter in a pan, add the flour and cook for 1 minute. Whisk in the reserved stock. Fold in the tomato

purée and cream. Season with cayenne pepper and salt to taste. Place the chayotes in a serving dish and pour over the sauce. Serve immediately.
Serves 4

NOTE: Chayotes are also tasty cooked in stock with a dash of vinegar and with a butter and chopped parsley.

Courgettes Provençal

4 tablespoons olive oil
1 onion, chopped
500 g/1 lb courgettes, thinly sliced
1 clove garlic, chopped
4 tomatoes, skinned and chopped
1 teaspoon tomato purée
salt
freshly ground black pepper

Heat the oil in a large pan, add the onion and courgettes and fry gently for 8 to 10 minutes, stirring occasionally. Stir in the garlic, tomatoes, tomato purée, and salt and pepper to taste. Cover and cook for 5 minutes. Transfer to a warmed serving dish to serve.
Serves 4

NOTE: Serve as a delicious accompaniment to grilled steak or lamb chops, or as a light starter with garlic bread.

Creole Okra Rice; Courgette Provençal;
Arabian Aubergines

Sweet Peppers with Tomatoes and Bacon

750 g/1½ lb sweet peppers
3 tomatoes, skinned
2 tablespoons oil
50 g/2 oz streaky bacon, derinded and
  chopped
1 clove garlic, peeled and crushed
3–4 tablespoons meat stock
salt
freshly ground black pepper
1 sprig of basil or dill, chopped
1–2 tablespoons soured cream

Cut the peppers in half lengthwise and remove the core and seeds. Chop the peppers into fairly large pieces. Cut the tomatoes into wedges.

Heat the oil in a pan, add the bacon and fry until crisp. Add the peppers, tomatoes and garlic and cook for 5 minutes, stirring continuously. Add the stock, salt and pepper to taste, and herbs. Simmer, over a low heat, for a further 3 to 4 minutes.

Add the soured cream and heat gently until thickened. Serve immediately.
Serves 4

NOTE: This accompaniment is delicious served with poached fish. Use red, green or yellow sweet peppers, or a mixture of these.

Sweet and Sour Cucumber

1 cucumber
4 tablespoons olive oil
1 onion, peeled and finely chopped
4 tomatoes, skinned and cut into wedges
1 small stick celery, chopped
300 ml/½ pint meat stock
ground paprika
pinch of dried rosemary
salt
freshly ground black pepper
1 tablespoon chopped dill
pinch of sugar
juice of ½ lemon
2–3 tablespoons double cream
dill sprigs to garnish

Peel and chop the cucumber, removing the seeds.

Heat the olive oil in a large pan, add the onion and cook for 5 minutes. Add the cucumber and cook for a further 2 to 3 minutes. Add the tomatoes and cook for about 5 minutes. Add the celery, stock, rosemary, dill, salt, pepper and paprika to taste.

Cover and simmer over a low heat for about 20 minutes, stirring occasionally. Stir in the sugar, lemon juice and cream. Serve immediately, garnished with sprigs of dill.
Serves 4

NOTE: Sweet and Sour Cucumber makes a tasty accompaniment to rissoles or fried fish.

Green Tomato Chutney; Pickled Mustard Cucumber; Pickled Dill Cucumber

Green Tomato Chutney

1 kg/2 lb green tomatoes, chopped
2 green peppers, cored, seeded and chopped
1 large onion, peeled and chopped
250 ml/8 fl oz distilled white vinegar
275 g/9 oz caster sugar
1 teaspoon curry powder
1 tablespoon mustard powder
1 teaspoon ground ginger
1 teaspoon allspice seasoning (or a mixture of ground cloves, cinnamon and allspice)
½ teaspoon ground black pepper
pinch of chilli powder

Place the chopped tomatoes, peppers and onion in a bowl, add the vinegar and toss well. Cover and leave to stand at room temperature overnight.

Place the mixture in a pan, add the sugar and heat until dissolved. Add the spices and cook, over a low heat, for about 7 minutes.

Spoon the chutney into hot sterilized jars and seal with vinegar-proof preserving paper while the chutney is still hot.
Makes about 1.5 kg/3 lb

NOTE: Green Tomato Chutney is a delicious thick chutney to serve with cold roast meat or grills. If you prefer a less thick chutney, do not soak the vegetables, but cook in the vinegar and sugar, over a low heat, for about 1½ hours, stirring occasionally. Add the spices 5 minutes before the end of the cooking time.

Pickled Mustard Cucumber

3 cucumbers, weighing about 2 kg/ 4½ lbs in total
4–5 tablespoons salt
600 ml/1 pint red wine vinegar
5 tablespoons sugar
4 bay leaves
1 tablespoon peppercorns
125 g/4 oz mustard seeds
few dill sprigs, chopped (optional)
pinch of ground coriander

Peel and halve the cucumbers, remove the seeds and cut into fairly large pieces. Place in a bowl, sprinkle with the salt and leave to stand overnight.

Place the vinegar in a pan with the sugar, bay leaves, peppercorns, mustard seeds, dill if using, and coriander. Bring to the boil, then leave to cool.

Drain the cucumbers thoroughly and dry on kitchen paper, then transfer to a large sterilized earthenware pot or preserving jars. Cover with the seasoned vinegar and seal with cling film.

After 3 to 4 days, pour off the vinegar wine into a pan, boil up once more, leave to cool, then pour back over the cucumber. Carefully reseal the pot or jars.
Makes about 2 kg/4½ lb

Piquant Okra

325 g/11 oz okra
150 ml/¼ pint dry white wine
2 bay leaves
1 × 227 g/8 oz can peeled tomatoes
pinch of sugar
pinch of ground ginger
salt
freshly ground black pepper
15 g/½ oz butter
1 tablespoon chopped parsley

Place the okra in a pan with the white wine and bay leaves. Bring to the boil, lower the heat and cook gently for about 8 minutes. Add the tomatoes with a little of their juice, the sugar, ginger, and salt and pepper to taste. Stir well and cook for a further 5 minutes. Add the butter and parsley, stirring well. Remove the bay leaves before serving.
Serves 4

NOTE: Serve this quick vegetable dish as an unusual accompaniment to veal or fried fish.

Pickled Dill Cucumber

2 medium cucumbers, thinly peeled
5 tablespoons wine vinegar
5 tablespoons oil
1 teaspoon salt
½ teaspoon dill seeds
pinch of celery salt
1 teaspoon black peppercorns
1 tablespoon sugar
2 cloves garlic, peeled and halved

Slice the cucumbers very finely and place in a large bowl.

Mix the vinegar with the oil, salt, dill seeds, celery salt, peppercorns, sugar and garlic and pour the mixture over the cucumber. Cover and chill overnight in the refrigerator. Toss well to mix before serving.

Serves 6 to 8

NOTE: Pickled Dill Cucumber will keep in screw-top jars in the refrigerator for 3 to 4 days.

STEMS & SHOOTS

Stems and shoots feature on the haute cuisine menus of the world.
Tender succulent asparagus, braised fragrant celery and delicately mild globe
artichokes have become gourmet dishes. Asparagus is the indisputable aristocrat
of this family but it has to compete with the globe artichoke and exotic palmito,
often known as palm hearts.

All stems and shoots should be cooked until just tender and barely crisp which varies
dramatically from one member to another. Bamboo shoots and beansprouts hardly
need 2 to 3 minutes stir-frying over high heat, while artichokes may need
30 to 45 minutes until the leaves will pull away easily.

Whether it be asparagus, palm hearts or globe artichokes, stems and shoots
make ideal starters, such as Cream of asparagus soup, Italian fennel
hors d'oeuvre and Celery dip; or tasty vegetable dishes like Bamboo shoots
with broccoli and Fennel fritters; or delicious crisp salads such as
Gourmet asparagus salad, Celery salad flavia and
Greek fennel salad.

GLOBE ARTICHOKES

Origin: The globe artichoke (*Cynara scolymus*) is a member of the Compositae family. Native to Asia Minor, this vegetable has won favour almost everywhere. It has been regularly grown in Italy since the 15th century and in France since the 16th century.

In appearance globe artichokes look like large flower buds, shaped rather like fat pine cones, with overlapping fleshy green leaves and stalks which measure up to 5 to 12 cm (2 to $4\frac{1}{2}$ inches) long. Size and weight vary a great deal, since there are many different varieties of globe artichoke.

Availability: Artichokes are in season from June to October, but occasionally they can be found during the winter months. They are grown extensively in France, Italy, Israel, Morocco, Egypt, Algeria and Spain. The main exporting countries are France, Italy and Israel.

Buying: Buy globe artichokes with the buds still closed, the leaves fleshy and lying close together. They are sold individually but size is not a good sign of quality so choose carefully.

Preparation and serving: Rinse the artichokes, cut off the stalks where they join the buds and sprinkle the cut surface with lemon juice. Boil in salted water, with a little vinegar, for 30 to 45 minutes, according to size and variety. You can test to see if they are cooked by pulling out one of the leaves; it should come away easily.

The bud opens out during cooking to enable you to remove the inedible choke. This is best done with a small pointed spoon. However, be careful not to scrape too energetically, or you may harm the fleshy artichoke bottom.

Artichokes make delicious starters. Stand cooked globe artichokes in the middle of a fairly large plate and pour the chosen sauce or dressing into the middle and around them. To eat, pull off the leaves, one by one, and dip them into the sauce or dressing. The fleshy part of each leaf is then stripped off with the teeth and the resulting leaf discarded.

Globe artichokes can also be boiled and then stuffed; or boiled, stuffed and then baked. Very young, tender artichokes are also delicious fried or cooked in a casserole.

Stuffed artichoke bottoms make an excellent starter or dish to serve in a cold buffet spread. It is often not worth the expense of using fresh artichokes for this purpose; canned artichoke bottoms will do. The same applies to artichoke hearts, which are especially good in salads, or served as part of an antipasta platter.

Never boil artichokes in aluminium pans, they will turn the pans black.

Nutritional value: Globe artichokes contain Vitamins A and B_1, plenty of calcium, a little protein and carbohydrate. Low in calories they contain 15 Calories (62 kj) per 100 g/$3\frac{1}{2}$ oz.

ASPARAGUS

Origin: Asparagus (*Asparagus officinalis*) is a member of the Liliaceae family. The plant originated in the Eastern Mediterranean, where it was used just as much as a cure for bee stings, heart trouble and toothache as a source of food! The ancient Egyptians thought very highly of asparagus, and used it mainly as a medicinal plant and in their rituals.

It has been grown in the more northerly parts of Europe since the 15th century, and is popular and much-sought after in Britain, France, Italy and America.

Availability: Fresh white asparagus is available from the middle of May to the end of June; French asparagus for rather longer.

Italy and France export asparagus, particularly green asparagus, almost all year round. The English asparagus season is from early May to the end of June.

Buying: There are three main kinds of asparagus to choose from: white asparagus, often considered the best and most tender which has a mild flavour and creamy white stems; French asparagus, with violet or bluish tips and a stronger, rather more astringent flavour; and green asparagus, the favourite in Britain, where the stalks are not cut underground, but grow to their full height above ground, and have an aromatic flavour.

White asparagus is the fattest, sturdiest variety. French asparagus is smaller and not so thick, while green asparagus is considerably thinner and smaller than the other varieties.

Choose asparagus according to the way you intend to use it. The very best quality, consisting of stems graded to the same length and thickness and with firm white tips, is only necessary for extra special dishes. Use those spears that have closed tips and white stalks which may not be all the same size for vegetable dishes. Thin asparagus or 'sprue' is adequate for soups and mixed vegetable dishes, where size and regularity is not important.

Whichever quality you are buying, freshness is all important. Choose asparagus with firm stems and juicy cut ends. Avoid those with cracked or woody stems.

Preparation and serving: Peel white and French asparagus before cooking. Peel the top third of each stem thinly, then the rest quite thickly, so that the asparagus does not taste fibrous or bitter. Green asparagus need only have the bottom third of the stems peeled very thinly. Cut away 1 to 2.5 cm ($\frac{1}{2}$ to 1 inch) of the woody stems from all three varieties to ensure tenderness.

The peelings can be used as the base for many delicious soups and sauces if you cook them with a little stock and lemon juice.

Tie asparagus stems in bundles and cook, tips uppermost, in boiling salted water with a small knob of butter. Cook white or French asparagus for 20 to 35 minutes, according to the thickness of the stems. Cook green asparagus for 15 to 20 minutes, according to thickness.

Serve boiled asparagus with melted butter and finely chopped parsley or dill. It makes a classic accompaniment to meat roasts, steaks, ham and white fish. It is also very popular as a salad ingredient, with a piquant, aromatic or mildly-flavoured dressing.

Asparagus makes an excellent vegetable dish, especially in a butter or cream sauce. It also makes good soups, aspic dishes, gratin dishes, an omelette filling and a vegetable to serve with

BEAN SPROUTS

BAMBOO SHOOT

eggs, scrambled or hard-boiled.

Asparagus is a highly perishable food but will keep for 2 to 3 days in the refrigerator if wrapped in cling film.

Nutritional value: Asparagus is a good source of Vitamins C and B, and potassium. Low in calories it contains 18 Calories (75 kj) per 100 g/3½ oz.

BAMBOO SHOOTS

Origin: Bamboo shoots (*Bambusa vulgaris*) are a member of the Gramineae family. Native to Asia, they are the white inner conical shoots of the tropical bamboo plant.

Bamboo shoots are picked when they are about 7.5 to 9 cm (3 to 3½ inches) thick and about 10 to 14 cm (4 to 5½ inches) long.

Availability: Fresh bamboo shoots are generally only found in the Far East where they are also known as Chinese asparagus. They have a very delicate and aromatic flavour and creamy white appearance. They are available canned in almost every country. Canned bamboo shoots taste a little like celery, but they were much milder.

Buying: Canned bamboo shoots are available in whole pieces or thin strips.

Preparation and serving: Fresh bamboo shoots should have their outer covering stripped before slicing thinly for use. Cook for about 4 to 5 minutes in boiling salted water or stir-fry over a high heat for about 2 to 3 minutes. Canned bamboo shoots are pre-cooked and simply need draining before use. Reheat them gently if serving hot.

Use bamboo shoots in stir-fried and braised dishes with other vegetables, meat, fish or poultry. They are delicious in salads with other crisp vegetables. They can be served as a vegetable in their own right with meat dishes. Rather bland in flavour, they appreciate spicy seasonings and flavourings such as soy sauce, ground or root ginger, curry powder, sherry, Tabasco sauce, powdered galingale root and chilli powder.

Nutritional value: Bamboo shoots do not provide nutrients in significant quantities. They are, however, low in calories, containing only 9 Calories (40 kj) per 100 g/3½ oz.

BEANS SPROUTS

Origin: Bean sprouts (*Phaseolus aureus*) are the tender young sprouts of the germinating soya or mung bean. They are used extensively in the Far East in stir-fried, braised and salad dishes. Creamy white in colour, with green to yellow sprouts, they grow to about 2.5 to 5 cm (1 to 2 inches) long.

Availability: Fresh bean sprouts are available all year round and because of their high perishability are generally sold in the country where they are grown. Canned bean sprouts are available in almost every country, the main exporter being China.

Buying: Choose fresh bean sprouts with a crisp, fresh appearance. Most on sale have been sorted and pre-packed into convenient quantities.

Canned bean sprouts are available plain or mixed with other Chinese-style vegetables like bamboo shoots and water chestnuts.

Preparation and serving: Rinse fresh bean sprouts thoroughly before use. Simply drain canned bean sprouts to use. Canned bean sprouts are already cooked and therefore need only a brief reheating time.

Use bean sprouts as a vegetable accompaniment, in stir-fried and braised dishes or as a crisp salad ingredient.

As they are highly perishable, store fresh or opened canned bean sprouts in the refrigerator for 2 to 3 days.

Nutritional value: Bean sprouts, despite their high water content, provide valuable protein. They contain only 9 Calories (40 kj) per 100 g/3½ oz.

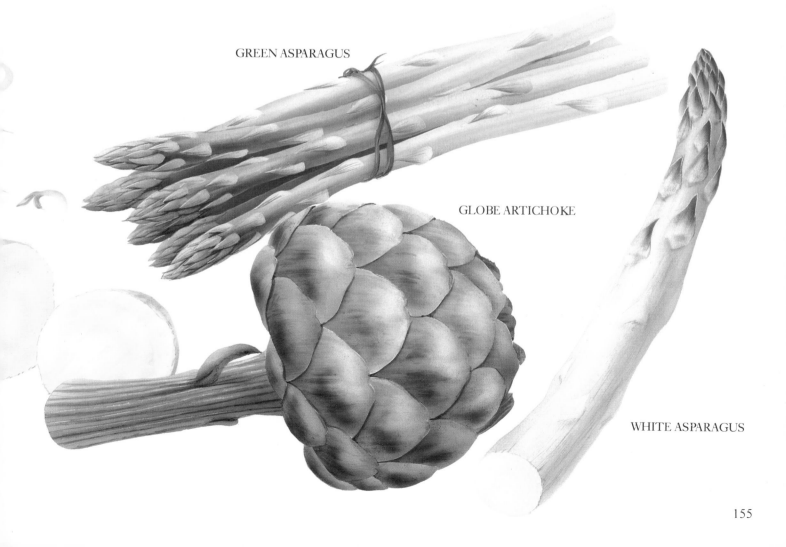

GREEN ASPARAGUS

GLOBE ARTICHOKE

WHITE ASPARAGUS

CARDOON

Origin: The cardoon (*Cynara cardunculus*) is a member of the Compositae family. It is a thistle-like plant that is related to the globe artichoke. It comes from southern Europe where it has been enjoyed since the 16th century. The Italians are particularly fond of it, eating it raw dipped into spicy sauces.

The cardoon is a longish plant, whose root and fleshy ribbed stalk is similar to celery but it has large, grey-green, laciniate leaves. The flavour of cardoon is aromatic and nutty, slightly reminiscent of globe artichokes.

Availability: Cardoons are grown extensively in Italy where they are in season during the winter months. Few are exported, and those that are, come almost exclusively from Italy.

Buying: Choose cardoons that have crisp stems, bright leaves and a fresh appearance. Reject any with damaged or wilting leaves or a limp appearance.

Preparation and serving: To prepare cardoons for cooking or serving, remove the leaves and stalks and cut the stems into smaller pieces. Cook in boiling salted water for about 20 to 25 minutes. Use as a plain vegetable accompaniment to meats and fish, baked in a sauce as an unusual starter, or raw in salads and to serve with dips.

Nutritional value: Cardoons contain a few vitamins and minerals but none in significant quantities. Low in calories they contain only 15 Calories (62 kj) per 100 g/$3\frac{1}{2}$ oz.

CELERY

Origin: Celery (*Apium graveolens*) is a relation of the celeriac root. The ancient Egyptians employed it mainly for ritual purposes, while the Greeks and Romans appreciated it as a cultivated vegetable. Italian gardeners cultivated blanched celery as early as the 19th century; they covered it with mounds of earth to keep out the light.

In appearance celery resembles long-stemmed bundles of fleshy, ribbed stalks, white to light green in colour. Pale yellow or light green leaves grow at the end of the stalks.

Availability: Celery is available most of the year but is at its best in season – generally from about September to April. It is grown extensively in Belgium, Spain, Italy, Israel, and many coastal areas of the Mediterranean. Britain grows a great deal of celery for home consumption. Imports come to Britain from Belgium, Israel and Spain.

Buying: There are two main varieties of celery to choose from: Pascal, or heavy green-ribbed celery; or golden, which has been blanched and has white to yellow ribs and leaves.

Choose celery with well-formed stems and a fresh appearance. Avoid pithy or woody-looking stalks.

A head of celery can weigh from 325 to 1200 g (11 oz to $2\frac{3}{4}$ lb), and grow up to 35 cm (14 inches) tall.

Preparation and serving: Rinse the celery thoroughly, remove the root end and any dark green leaves that may be bitter in taste. Leave whole or cut into pieces. Serve raw with dips, as part of a mixed salad, as a plain cooked vegetable, or stuffed and baked.

Cook individual stems of celery in boiling salted water for about 7 to 10 minutes, or solid celery hearts for about 20 minutes. Drain and serve with melted butter and a sprinkling of chopped herbs.

Nutritional value: Celery is rich in Vitamin A, especially Pascal celery. It also contains a good deal of Vitamin C, sodium and potassium. It is the slimmer's ideal vegetable containing only 8 Calories (36 kj) per 100 g/$3\frac{1}{2}$ oz.

FENNEL

Origin: Fennel (*Foeniculum vulgare*) is a member of the Umbelliferae family. It is also known as Florentine fennel or finocchio.

It originally came from the Near East where it was almost exclusively valued as a herbal plant. The ancient Romans and the ancient Greeks used it for religious and medicinal purposes. By the Middle Ages, fennel was being grown all over southern Europe for use as a vegetable. In northern Europe, the dried seeds of the plant were used (as they still are) as a seasoning and a herbal tea.

The fennel bulb may have been a popular vegetable in Italy from ancient times but it has only recently found popularity in Britain. In appearance it is a fist-sized, white bulb, consisting of fleshy, ribbed leaves, with pale green tubular stalks, and bright green feathery leaves. The flavour is fresh and crisp, highly aromatic and slightly sweet, with a strong taste of aniseed.

CELERY

CARDOON

PALM HEART

Availability: Fennel is available all year round, although it is often more difficult to find during the summer months. It is grown in all Mediterranean countries, especially Italy. Most of the fennel on sale in Britain is imported from Italy.

Buying: Fennel is sold in bulbs by weight. Choose bulbs that are fresh, solid and crisp. Avoid any with cut stalk surfaces that are yellow or show any signs of age.

Preparation and serving: Rinse fennel thoroughly before use. Slice the stalks into rings. Cut the bulbs into strips, chunks, halves or quarters as liked. The feathery green leaves can also be used chopped in salads, and as an attractive garnish.

Cooked fennel makes a delicious vegetable accompaniment, boiled, baked or in a gratin. Cook in boiling salted water for about 15 to 20 minutes until tender. Serve with melted butter or sprinkled with cheese.

Sprinkle fennel that is to be eaten raw with a little lemon juice to prevent discoloration.

Nutritional value: Fennel has a high Vitamin C content, plenty of calcium and phosphorus, a little protein, carbohydrate, iron, potassium and Vitamin E. Fennel contains 52 Calories (217 kj) per 100 g/3½ oz.

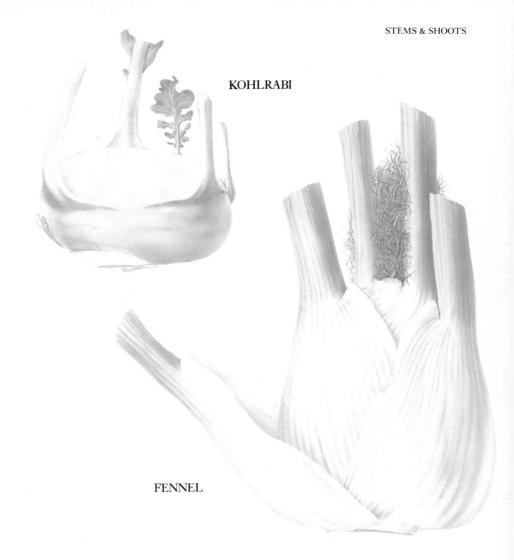

KOHLRABI

FENNEL

KOHLRABI

Origin: Kohlrabi (*Brassica oleracea* var. *gongylodes*) is a member of the Cruciferae family. It originated less than 500 years ago in northern Europe and by the end of the 16th century was known in Germany, England, Italy and Spain.

Kohlrabi is not a root as many think, but a stem which swells to a turnip shape above ground. The long and unswollen part of the stem is just as edible as the swollen part, at least for soups.

Availability: Kohlrabi is grown in many northern European countries, especially Germany. There are spring, summer and autumn varieties of kohlrabi, ensuring a good supply almost all year round. In winter and spring the kohlrabi on sale has often been grown under glass, and is rather milder in flavour than the outdoor kohlrabi.

Most of the kohlrabi on sale in Britain is home produced, but some imports do arrive from Germany.

Buying: You can choose from two main varieties of kohlrabi: the pale green kind which is grown under glass; and the purplish or violet outdoor kohlrabi. Sold individually, look for globes about the size of large eggs. Any stems that are much larger than this will

probably be woody and tough. The tops of kohlrabi will also show signs of age – look for tops that are green, young and fresh.

If you are catering for normal appetites, you will need 4 to 5 kohlrabi to feed 4 people.

Preparation and serving: Trim off the stems and leaves; use these for soups. Peel the kohlrabi thinly at the top end, more thickly at the root end. Rinse and cut into strips, slices or chunks. Simmer in stock for about 25 to 30 minutes until tender.

Serve cooked kohlrabi with a white sauce or add to casseroles and stews. Kohrabi can also be stuffed and baked.

Nutritional value: Kohlrabi provides an excellent source of Vitamin C. The tops are a good source of Vitamin A. Useful minerals include calcium and phosphorus. Kohlrabi is low in calories, containing only 17 Calories (71 kj) per 100 g/3½ oz.

PALM HEARTS

Origin: Palm hearts, also known as palmito, palmetto and palmetto cabbage, are a member of the Palmaceae family. They are the tender young terminal shoots of some tropical varieties

of palm trees, that grow wild in Brazil.

The Brazilians cut them out of the bark, remove the hard outer crust and then chop them into pieces of regular size for canning or bottling. In flavour, palm hearts taste rather like asparagus.

Availability: In Britain we generally can only buy palm hearts canned or bottled in brine. They can be found in most delicatessens, or the food halls of large department stores specialising in exotic foodstuffs.

Buying: Choose canned or bottled palm hearts with a reliable brand name for quality. Store for up to 6 months in a cool dry place.

Preparation and serving: Palm hearts of the canned or bottled variety are very simple to use. Simply drain and rinse before use. Canned palm hearts are already cooked so they will only need a short reheating period.

Palm hearts are excellent as a starter with a savoury dressing or sauce. They also make a good salad ingredient and tasty vegetable to include in a casserole.

Nutritional value: Rich in vitamins and minerals, palm hearts are valued mainly as an unusual vegetable ingredient rather than a staple food. Low in calories they contain only 14 Calories (60 kj) per 100 g/3½ oz.

Cream of Asparagus Soup

625 g/1¼ lb asparagus spears
600 ml/1 pint chicken stock
15 g/½ oz butter
2 teaspoons flour
300 ml/½ pint dry white wine
salt
pinch of cayenne pepper
2–3 tablespoons soured cream
1 tablespoon snipped chives

Wash the asparagus and trim off the woody stalk bases. Cut the stems into 2.5 to 4 cm/1 to 1¾ inch lengths. Bring the stock to the boil in a pan. Add the asparagus, lower the heat and cook gently for 20 minutes, or until tender. Drain, reserving the cooking liquid.

Meanwhile, melt the butter in a pan, add the flour and cook for 2 to 3 min-utes. Gradually whisk in the reserved cooking liquid, keeping the soup smooth. Add the wine and season with salt and cayenne pepper to taste. Add the asparagus and bring the soup to the boil, stirring. Cook for 2 to 3 minutes. Remove from the heat, stir in the cream and serve sprinkled with chives.
Serves 4

Artichoke Hors d'Oeuvre

4 globe artichokes
juice of 2 lemons
salt
3–4 tablespoons vinegar
2 tablespoons olive oil
75–125 g/3–4 oz butter
300 ml/½ pint double cream
2 egg yolks, beaten
grated nutmeg
sugar

Using a sharp knife, cut the stalks off the artichokes. Rinse thoroughly and rub the cut ends with a little of the lemon juice. Bring a large pan of water to the boil. Add a pinch of salt, the vinegar and oil. Add the artichokes, cover and simmer for 30 minutes, or until a leaf will pull away easily. Drain, reserving 6 tablespoons cooking liquid.

Melt the butter with the remaining lemon juice in a small pan. Add the reserved cooking liquid, blending well. Stir in the cream and simmer, stirring, for 2 to 3 minutes. Remove the pan from the heat and carefully whisk in the egg yolk. Return to the heat and cook gently, stirring, until the sauce is creamy; do not allow to boil. Season with salt, nutmeg and sugar to taste.

Using a sharp pointed spoon, re-move the chokes from the artichokes and discard. Place them on warmed individual serving plates. Spoon over a little of the sauce and pour the remain-der around the base of each artichoke.
Serves 4

Celery with Cream Cheese

1 small head celery
juice of ½ lemon
2 × 62.5 g/2.2 oz packets cream cheese
salt
freshly ground black pepper
2 tablespoons Grand Marnier
2 tablespoons coarsely chopped walnuts

Cut the bottom off the celery, separate the sticks and trim the ends. Reserve a few celery leaves. Rinse the celery sticks thoroughly and sprinkle with the lemon juice.

Beat the cream cheese with salt and pepper to taste, and the Grand Mar-nier. Spoon into a piping bag fitted with a star-shaped nozzle. Pipe cream cheese into the celery sticks and sprinkle with the chopped walnuts. Ar-range the celery on a serving dish and garnish with the celery leaves to serve.
Serves 4

Italian Fennel Hors d'Oeuvre

125 g/4 oz button mushrooms
40 g/1½ oz butter
3 cloves garlic, peeled and halved
2 anchovy fillets, cut into fine strips
4 tablespoons dry white wine
150 ml/¼ pint double cream
2 egg yolks
2 heads fennel, cut into strips

Slice the mushrooms very finely. Melt the butter in a pan, add the garlic and fry until golden brown. Remove the garlic and discard. Add the mushrooms to the pan and fry over a gentle heat for 2 to 3 minutes. Add the anchovies and wine and simmer for 2 to 3 minutes. Mix the cream with the egg yolks and stir into the mushroom mixture.

Place the uncooked fennel on a serv-ing dish. Spoon the hot sauce into a separate dish or into individual dishes. Each guest then dips the strips of fen-nel into the mushroom sauce to eat, as with a fondue.
Serves 4 to 6

Cardoon Hors d'Oeuvre

1 cardoon stem
salt
2 eggs
freshly ground black pepper
scant 2 tablespoons flour
120 ml/4 fl oz olive oil
50–75 g/2–3 oz Parmesan cheese, grated

Divide the cardoon into stalks. Remove the leaves, leaving the fleshy stalks. Rinse thoroughly. Cook the cardoon in boiling salted water for 15 to 20 minutes. Drain and peel off the fibrous skin.

Beat the eggs with salt and pepper to taste. Dip the cardoon stalks in the egg, then coat with the flour. Sprinkle with the olive oil and then the cheese. Cook under a preheated hot grill for 8 to 10 minutes. Serve immediately.
Serves 4

Cream of Asparagus Soup; Celery with Cream Cheese; Italian Fennel Hors d'Oeuvre

Artichokes alla Romana

4 artichokes
salt
1 tablespoon lemon juice
2 tablespoons oil
2–3 thick slices white bread
2 cloves garlic, peeled and crushed
1 tablespoon vinegar
1 tablespoon fresh or 1½ teaspoons dried
  mint
1–2 tablespoons olive oil

Using a sharp knife, cut the stalks off the artichokes. Rinse thoroughly. Bring a large pan of water to the boil. Add a pinch of salt, the lemon juice and oil. Add the artichokes, cover and simmer for 30 to 40 minutes, until a leaf can be pulled away easily. Remove with a slotted spoon and leave to drain. Reserve the cooking liquid.

Meanwhile, crumble the bread into a bowl, add the garlic, vinegar, mint and salt to taste. Mix thoroughly and use to stuff the artichokes.

Place the artichokes in an ovenproof dish, pour the reserved cooking liquid around them and sprinkle with the olive oil. Cook in a preheated hot oven (220°C/425°F, Gas Mark 7) for about 10 minutes. Serve immediately.
Serves 4

NOTE: Artichokes alla Romana are delicious served with cubed cheese, olives and a dry white wine.

Celery with Hazelnut Dip

1 head celery
juice of 1 lemon
150 ml/¼ pint mayonnaise
50 g/2 oz ground hazelnuts
25 g/1 oz chopped hazelnuts
pinch of sugar (optional)
radish roses to garnish (optional)

Cut the bottom off the celery, separate the sticks and trim ends. Stand in a jug.

Mix the lemon juice with the mayonnaise, ground hazelnuts, chopped nuts and sugar if liked. Spoon the dip into a small dish. Garnish with radish roses if liked, and serve with the celery.
Serves 4

Artichokes with Avocado and Cheese Dip

4 globe artichokes
salt
2 avocados
125 g/4 oz Gorgonzola or blue-veined cheese
1 egg yolk
300 ml/½ pint soured cream
pinch of curry powder

Cook the artichokes in boiling salted water until tender; drain.

Meanwhile, peel and stone the avocados and purée in an electric blender with the cheese. Stir in the egg yolk, cream, a pinch of salt and the curry powder. Serve with the hot artichokes.
Serves 4

Artichokes with Tomato Mayonnaise

4 globe artichokes
salt
3 tablespoons mayonnaise
1 tablespoon tomato purée
2 tablespoons Italian dressing
6 tablespoons double cream
dash of Tabasco sauce
freshly ground black pepper

Cook the artichokes in boiling salted water until tender; drain.

Beat the mayonnaise with the tomato purée, Italian dressing, cream, Tabasco and salt and pepper to taste. Serve the tomato mayonnaise cold with the hot artichokes.
Serves 4

Artichokes with Garlic Sauce

4 globe artichokes
4 cloves garlic, peeled and crushed with 1 teaspoon salt
4 egg yolks
200 ml/⅓ pint olive oil
1 tablespoon chopped herbs (e.g. parsley, thyme, sage)
pinch of cayenne pepper

Cook the artichokes in boiling salted water until tender; drain.

Meanwhile, place the garlic and egg yolks in an electric blender and blend for a few seconds, then add the oil slowly with the blender on a low speed. Season with the herbs and cayenne pepper. Serve cold with the hot artichokes.
Serves 4

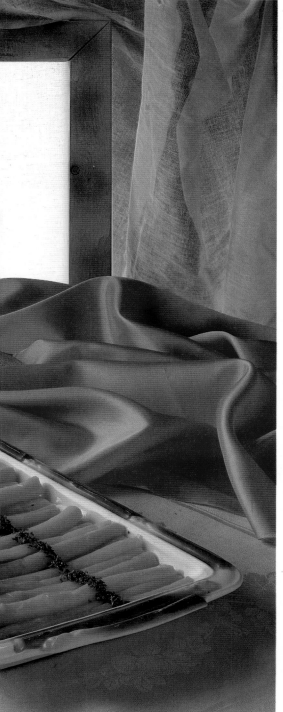

French-style Asparagus

750 g/1½ lb asparagus spears
lemon juice
pinch of salt
knob of butter
SAUCE:
2 tablespoons mayonnaise
1 teaspoon made mustard
1 teaspoon chopped fresh or ½ teaspoon dried tarragon.
150 ml/¼ pint whipping cream,
TO GARNISH:
1 tablespoon chopped parsley

Rinse the asparagus thoroughly under cold running water and trim off the woody bases of the stalks. Bring a large pan of water to the boil. Add the lemon juice, salt, butter and asparagus. Lower the heat and cook for 20 minutes, or until tender. Leave to cool in the cooking liquid.

To make the sauce, combine the mayonnaise, mustard and tarragon in a bowl. Lightly whip the cream and fold into the sauce.

Drain the asparagus and transfer to a serving dish. Sprinkle with the parsley and serve immediately, with the tarragon sauce in a separate dish.
Serves 4

Artichokes with Tomato Mayonaise; Artichokes with Avocado and Cheese Dip; French-style Asparagus

Palm Heart Spring Salad

*1 × 398 g/14 oz can palm hearts,
   drained*
1 bunch small radishes
*2 hard-boiled eggs, shelled and cut into
   wedges*
1 tablespoon stuffed olives, sliced
4 tablespoons oil
juice of 1 lemon
salt and freshly ground black pepper
pinch of sugar
1–2 tablespoons snipped chives

Cut the palm hearts into 2.5 cm/1 inch lengths and place in a serving bowl. Cut the radishes into rosettes and add to the palm hearts with the eggs and olives.

To make the dressing, beat the oil with the lemon juice, salt and pepper to taste, and the sugar. Fold in the chives, blending well. Leave the dressing to chill in the refrigerator for about 10 minutes to allow the flavours to de-velop. Pour the dressing over the salad and toss well. Serve immediately.
Serves 4

NOTE: To give this salad extra flavour, rub the salad bowl with the cut side of half a clove of garlic before adding the salad ingredients.

Palm hearts wrapped in slices of tongue spread with mayonnaise or pic-calilli make an excellent hors d'oeuvre.

Artichoke Hearts with Dill Butter

75 g/3 oz butter
1 egg yolk
1 teaspoon tomato purée
salt
pinch of cayenne pepper
1–2 small dill sprigs, chopped
*1 × 396 g/14 oz can artichoke hearts in
   brine, drained*

Cream the butter with the egg yolk, tomato purée, salt to taste and cayenne pepper. Fold in the dill and spread over the artichoke hearts to serve.
Serves 4

NOTE: This is a delicious hors d'oeuvre, served with salami or salmon and toast.

Bamboo Shoot Salad

*1 × 227 g/8 oz can bamboo shoots,
   drained*
125 g/4 oz peeled shrimps or prawns
*2 tablespoons chopped fresh or canned
   pineapple*
*1 green pepper, cored, seeded and
   chopped*
1 tablespoon chopped parsley
3 tablespoons salad oil
2 tablespoons dry white wine
1 tablespoon soy sauce
pinch of ground ginger
salt
freshly ground black pepper
pinch of sugar (optional)

Cut the bamboo shoots into thin strips and place in a serving bowl. Add the shrimps or prawns, pineapple, green pepper and parsley.

To make the dressing, beat the oil with the wine, soy sauce, ginger, salt, pepper and sugar to taste, if using. Pour the dressing over the salad and toss well to mix.

Cover and leave to stand in the re-frigerator for 30 minutes to 1 hour to allow the flavours to develop. Toss again before serving.
Serves 4

Garnished Artichoke Hearts

*2 × 85 g/3½ oz packets soft cream
   cheese*
1 clove garlic, peeled and crushed
1 egg yolk
*6 tablespoons double cream, lightly
   whipped*
ground paprika
*2 tablespoons chopped herbs (e.g.
   parsley, thyme, sage)*
salt
freshly ground white pepper
*1 × 396 g/14 oz can artichoke hearts in
   brine, drained*
TO GARNISH:
shredded lettuce
red pepper slices

Beat the cream cheese with the garlic, egg yolk, cream, paprika, herbs and salt and pepper to taste. Spoon into a pip-ing bag fitted with a star-shaped nozzle and pipe swirls of the mixture onto the artichoke hearts.

Chill the artichoke hearts lightly before serving, on a bed of lettuce, garnished with red pepper slices.
Serves 4

NOTE: Garnished Artichoke Hearts make a delicious party snack, or hors d'oeuvre. Serve with garlic bread and a light dry red wine.

Artichokes Tuscan-style

4–6 small young artichokes
juice of 1 lemon
salt
freshly ground black pepper
4 tablespoons olive oil
4 eggs, beaten
2 sprigs of parsley, chopped
25 g/1 oz grated Parmesan cheese

Rinse the artichokes thoroughly under cold running water. Cut them in half and sprinkle with lemon juice and salt and pepper to taste. Heat the olive oil in a pan until very hot and quickly fry the artichokes on all sides.

Transfer the artichokes to an oven-proof dish. Mix the eggs with the parsley and salt to taste. Pour over the artichokes and sprinkle with the cheese. Cook in a preheated hot oven (200°C/400°F, Gas Mark 6) for 15 to 18 minutes. Serve immediately.
Serves 4

NOTE: This recipe is only suitable for very young chokeless artichokes. It is ideal to serve as an hors d'oeuvre.

Palm Heart Spring Salad; Bamboo Shoot Salad; Garnished Artichoke Hearts

163

Celery and Orange Salad

1 head celery, cut into small strips
1 apple, cored and chopped
1 red pepper, cored, seeded and sliced
1 small orange
3 tablespoons mayonnaise
1 tablespoon orange juice
salt
pinch of cayenne pepper

Mix the celery with the apple and red pepper in a salad bowl. Peel the orange and divide into segments, discarding all pith.

To make the dressing, beat the mayonnaise with the orange juice, salt and cayenne pepper to taste. Pour the dressing over the salad and toss to mix.

Cover and chill for about 30 minutes to allow the flavours to develop.
Serves 4

NOTE: This salad looks most attractive served in individual dessert glasses, garnished with pared cucumber slices.

Palm Heart Salad with Dill Mayonnaise

1 × 425 g/15 oz can palm hearts, drained
2 hard-boiled eggs, shelled and finely chopped
1 tablespoon mayonnaise
4–5 tablespoons soured cream
pinch of cayenne pepper
1–2 teaspoons chopped dill

Cut the palm hearts into 2.5 cm/1 inch lengths. Spread the chopped eggs over the palm hearts and place in a serving dish.

To make the dressing, beat the mayonnaise with the soured cream, cayenne pepper and dill. Pour the dressing over the palm hearts and toss

well to mix. Leave to stand for about 10 minutes to allow the flavours to develop.
Serves 4

NOTE: Palm Heart Salad with Dill Mayonnaise makes an appetising hors d'oeuvre or vegetable dish.

Waldorf Salad

150 ml/¼ pint mayonnaise
2 tablespoons single cream
3 dessert apples, cored and chopped
4 sticks celery, chopped
25 g/1 oz walnut pieces
few lettuce leaves
1 tablespoon snipped chives, to garnish

Blend the mayonnaise with the cream in a bowl. Add the apples, celery and walnuts, tossing well to coat. Arrange the lettuce leaves in a salad bowl. Spoon the salad into the centre of the bowl and sprinkle with the chives.
Serves 6 to 8

NOTE: This American salad is ideal to serve with cold roast meats.

RIGHT: *Gourmet Asparagus Salad; Fennel Salad Milano*
BELOW: *Waldorf Salad; Palm Heart Salad*

Gourmet Asparagus Salad

625 g/1¼ lb asparagus spears
salt
knob of butter
1 teaspoon herb-flavoured vinegar
1 tablespoon orange juice
1 dash of vodka
cayenne pepper
2 tablespoons snipped chives to
    garnish

Wash the asparagus under cold running water and trim off the woody bases of the stalks. Bring a large pan of water to the boil. Add a pinch of salt, the butter and asparagus. Lower the heat and cook gently for about 20 minutes, until tender. Leave to cool in the cooking liquid.

To make the marinade, whisk 6 tablespoons of the cooking liquid with the vinegar, orange juice, vodka, salt and cayenne pepper to taste.

Drain the asparagus, pour over the marinade and leave to stand for at least 1 hour to allow the flavours to develop. Garnish with chives before serving.
Serves 4

NOTE: Serve as a delicious hors d'oeuvre or accompaniment.

Fennel Salad Milano

2 heads fennel
1 apple, peeled, cored and chopped
1 orange, peeled, pith removed, and
    coarsely chopped
50 g/2 oz cooked ham, finely chopped
125 g/4 oz canned mussels or shrimps,
    drained
4 tablespoons olive oil
1 egg yolk
1 clove garlic, peeled and crushed
salt and freshly ground black pepper

Cut the fennel heads into strips and the stalks into rings, reserving the feathery leaves. Place the fennel in a sieve, rinse and drain thoroughly. Place in a serving bowl. Add the apple, orange, ham and mussels or shrimps.

To make the dressing, beat the olive oil with the egg yolk, garlic and salt and pepper to taste. Pour over the salad and toss to mix. Cover and chill for about 10 minutes to allow the flavours to develop. Garnish with the fennel leaves before serving.
Serves 4

NOTE: Fennel Salad Milano is a delicious hors d'oeuvre or vegetable dish to serve with fish.

165

Bean Shoot Omelette

200 g/7 oz fresh bean shoots
125 g/4 oz mushrooms, sliced
juice of 1 lemon
15 g/½ oz butter or 1 tablespoon oil
1 onion, peeled and chopped
6–8 eggs
1 parsley sprig chopped
salt
freshly ground black pepper
ground paprika
oil for frying

Place the bean shoots in a bowl. Cover with water and soak until the husks rise to the surface. Remove these and drain the bean shoots thoroughly.

Meanwhile, place the mushrooms in a bowl and sprinkle with the lemon juice. Melt the butter or oil in a pan. Add the bean shoots, mushrooms and onion. Lower the heat and cook gently for about 5 minutes.

Meanwhile, beat the eggs with the herbs, salt, pepper and paprika to taste. Heat a little oil in an omelette or frying pan. Add one quarter of the bean shoot and mushroom mixture and one quarter of the egg mixture. Cook, over a moderate heat, until the eggs have just set, drawing the cooking mixture from the outside of the pan to the centre during cooking. Remove and keep warm. Cook three more omelettes in the same way with the remaining mixtures. Serve immediately.
Serves 4

NOTE: Serve this light main course with French bread and a dry white wine.

Fresh bean shoots are also delicious cooked with thin strips of cooked meat or minced beef and a little soy sauce. If you can't get fresh bean shoots for either dish, canned ones are almost as good and need only be reheated according to the manufacturer's instructions.

Greek Fennel Salad

1 head fennel
325 g/11 oz tomatoes, cut into wedges
125 g/4 oz raw smoked ham, chopped
1 tablespoon black olives, stoned
1 small onion, peeled and cut into thin
   rings
salt
freshly ground black pepper
½ teaspoon dried oregano
4 tablespoons olive oil

Cut the fennel head into strips and the stalks into rings, reserving the feathery leaves. Place the fennel in a sieve, rinse and drain thoroughly.

Transfer the fennel to a serving bowl and mix with the tomatoes, ham, olives and onion. Sprinkle with salt and pepper to taste and the oregano. Add the olive oil and toss well to mix. Garnish the salad with the reserved fennel leaves and serve immediately.
Serves 4

NOTE: This Greek Fennel Salad is even more delicious if you rub the inside of the salad bowl with the cut side of half a garlic clove before filling it with the salad. It is delicious served with meat or fish kebabs.

Baked Asparagus and Ham Rolls

1 kg/2 lb asparagus spears
salt
knob of butter
pinch of sugar
350 g/12 oz cooked ham, thickly sliced
50 g/2 oz cheese, grated
SAUCE:
50 g/2 oz butter
1 tablespoon flour
1 egg yolk, beaten
freshly ground white pepper
grated nutmeg
TO GARNISH:
chopped parsley

Wash the asparagus stems under cold running water and trim off the woody bases of the stalks. Bring a large pan of water to the boil. Add a pinch of salt, the butter, sugar and asparagus. Lower the heat and simmer for about 15 minutes, until almost cooked but still crisp. Drain, reserving 300 ml/½ pint liquid.

Meanwhile, make the sauce. Melt 40 g/1½ oz of the butter in a pan, add the flour and cook for 2 to 3 minutes. Gradually stir in the reserved asparagus cooking liquid. Cook, stirring, for 2 to 3 minutes to make a smooth sauce. Remove from the heat and stir in the egg yolk. Season with salt, pepper and nutmeg to taste.

Place 4 to 5 asparagus spears on each slice of ham and roll up. Place the rolls in a greased ovenproof dish, pour over the sauce and sprinkle with the cheese. Dot with the remaining butter. Cook in a preheated moderately hot oven (200°C/400°F, Gas Mark 6) for 15 to 20 minutes. Garnish with parsley and serve immediately.
Serves 6

Celery Salad Flavia

1 clove garlic, peeled and halved
1 head celery, cut into small strips
1 × 200 g/7 oz can artichoke hearts in brine, drained and halved
1 tablespoon black olives, stoned
1 tablespoon chopped parsley
3 tablespoons olive oil
1 tablespoon lemon juice
dash of Tabasco sauce
½ teaspoon made mustard
pinch of dried oregano
salt
few celery leaves to garnish

Using the cut side of the garlic, vigorously rub the inside of a salad bowl, then discard. Add the celery, artichoke hearts, olives and parsley to the bowl.

To make the dressing, beat the olive oil with the lemon juice, Tabasco sauce, mustard, oregano and salt to taste.

Pour the dressing over the salad and toss well. Cover and chill for 30 minutes to allow the flavours to develop.

Toss the salad again before serving and garnish with a few celery leaves.
Serves 4

NOTE: For special occasions, this salad can be garnished with a ring of hard-boiled egg slices and tomato wedges.

Greek Fennel Salad; Celery Salad Flavia; Baked Asparagus and Ham Rolls

Stuffed Celery

1 head celery
300 ml/½ pint beef stock
150 g/5 oz cooked minced beef
1 egg yolk
50 g/2 oz streaky bacon, derinded and
   chopped and fried
50 g/2 oz cooked ham, chopped
2 tablespoons fresh white breadcrumbs
250 ml/8 fl oz tomato ketchup
150 ml/¼ pint double cream
pinch of cayenne pepper
15 g/½ oz butter
parsley sprigs to garnish

Cut the celery head in half vertically. Remove the leaves, chop them finely and reserve 1 tablespoon. Remove the woody base, but do not separate the sticks. Scrub thoroughly under cold running water. Bring the stock to the boil in a pan. Add the celery, lower the heat and cook gently for about 10 minutes until almost cooked, but still crisp. Drain thoroughly.

Meanwhile, make the stuffing. Mix the beef with the egg yolk, bacon, ham, breadcrumbs and celery leaves.

Fill the two celery halves with the stuffing. Beat the tomato ketchup with the cream and cayenne pepper. Place the stuffed celery in an ovenproof dish, pour over the sauce, dot with the butter and cook in a preheated moderately hot oven (200°C/400°F, Gas Mark 6) for 15 to 20 minutes. Garnish with the parsley and serve immediately.
Serves 4

NOTE: Stuffed Celery is delicious served with boiled potatoes or rice.

Chinese Pork with Bamboo Shoots

3–4 tablespoons groundnut oil
325 g/11 oz pork, shredded
salt and freshly ground white pepper
1 small Chinese cabbage, shredded
1 tablespoon coarsely chopped hazelnuts
1 × 227 g/8 oz can bamboo shoots,
   drained with juices reserved, and
   sliced
2 tablespoons soy sauce
1 teaspoon curry powder
pinch of chilli powder
small pinch of sugar

Heat the oil in a pan, add the pork and stir fry quickly until lightly browned. Season with salt and pepper to taste. Add the cabbage, hazelnuts and a few tablespoons of liquid from the can of bamboo shoots. Cook, stirring, for about 5 minutes.

Add the bamboo shoots, soy sauce, curry powder, chilli powder and sugar, mixing well. Cook gently for a further 10 minutes. Serve immediately.
Serves 4

NOTE: Serve Chinese Pork with Bamboo Shoots with cooked long-grain rice and a glass of rosé wine or a beer.

Celebration Asparagus on Toast

500 g/1 lb cooked asparagus spears
4 thick slices white bread
40 g/1½ oz butter
4 slices cooked ham
4 slices Gouda cheese
2 tomatoes, thickly sliced
salt
freshly ground black pepper
few basil sprigs

Cut the asparagus spears in half, if large. Toast the bread lightly on both sides and spread lightly with the butter. Place a slice of ham on each piece of toast and cover with the asparagus spears. Lay the cheese slices on the asparagus and top with the tomato slices. Season with salt and pepper to taste. Chop a few of the basil leaves and sprinkle over the tomatoes.

Cook under a preheated hot grill until the cheese has melted, about 5 to 8 minutes. Serve immediately, garnished with the remaining basil.
Serves 4

NOTE: Asparagus on Toast makes a filling hors d'oeuvre or light supper dish if served with a green salad.

Mediterranean Fennel Casserole

2 heads fennel
25 g/1 oz butter
3 cloves garlic, peeled and halved
200 g/7 oz mushrooms, chopped
275 g/9 oz tomatoes, quartered
300 ml/½ pint meat stock
275 g/9 oz white fish fillet (e.g. cod,
   haddock, plaice)
salt
freshly ground black pepper
1 tablespoon tomato purée
1 teaspoon made mustard
1 tablespoon double cream (optional)
1 tablespoon chopped mixed herbs (e.g.
   chives, parsley, thyme (optional)

Remove the stalks and leaves from the fennel and cut the heads into quarters or large pieces. Melt the butter in a pan, add the garlic and fry until brown. Remove and discard the garlic.

Add the mushrooms, tomatoes and fennel to the garlic butter and cook, over a low heat, for 4 to 5 minutes. Add the stock, stirring well.

Cut the fish into 2.5 cm/1 inch cubes or strips and add to the pan. Season with salt and pepper to taste and simmer, over a low heat, for about 15 minutes. Add the tomato purée, mustard and cream if using, blending

well. Transfer to a warmed serving dish and sprinkle with chopped herbs before serving, if liked.
Serves 4

Stuffed Celery; Chinese Pork with Bamboo Shoots; Mediterranean Fennel Casserole; Celebration Asparagus on Toast

Artichokes with Prawn Stuffing

4 globe artichokes
1 tablespoon lemon juice
salt
3 tablespoons vinegar
2 tablespoons olive oil
15 g/½ oz butter
scant 1 tablespoon flour
125 g/4 oz peeled prawns
1 × 283 g/10 oz can asparagus spears,
   drained and chopped
1 egg yolk
2 tablespoons double cream
freshly ground white pepper
1 tablespoon chopped dill or basil

Using a sharp knife, cut the stalks off the artichokes and rub the cut ends with a little of the lemon juice. Bring 1 litre/1¾ pints water to the boil in a large pan with the salt, vinegar and olive oil added. Put the artichokes in the pan and cook for 20 minutes or until a leaf can be pulled away easily. Drain thoroughly, reserving 150 ml/¼ pint of the cooking liquid.

Meanwhile, melt the butter in a frying pan. Add the flour and gradually whisk in the reserved liquid. Bring to the boil, stirring. Add the prawns and asparagus and heat through.

Beat the egg yolk with the cream. Remove the pan from the heat and add the egg mixture, stirring well. Season with salt and pepper to taste.

Using a sharp pointed spoon, remove the chokes from the cooked artichokes. Fill with the prawn and asparagus mixture. Sprinkle with the dill or basil and serve immediately.
Serves 4

NOTE: These artichokes are delicious served with herb-flavoured rice.

Fennel with Cheese Sauce

2–3 heads fennel
juice of 1 lemon
300 ml/½ pint meat stock
salt
freshly ground black pepper
pinch of sugar
pinch of ground coriander
140 g/4½ oz cheese (Emmenthal, Swiss
   or Parmesan), grated
150 ml/¼ pint double cream
150 g/5 oz cooked ham, chopped
15 g/½ oz butter

Remove the stalks and leaves from the fennel and cut the heads into large pieces or thick strips. Sprinkle with the lemon juice. Bring the stock to the boil in a large pan, add the fennel, salt and pepper to taste, sugar and coriander. Lower the heat and simmer for about 15 minutes.

Add the grated cheese and cream. Simmer, stirring vigorously, until the cheese has melted. Dot with the ham and butter and cook under a preheated hot grill for 2 to 3 minutes, until bubbling. Serve immediately.
Serves 4 to 6

NOTE: Serve with French bread and a light dry white wine.

RIGHT: *Country-style Asparagus Platter; Stuffed Kohlrabi*
BELOW: *Artichokes with Prawn Stuffing; Fennel with Cheese Sauce*

Stuffed Kohlrabi

8 kohlrabi, peeled
salt
2 slices white bread, crusts removed
2–3 tablespoons beer
275 g/9 oz calves liver, minced
150 g/5 oz cooked ham, chopped
freshly ground black pepper
pinch of grated nutmeg
pinch of dried marjoram
SAUCE:
15 g/½ oz butter
1 tablespoon flour
300 ml/½ pint meat stock
2 teaspoons made mustard
pinch of sugar
150 ml/¼ pint double cream

Place the kohlrabi in a pan, add enough water to cover, a pinch of salt and bring to the boil. Lower the heat and cook for about 10 minutes. Drain and leave to cool. Cut a 1 cm/½ inch slice from the top of each kohlrabi and reserve. Hollow out the centre of each kohlrabi with a sharp knife or spoon.

Cut the bread into cubes, moisten with the beer and then squeeze out any excess. Mix the bread with the liver, ham, salt and pepper to taste, nutmeg and marjoram. Stuff the kohlrabi with this mixture.

Melt the butter in a pan. Add the flour and cook for 2 to 3 minutes.

Gradually add the stock, blending well to make a smooth sauce. Add the mustard, salt to taste, the sugar and the cream. Bring to the boil, stirring constantly. Pour the sauce into an ovenproof dish.

Stand the stuffed kohlrabi in the sauce and replace the reserved lids. Cover and cook in a preheated moderately hot oven (190°C/375°F, Gas Mark 5) for about 30 to 40 minutes. Serve immediately.
Serves 4

NOTE: Stuffed Kohlrabi is delicious served with boiled long-grain rice.

Country-style Asparagus Platter

1 kg/2 lb asparagus spears
salt
15 g/½ oz butter
1 teaspoon lemon juice
SCRAMBLED EGG AND HAM:
2 tablespoons oil
200 g/7 oz smoked ham, chopped
8 eggs
4 tablespoons cream
pinch of ground paprika
freshly ground white pepper
1 sprig of parsley, chopped

Rinse the asparagus spears and trim off the woody bases from the stalks. Bring 600 ml/1 pint water to the boil in a pan. Add a pinch of salt, the butter, lemon juice and asparagus. Lower the heat and cook, for about 20 minutes until tender. Drain thoroughly, arrange on a large flat dish and keep warm.

To make the scrambled egg and ham, heat the oil in a large frying pan. Add the ham and cook for 1 minute. Beat the eggs with the cream, paprika,

salt and pepper to taste, and the parsley. Pour the mixture over the ham and stir, over a gentle heat, until the eggs are scrambled. Spoon the scrambled egg and ham over the asparagus and serve immediately.
Serves 4

Kohlrabi in Cream Sauce

15 g/½ oz butter
1 tablespoon chopped smoked bacon
½ onion, peeled and chopped
4–5 kohlrabi, peeled and thinly
  sliced
300 ml/½ pint water
salt
pinch of cayenne pepper
pinch of sugar
150 ml/¼ pint double cream
1 parsley sprig, chopped

Melt the butter in a pan, add the bacon and onion and cook, stirring, for 4 to 5 minutes. Add the kohlrabi and cook over a low heat for 4 to 5 minutes. Add the water and season with salt to taste, the cayenne pepper and sugar, blending well. Cover and simmer over a low heat for about 25 minutes, until the kohlrabi is tender.

Pour in the cream and stir well. Transfer to a warmed serving dish and

sprinkle with the chopped parsley. Serve immediately.
Serves 4

NOTE: Kohlrabi in Cream Sauce is a tasty vegetable dish to serve with grilled chops or sausages.

Celery with Sweetcorn

2 tablespoons vegetable oil
½ head celery, cut into 5 cm/2 inch
   lengths
3 tomatoes, chopped
250 ml/8 fl oz meat stock
1 × 198 g/7 oz can sweetcorn kernels,
   drained
pinch of chilli powder
salt
freshly ground black pepper
1 tablespoon chopped parsley
pinch of cayenne pepper (optional)

Heat the oil in a pan. Add the celery and cook over a low heat for 7 to 8 minutes. Add the tomatoes and stock and cook over a low heat for about 8 minutes. Add the sweetcorn, chilli powder and salt and pepper to taste. Bring to the boil.

Transfer to a warmed serving dish and sprinkle with the chopped parsley, and cayenne pepper if liked. Serve immediately.
Serves 4

NOTE: Celery with Sweetcorn is tasty served with any type of roast meat.

Kohlrabi au Gratin

5–6 kohlrabi, peeled, finely sliced or
   chopped
15 g/½ oz melted butter
1 parsley sprig, coarsely chopped
125 g/4 oz Camembert cheese, cubed
50 g/2 oz cooked ham, cut into strips
300 ml/½ pint milk, warmed
½ teaspoon salt
grated nutmeg

Place the kohlrabi in a casserole dish and sprinkle with the melted butter. Add the parsley, Camembert cheese, ham, milk, salt and nutmeg to taste. Mix well and cook in a preheated moderately hot oven (200°C/400°F, Gas Mark 6) for 20 to 30 minutes.
Serves 4

NOTE: This dish is almost a meal in itself, but it can be served as a vegetable dish to accompany grilled meat.

Braised Fennel

3 heads fennel, trimmed
25 g/1 oz butter
150 ml/¼ pint light stock
1 tablespoon lemon juice
salt
freshly ground black pepper
2 tablespoons grated Parmesan cheese

Cut the fennel heads into quarters lengthwise. Melt the butter in a large heavy-based pan, add the fennel and cook, stirring carefully until well coated in the butter.

Pour in the stock and lemon juice, adding salt and pepper to taste. Cover and simmer gently for 35 to 40 minutes. Sprinkle with the cheese and place under a preheated hot grill until golden brown. Serve immediately.
Serves 4

Braised Fennel; Celery with Sweetcorn;
Kohlrabi in Cream Sauce; Bamboo Shoots with
Broccoli

Bamboo Shoots with Broccoli

375 g/12 oz broccoli
½ × 227 g/8 oz can bamboo shoots,
   drained with juice reserved
3–4 tablespoons oil
1 onion, peeled and chopped
pinch of ground cinnamon
salt
cayenne pepper
2 egg yolks
2 tablespoons cream
dash of Tabasco sauce

Divide the broccoli into tiny florets. Cut the bamboo shoots into thin strips.

Heat the oil in a frying pan. Add the broccoli, onion and bamboo shoots and fry for 3 to 4 minutes. Add a little of the reserved bamboo shoot juice, the cinnamon and salt and cayenne pepper to taste, blending well. Simmer, over a low heat, for 2 to 3 minutes.

Beat the egg yolks with a little salt, the cream and Tabasco sauce. Remove the pan from the heat and when off the boil, add the egg mixture, blending well. Transfer to a serving dish and serve immediately.
Serves 4

NOTE: Bamboo Shoots with Broccoli is an excellent vegetable dish to serve with fried fish, chops or minced meat and cooked long-grain rice.

Fennel in Wine Sauce

2–3 large heads fennel
4 tablespoons olive oil
2 cloves garlic, peeled and halved
300 ml/$\frac{1}{2}$ pint meat stock
300 ml/$\frac{1}{2}$ pint dry white wine
3 tomatoes, cut into wedges
1 bay leaf
3 peppercorns
salt
sugar
pinch of curry powder
2 tablespoons coarsely chopped parsley
1 teaspoon cornflour

Remove the stalks from the fennel and cut the heads into quarters. Heat the oil in a pan. Add the garlic and fry until golden brown. Remove and discard the garlic.

Add the stock and wine to the pan, stirring well. Add the fennel, tomatoes, bay leaf and peppercorns. Season with salt and sugar to taste. Simmer over a low heat for 15 to 20 minutes. Add the curry powder and parsley, blending well. Discard the bay leaf.

Dissolve the cornflour in 2 tea-spoons water. Add to the fennel mixture stirring constantly. Cook, stirring, for 1 to 2 minutes. Transfer to a warmed serving dish and serve immediately.
Serves 4

NOTE: Fennel in Wine Sauce is particularly delicious served with grilled meat or fish dishes.

Celery au Gratin

1 head celery
50 g/2 oz butter
salt
freshly ground black pepper
125 g/4 oz Pecorino or Parmesan cheese, sliced

Cut the leaves from the celery and chop them very finely. Cut the stalks into 5 to 6 cm/2 to 2$\frac{1}{2}$ inch lengths. Melt the butter in a pan, add the celery and salt and pepper to taste. Cook over a low heat for about 15 minutes.

Transfer the celery to an ovenproof dish and top with the chopped celery leaves and cheese. Cook in a preheated hot oven (220°C/425°F, Gas Mark 7) for about 10 minutes, or alternatively brown under a preheated hot grill. Serve immediately.
Serves 4

NOTE: Celery au Gratin is delicious served with fish. It also makes a good light hors d'oeuvre.

Fennel Fritters

2 heads fennel
lemon juice
2 eggs
salt
grated nutmeg
2 tablespoons flour
50 g/2 oz dry white breadcrumbs
oil for deep frying
2 tablespoons mayonnaise
150 ml/$\frac{1}{4}$ pint soured cream
pinch of salt
pinch of curry powder
TO GARNISH:
lemon slices

Remove the stalks and leaves from the fennel and cut the heads lengthways into 5 mm/$\frac{1}{4}$ inch slices. Sprinkle with a little lemon juice. Beat the eggs with a little salt and nutmeg to taste. Dip the fennel slices in the flour, then into the egg mixture and finally coat in the breadcrumbs.

Heat the oil in a pan. Add the coated fennel slices and fry until golden brown. Drain on kitchen paper.

Meanwhile, make the dressing. Beat the mayonnaise with the soured cream, salt and curry powder. Serve the hot fritters accompanied by the sauce and lemon slices.
Serves 4

NOTE: Fennel Fritters can be served as an hors d'oeuvre or snack. With ham or cheese they make a light supper dish, or they can be served as a vegetable dish to accompany grilled meat or sausages.

Asparagus with Cream Sauce

750 g/1$\frac{1}{2}$ lb asparagus spears
20 g/$\frac{3}{4}$ oz butter
$\frac{1}{2}$ teaspoon salt
1 teaspoon sugar
SAUCE:
150 ml/$\frac{1}{4}$ pint milk
30 g/1$\frac{1}{2}$ oz butter
1 teaspoon cornflour, blended with 2 teaspoons water
2 egg yolks
150 ml/$\frac{1}{4}$ pint double cream
1 tablespoon lemon juice
salt
pinch of grated nutmeg

Rinse the asparagus thoroughly and trim off the woody bases of the stalks. Bring 600 ml/1 pint water to the boil in a pan. Add the butter, salt, sugar and asparagus. Lower the heat and cook for 20 minutes, or until tender.

Meanwhile make the sauce. Mix the milk, butter and cornflour in a pan. Bring to the boil, stirring constantly. Beat the egg yolks with the cream. Remove the pan from the heat and stir in the cream and egg mixture, blending well. Add the lemon juice, salt to taste and nutmeg, mixing well.

Drain the asparagus and place in a serving dish. Pour the sauce over, or serve separately. Serve immediately.
Serves 4

NOTE: Asparagus with Cream Sauce is a tasty vegetable to accompany grilled fillet steaks or grilled gammon steaks.

Asparagus with Cream Sauce; Fennel Fritters; Fennel in Wine Sauce; Celery au Gratin

MUSHROOMS

Mushrooms seem like magic, they spring up under trees, in fields and in some of the most unexpected dark and damp places, literally overnight. If you are lucky you can still gather wild mushrooms by the basketful during the late summer, autumn and winter months, but there are plenty of cultivated mushrooms for all. Those that are cultivated on a large scale range from the small, neat button mushroom, ideal for sautéing, slicing and eating raw, to the large flat mushroom with fully open and flat cap, ideal for stuffing and braising.

Beyond the cultivated mushrooms, so often taken for granted, are the often forgotten fragrant and rarer Chanterelles, earthy cèpes, pungent yet delicate morels, to the rarest of all – the truffles. Fresh or canned they can prove prohibitively expensive, but their aromatic fragrance is exquisite. Even a little goes a long way, a few slices will add a touch of luxury to the simplest of dishes.

MUSHROOMS

Origin: Mushrooms, as spore-bearing plants, are among the oldest plants in the world. Long ago, mushrooms grew far and wide. Today, there are so few woods and tracts of natural meadowland, that field mushrooms have become a rarity.

Mushrooms figure large in history and legend. They appear in many fairy tales, and feature in the history of the Roman Emperors: the Emperor Claudius was poisoned with inedible mushrooms by his wife.

There are over 250 varieties of edible mushrooms, differing in appearance, flavour and nutritional value.

Among the finest of the edible mushrooms and fungi are cèpes, chanterelles, field mushrooms, cultivated mushrooms, oyster mushrooms, morels and truffles. Other edible fungi include orange agaric, chestnut boletus, the rough-stemmed boletus, red boletus, honey agaric and the ringed boletus.

Cèpes (*Boletus edulis*) are superior-tasting wild mushrooms widely eaten in Europe. They are found in woodland clearings in late summer and autumn, usually under conifers. They have short, stout stalks with slightly raised veins and tubes underneath the cap in which the brown spores are produced.

Chanterelles (*Cantharellus cibarius*) are wild, funnel-shaped, yellow-capped mushrooms that can be found mainly under beech trees. They have a slightly ribbed stalk which runs up under the edge of the cap. They cannot be artificially cultivated but are found in season from July to December.

Field mushrooms (*Agaricus campestris*) are found in meadows from late summer to autumn. They have a creamy white cap and stalk.

Cultivated mushrooms (*Agaricus bisporus*) can be picked young as button mushrooms, where the cap is tight and round; as a cup, where the cap is partially opened; or as a flat mushroom, where the cap is fully opened to reveal dark brown gills.

The oyster mushroom (*Pleurotus ostreatus*) is a wild mushroom with a bluish-grey cap. It is popular in France.

Availability: There is a mushroom available for every month and season of the year; cultivated mushrooms ensure this good supply. Cultivated mushrooms are grown in sheds with controlled temperatures, in specially prepared beds enriched with compost plant waste or manure. Most of the fresh mushrooms on sale here are produced in this country. We do however, import canned mushrooms from other countries, such as Taiwan, France and Belgium.

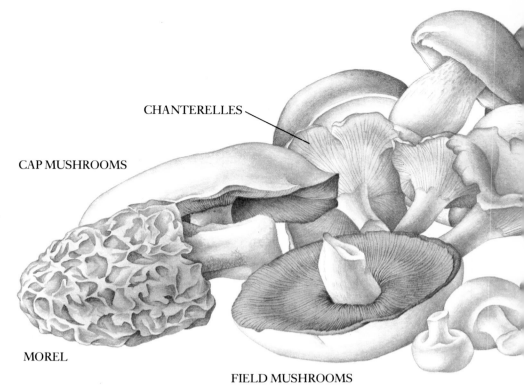

CHANTERELLES

CAP MUSHROOMS

MOREL

FIELD MUSHROOMS

Occasionally, fresh field mushrooms can be bought in vegetable markets during the autumn. It is also becoming increasingly easier to obtain oyster mushrooms from delicatessens.

Buying: Buy fresh field or woodland mushrooms only from shops, stalls and markets which you know have been officially inspected. Make sure they are really fresh; they must be pale in colour if cut or broken, and the skins should be dry. If in any doubt at all, then reject the mushrooms.

Cultivated open and button mushrooms are usually sold by weight or pre-packed into convenient quantities. The size of the mushrooms will tell you nothing about their flavour. Choose button mushrooms with closed caps, if the caps have opened they will probably be a few days old.

If you are gathering your own wild field or woodland mushrooms, take a penknife with you so that you can cut the mushroom stalks close to the ground. The trick of carefully twisting the mushrooms off at the stalk requires skill. They should never be torn out of the ground; this destroys the delicate root network, which will then dry out. Mushrooms are sensitive to pressure, so they should be laid side by side and then on top of each other gently and carefully. They also need air so it is best to use a wicker or wooden basket for collecting them. Plastic bags are unsuitable since they encourage the mushrooms to decay quickly.

Preparation and serving: Always cook mushrooms as soon as possible; they spoil easily, and lose flavour by the hour. If you cannot cook them the same day as you pick them, then store in the salad drawer of the refrigerator.

To clean, remove all earth, sand, bits of grass or other vegetation. If you are cleaning the rough-stemmed boletus or any mushroom type that has tubes or thick gills, then check carefully for dirt. **Always check and identify the mushrooms you have picked to ensure that they are an edible variety – if in any doubt then do not eat.**

Cook mushrooms with the minimum of seasonings to preserve their delicate flavour. All fine mushrooms can be sliced and cooked in butter in their own juices with just a little salt and pepper and garlic if liked. Sturdy mushrooms, such as the orange agaric, chestnut boletus and chanterelle, also taste good fried with chopped bacon and onion; in stews, sauces and soups; or combined with meat or eggs. They also make a good base for a soufflé and an ideal ingredient in a mixed salad.

Cultivated mushrooms should also be rinsed thoroughly and then drained in a sieve. Cut off the stalk ends, halve, quarter or slice, according to their size. Sprinkle immediately with lemon juice to prevent discoloration.

Button mushrooms can be eaten raw, served with dressings and dips, or in many salads. They can be cooked gently in butter with just a little salt

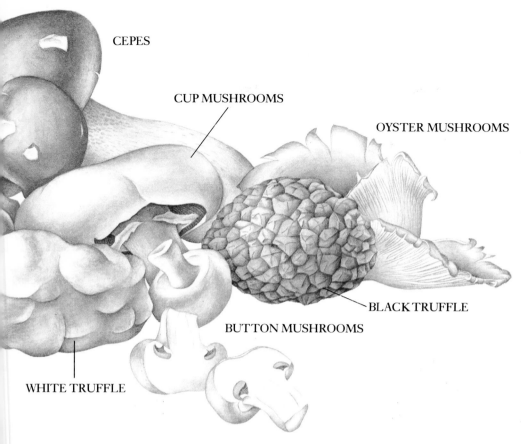

CEPES

CUP MUSHROOMS

OYSTER MUSHROOMS

BLACK TRUFFLE

BUTTON MUSHROOMS

WHITE TRUFFLE

and pepper and chopped parsley. They make delicious soups, stews, soufflés, casserole dishes and garnishes. They can be made into a sauce, used as a pizza topping, stuffed or baked in puff pastry. They are particularly good in omelettes, cream soups and dishes with delicately flavoured meats, such as veal. They are excellent baked in scallop shells, in mushroom tarts and kebabs. They will take 12 to 25 minutes to cook, according to size and variety.

Nutritional value: All mushrooms have a high water and protein content, which is why they decay so quickly. They contain scarcely any vitamins, but provide valuable minerals. Chanterelles and cèpes contain large quantities of phosphorus.

All mushrooms are low in calories, varying between about 15 to 30 Calories (65 to 128 kj) per 100 g/3½ oz.

MORELS

Origin: Morels (*Morchella esculenta*) are also known as sponge mushrooms because they have sponge-like caps with a honeycomb texture and longish stalks. They are full of flavour, and are known as 'cloud ears' in their native China.

Availability: Morels can be found in woodland clearings during spring and early summer but are generally bought dried or canned. Chinese morels can be bought fresh in some delicatessens and specialist food shops.

Buying: In Europe most morels are sold dried. They are dark in colour, almost black. They are expensive but a little goes a long way. Store any opened packets of dried morels in a tin with a close-fitting lid. Stored this way they will keep fresh for months.

Preparation and serving: Rinse and drain fresh morels before use. Soak dried morels in warm water for at least 1 hour.

Use morels to add flavour to soups, casseroles, vegetable and meat dishes, in sauces, chopped in rice mixtures and with lightly-scrambled eggs. They are extensively used in many East Asian dishes.

Nutritional value: Nutritionally, morels have little to recommend them other than a few minerals; they are valued more for their delicious flavour. Fresh or rehydrated morels contain about 12 Calories (51 kj) per 100 g/3½ oz.

TRUFFLES

Origin: Truffles are edible fungi tubers that only grow underground, at about a depth of 10 to 30 cm/4 to 10 inches, although some can be found as deep as 100 cm/40 inches. They grow in limey soil, among the roots of oaks and maples, especially the former. They can only be found with the help of pigs or specially-trained dogs who sniff them out. These exquisite fungi have been regarded as a delicacy in Europe since the Middle Ages.

The two main varieties, and the most highly prized, are the black or winter truffle called Périgord (*Tuber melanosporum*) and the white summer Piedmontese (*Tuber magnatum*). There is also a red-grained black truffle native to England (*Tuber aestivum*) but it is largely ignored.

Availability: Fresh truffles are gathered mainly in the autumn, and are generally only marketed locally. They are only cultivated in as much as oak trees are planted to encourage them, but new research methods are constantly tried. The latest involves injecting truffle purée into the roots of oak trees. For the time being, therefore, truffles remain prohibitively expensive.

Fresh truffles are seldom sold in this country, and then only in the most exclusive specialist shops, starting with 50 g/2 oz quantities. We do however, find expensive preserved truffles in jars and cans.

The main areas for truffles are in the Périgord region of France and the Spoleto and Norcia regions of Italy. Imports mainly come from these areas.

Buying: Fresh truffles have a powerful taste and aroma, similar to liver pâté or truffled calves' liver sausage.

Preserved truffles, in jars and cans, can be bought in 25 g/1 oz, 50 g/2 oz or 125 g/4 oz quantities. They are available prepared in the following ways: brossées, brushed and left whole; en morceaux, in pieces or slices; and pelées, peeled.

Preparation and serving: Fresh truffles should be soaked in cold water for a few hours, then rinsed well, brushed and peeled very thinly. Pounded with a little salt, the truffle peel makes a fine flavouring for delicate sauces, meat, fish or poultry. Whole truffles can be marinated in brandy or armagnac, wrapped in bacon and then cooked in a foil parcel, preferably in the hot ashes of a wood fire, or briefly simmered in wine and baked in puff or flaky pastry.

Sliced truffles can be scrambled with egg or made into a truffle omelette. They are also used in unusual sauces and salads. Canned or bottled truffles are generally used in soups and pies.

Black truffles can also be used as a decorative garnish, in pâté de foie gras or in aspic dishes.

Nutritional value: Like all other mushrooms and fungi, truffles have a high water content, a few valuable minerals and salts but few vitamins. They are generally valued for their taste rather than their nutritional value. Low in calories they contain about 21 Calories (88 kj) per 100 g/3½ oz.

Champagne Truffles en Croûte

4–6 fresh truffles
300 ml/½ pint dry champagne
½ × 215 g/7½ oz packet frozen puff
    pastry, thawed
4–6 very thin rashers bacon
1 egg yolk
parsley sprigs to garnish

Scrub the truffles and peel very thinly (you can keep the skins to use in sauces if you crush them with salt and store in a small screw-top jar). Simmer over a low heat in the champagne for about 20 minutes.

Roll out the pastry on a lightly floured surface until very thin. Cut out 4 to 6 star shapes, using a canapé cutter. Drain the truffles and wrap each one in a rasher of bacon, place each truffle on a pastry star and fold the pastry over so that the points of the stars interlock. Brush the pastry with egg yolk to seal well and to glaze.

Place the champagne truffles on a dampened baking sheet and cook in a preheated hot oven (220°C/425°F, Gas Mark 7) for about 20 minutes. Serve immediately, garnished with parsley.
Serves 4 to 6

NOTE: Truffles are prohibitively expensive to buy. If you are lucky enough to obtain any, this is an appropriate way to treat them.

Quick Chinese Morel Soup

1 tablespoon oil
2–3 tablespoons dried morel mushrooms,
 soaked for 30 minutes in warm water
2 tablespoons chopped parsley
750 ml/1¼ pints rich chicken stock
scant 1 tablespoon Patna rice
pinch of cayenne pepper

Heat the oil in a pan, add the mushrooms and parsley and cook for 5 minutes. Add the stock and rice, bring to the boil, then reduce the heat and simmer, over a low heat, for 20 to 25 minutes, stirring occasionally. Season with cayenne pepper before serving.
Serves 4

Wild Mushroom Soup

1 tablespoon oil
500–750 g/1–1½ lb wild mushrooms,
 rinsed, trimmed and cut into strips or
 chopped
½ onion, peeled and chopped
1 bunch watercress, chopped
½ clove garlic, peeled and crushed
scant 1 litre/1¾ pints meat stock
1 tablespoon coarsely chopped parsley
2 egg yolks
2 tablespoons double cream

Heat the oil in a pan. Add the mushrooms and onion and fry gently for 5 minutes. Add the watercress, garlic and stock and simmer, over a low heat, for 20 minutes.
 Add the parsley, mixing well. Beat the egg yolks with the cream. Stir into the soup and cook gently to thicken but do not allow to boil. Serve hot.
Serves 4 to 6

Mushroom Kebabs

325 g/11 oz button mushrooms
juice of ½ lemon
2 tablespoons dry or medium dry sherry
200 g/7 oz turkey or chicken liver
salt
freshly ground black pepper
1 teaspoon dried sage
125 g/4 oz streaky bacon rashers,
 · derinded and halved lengthwise
1 onion, peeled and cut into wedges
olive oil for basting
chopped parsley to garnish

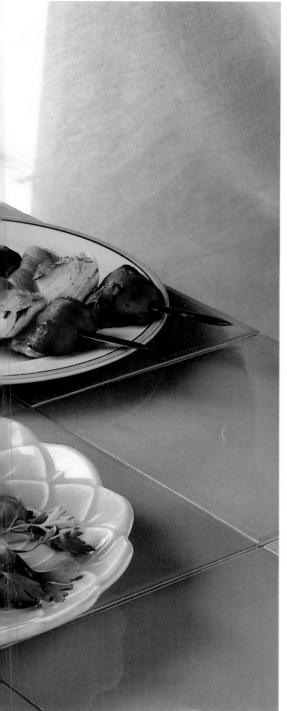

*Marinated Mushrooms; Mushroom Kebabs;
Champagne Truffles en Croûte*

Trim the stalks from the mushrooms (they can be used for a soup or sauce). Place the caps in a sieve, rinse and drain thoroughly. Sprinkle with lemon juice and sherry. Leave to marinate for about 5 minutes to allow the flavours to develop.
 Cut the turkey liver into bite-sized cubes or strips and season with salt and pepper to taste, and the sage. Stretch the bacon slices and roll up. Arrange the mushrooms on 4 skewers alternating with bacon rolls, onion wedges and the turkey liver. Brush well with oil and cook under a preheated hot grill for 4 to 6 minutes, basting frequently. Serve immediately, garnished with parsley.
Serves 4

Marinated Mushrooms

400–500 g/14 oz–1 lb button
 mushrooms
15 g/½ oz butter
juice of ½ lemon
1 parsley sprig, chopped
150 ml/¼ pint dry red wine
2 cloves garlic, peeled and crushed with
 salt
freshly ground black pepper
1 bay leaf
pinch of ground allspice
parsley sprig to garnish

Trim the mushroom stalks level with the caps. Place in a sieve, rinse and drain thoroughly.
 Melt the butter in a pan. Add the mushrooms, sprinkle with the lemon juice and parsley and cook for 2 to 3 minutes. Add the red wine, garlic, pepper to taste, bay leaf and allspice. Bring to the boil and cook for 2 minutes. Remove and discard the bay leaf.
 Transfer the mushrooms and their cooking liquor to a bowl, cover and chill in the refrigerator for 2 to 3 hours. Garnish with parsley and serve chilled, in the marinade.
Serves 4 to 6

NOTE: This makes a delicious starter, served with crusty garlic bread. It is also an excellent accompaniment for fish, poultry and grilled meat dishes.

Crispy Fried Mushrooms

500 g/1 lb medium flat mushrooms
1 egg
1 egg yolk
½ tablespoon finely chopped parsley
salt
freshly ground black pepper
3 tablespoons dry white breadcrumbs
25 g/1 oz butter
1 clove garlic, peeled and halved

Trim the mushroom stalks level with the caps. Place the mushrooms in a sieve, rinse and drain thoroughly and slice thickly.

Beat the egg with the egg yolk, parsley, and salt and pepper to taste. Dip the mushrooms in the egg mixture and coat in the breadcrumbs.

Melt the butter in a large frying pan, fry the garlic until golden brown, remove and discard. Add the mushrooms and fry until golden brown on all sides. Serve immediately.
Serves 4 to 6

NOTE: Crispy Fried Mushrooms are delicious served with a herb-flavoured mayonnaise and French bread.

Stuffed Mushrooms

625 g/1¼ lb large flat mushrooms
lemon juice for sprinkling
125 g/4 oz carrots, peeled and diced
120 ml/4 fl oz meat stock
15 g/½ oz butter
1 tablespoon plain flour
salt
freshly ground black pepper
pinch of grated nutmeg
pinch of curry powder
125 g/4 oz peeled shrimps
125 g/4 oz cooked ham, chopped
125 g/4 oz Bonbel cheese, diced
1 red pepper, cored, seeded and sliced
125 g/4 oz Parmesan cheese, grated

Trim the stalks from the mushrooms and reserve. Place the caps in a sieve, rinse and drain thoroughly. Sprinkle with a little lemon juice and place, hollowside up, in a greased baking dish.

Finely chop the mushroom stalks and keep to one side. Place the carrots in a pan with the stock. Bring to the boil, then lower the heat and cook gently for 8 to 10 minutes. Drain and reserve the stock.

Melt the butter in a pan. Add the flour and cook, stirring, for 1 minute. Whisk in the reserved stock. Season with salt and pepper to taste, nutmeg and curry powder. Add the carrot, shrimps, ham, cheese, red pepper and chopped mushroom stalks. Bring to the boil, stirring constantly.

Fill the mushroom caps with this mixture and arrange any remaining stuffing between the mushrooms. Sprinkle with the Parmesan cheese and cook in a preheated hot oven (220°C/425°F, Gas Mark 7) for about 12 minutes, until golden and bubbling. Serve immediately.
Serves 4 to 6

NOTE: This dish makes a delicious hors d'oeuvre or, served with French bread and a salad, an unusual main course.

Mushroom Salad

275 g/9 oz button mushrooms
juice of ½ lemon
2 tablespoons sliced gherkins
175 g/6 oz tomatoes, finely chopped
1 clove garlic, peeled and crushed with
 salt
1 parsley sprig, finely chopped
freshly ground black pepper
pinch of sugar
4–5 tablespoons olive oil

Trim the mushroom stalks level with the caps. Place in a sieve, rinse and drain thoroughly. Cut into thin slices, place in a bowl and sprinkle with the lemon juice. Add the gherkins and tomatoes and mix well to blend.

To make the dressing, beat the garlic with the parsley, pepper to taste, sugar and oil. Pour over the mushroom salad and toss well to mix. Leave to marinate in the refrigerator, for about 10 to 15 minutes, to allow the flavours to develop. Serve lightly chilled.
Serves 4

NOTE: This piquant salad makes a delicious accompaniment to cold roast chicken or lamb. It can also be served as a light starter.

Creamed Chanterelles or Mushrooms

30 g/1¼ oz butter
750 g/1½ lb chanterelles or other wild
 mushrooms, washed, trimmed and
 coarsely chopped
75 g/3 oz streaky bacon, derinded and
 chopped
salt
freshly ground black pepper
120 ml/4 fl oz double cream
1 egg yolk
1 egg
2 tablespoons chopped parsley, to
 garnish

Melt the butter in a large pan, add the chanterelles or other mushrooms and bacon. Fry, stirring, over a moderate heat, for 5 minutes. Reduce the heat and cook gently for 15 to 20 minutes. Season with salt and pepper to taste and stir in the cream. Remove the pan from the heat and allow the mixture to cool slightly.

Beat the egg yolk and egg together in a bowl with a little salt to taste. Carefully fold into the mushroom mixture. Return the pan to the heat and cook gently for 3 to 4 minutes, stirring constantly.

Transfer to a warmed serving dish and serve immediately, sprinkled with the parsley.
Serves 6

NOTE: Creamed Mushrooms are delicious served with buttered new potatoes, or Melba toast if serving as a starter.

*Mushroom Salad; Stuffed Mushrooms;
Creamed Chanterelles or Mushrooms*

Braised Chanterelles

750 g/1½ lb chanterelles
15 g/½ oz butter
50 g/2 oz bacon, derinded and chopped
2 teaspoons plain flour
150 ml/¼ pint meat stock
120 ml/4 fl oz dry red wine
salt
pinch of cayenne pepper
1 parsley sprig, chopped

Rinse and clean the chanterelles thoroughly. Trim and cut any large ones into smaller pieces.

Melt the butter in a pan and fry the bacon until crisp. Add the chanterelles and cook for 5 minutes. Add the flour and cook, stirring, for 1 minute. Gradually stir in the stock and wine. Season with salt to taste and the cayenne pepper. Simmer, over a low heat, for about 20 minutes. Stir in the parsley and serve immediately.
Serves 6

NOTE: Braised Chanterelles can be served in a ring of boiled long-grain rice.

Chicken with Mushrooms

4 chicken quarters
salt and freshly ground black pepper
dried oregano
ground paprika
3 tablespoons olive oil
1 tablespoon plain flour
400 g/14 oz mushrooms, washed,
  trimmed and quartered
300 ml/½ pint chicken stock
½ onion, peeled and grated
1 green pepper, cored, seeded and cut
  into fine strips
300 ml/½ pint double cream
50 ml/2 fl oz Cognac
cayenne pepper (optional)

Season the chicken quarters with salt, pepper, oregano and paprika to taste.

Heat the olive oil in a pan. Add the chicken and cook until golden brown on all sides. Remove with a slotted spoon. Add the flour and mushrooms and cook for 1 to 2 minutes. Stir in the chicken stock, onion and green pepper. Return the chicken to the pan. Cover and simmer, over a low heat, for about 30 minutes, until the chicken is tender, stirring occasionally.

About 10 minutes before the end of the cooking time add the cream and Cognac, stirring well to combine.

Season to taste with a little more salt and cayenne, if liked. Serve immediately.
Serves 4

NOTE: Any mushrooms can be used for this casserole, but field ones give the best flavour. If button mushrooms are used, they should be sautéed and added 15 minutes before the end of cooking.

RIGHT: *Chicken with Mushrooms; Trout with Morel Cream Sauce*
BELOW: *Braised Chanterelles; Cèpes with Herb Sauce*

Cèpes with Herb Sauce

40 g/1½ oz butter
1 clove garlic, peeled and halved
750 g/1½ lb cèpes or other wild
  mushrooms, washed, trimmed and cut
  into bite-sized pieces
1 tablespoon chopped parsley
1 tablespoon chopped chervil
1 tablespoon chopped basil
1 tablespoon plain flour
4 tablespoons dry white wine
150 ml/¼ pint double or soured cream
salt
freshly ground white pepper

Melt the butter in a pan. Add the garlic and fry until golden brown. Remove and discard the garlic. Add the cèpes or other mushrooms to the pan and cook over a low heat for about 20 minutes.

Add half of the chopped herbs to the pan and mix well. Stir in the flour and cook for 2 to 3 minutes, stirring well. Gradually add the wine, blending well after each addition to make a smooth sauce. Simmer, over a low heat, for about 3 minutes. Fold in the double or soured cream and season with salt and

pepper to taste. Transfer to a serving dish, sprinkle with the remaining herbs and serve immediately.
Serves 6

NOTE: Cèpes with Herb Sauce is particularly delicious served with French bread and a light dry white wine.

Trout with Morel Cream Sauce

4 trout, each weighing about 175 g/
  6 oz, gutted and cleaned
juice of 1 lemon
salt and freshly ground white pepper
1 bunch mixed herbs (e.g. parsley,
  chives, thyme)
300 ml/½ pint water
300 ml/½ pint dry white wine
2 tablespoons dried morel mushrooms,
  soaked for 45 minutes in warm water
2 juniper berries, crushed
2 black peppercorns, crushed
1 teaspoon cornflour
150 ml/¼ pint double cream
knob of butter

Sprinkle the fish with the lemon juice and leave to stand for 5 minutes. Season the fish, inside and out, with salt and pepper to taste. Stuff each fish with whole sprigs of herbs.

Pour the water and wine into a large pan with a scant ½ teaspoon of salt and heat until almost boiling. Add the trout and drained morels to the pan, reduce the heat and simmer over a low heat for 20 to 25 minutes, turning the fish once.

Transfer the trout to a warmed serving dish; keep warm. Stir the juniper berries and peppercorns into the pan. Blend the cornflour with a little water

to form a thin paste. Whisk into the stock, blending well, and cook, stirring, for 1 to 2 minutes. Add the cream and butter, mixing well. Pour the morel cream sauce over the fish or serve separately, if liked.
Serves 4

NOTE: Serve Trout with Morel Cream Sauce with fresh garden peas and plain boiled rice.

Mushrooms on Toast

400 g/14 oz button mushrooms, rinsed,
  trimmed and sliced
1 tablespoon lemon juice
15 g/½ oz butter
½ tablespoon chopped basil
2 tablespoons chopped parsley
2 tablespoons double cream
salt and freshly ground black pepper
2 tablespoons olive oil
4 slices white bread
50 g/2 oz Gouda cheese, sliced

Sprinkle the mushrooms with the lemon juice and leave to stand for 5 minutes.

Melt the butter in a pan. Add the mushrooms and cook, over a moderate heat, for 2 minutes. Add the basil, parsley, cream and salt and pepper to taste. Reduce the heat and simmer, over a low heat, for about 7 minutes or until the mushrooms are cooked.

Meanwhile, heat the oil in a frying pan, add the bread and fry until golden brown on both sides, then drain on kitchen paper. Divide the mushrooms equally between the slices of bread and top with the cheese. Place under a preheated hot grill until the cheese is bubbling. Serve immediately.
Serves 4

NOTE: Mushrooms on Toast makes an ideal snack or light supper dish.

Mushrooms in Garlic Cream

500 g/1 lb blue-cap or other wild
* mushrooms*
15 g/½ oz butter
30 g/1¼ oz streaky bacon, derinded and
* chopped*
2 cloves garlic, peeled and halved
salt
freshly ground white pepper
2–3 tablespoons hot water
2 tablespoons chopped parsley
150 ml/¼ pint double cream

Trim the mushrooms, rinse and drain thoroughly. Cut them into bite-sized pieces. Melt the butter in a pan. Add the chopped bacon and the garlic and fry gently until golden brown. Remove and discard the garlic. Set aside a little of the bacon.

Add the mushrooms to the pan with salt and pepper to taste. Stir in the water and parsley and cook, over a low heat, for about 8 minutes. Stir in the double cream and simmer over a low heat for a further 2 to 4 minutes. Serve immediately, garnished with the reserved bacon.
Serves 4

NOTE: Mushrooms in Garlic Cream makes a delicious accompaniment for veal schnitzel or fillet steaks.

Mushroom Casserole

15 g/½ oz butter
1 kg/2 lb mushrooms (wild mushrooms,
* cup or button mushrooms), washed,*
* trimmed and roughly chopped if large*
1 small onion, peeled and chopped
2 tomatoes, peeled and cut into wedges
½ cucumber, chopped
salt
freshly ground white pepper
1 tablespoon lemon juice
1 small bunch herbs (e.g. parsley, dill,
* thyme), chopped*

Melt the butter in a pan. Add the mushrooms and onion and cook, over a moderate heat, for 5 minutes. Reduce the heat and cook gently for 20 minutes or until tender.

Add the tomatoes and cucumber and cook for 3 to 5 minutes. Season with salt and pepper to taste and add the lemon juice, blending well. Fold in the chopped herbs and serve immediately.
Serves 6 to 8

NOTE: This is delicious served with saffron or herb-flavoured rice.

Mushrooms Gourmet-style

4 tablespoons olive oil
125 g/4 oz shallots, peeled
4 tomatoes, chopped
2 bay leaves
1 tablespoon vinegar
50 ml/2 fl oz dry white wine
salt and freshly ground black pepper
pinch of ground paprika
500 g/1 lb button mushrooms
50 g/2 oz uncooked ham, finely chopped
1 tablespoon chopped parsley

Heat the oil in a pan. Add the shallots and fry for about 5 minutes until golden brown. Add the tomatoes, bay leaves, vinegar, wine, salt and pepper to taste, and paprika, stirring well. Add the mushrooms and cook over a low heat for about 15 minutes. Stir in the ham and parsley and cook for a further 3 to 5 minutes. Discard the bay leaves. Serve immediately.
Serves 4

Mushroom Sauce

275 g/9 oz button mushrooms
juice of ½ lemon
25 g/½ oz butter
salt
freshly ground white pepper
200 ml/⅓ pint double cream
1 parsley sprig, chopped

Trim the mushroom stalks level with the caps. Place in a sieve, rinse and drain. Sprinkle with the lemon juice and leave to stand for about 5 minutes.

Melt the butter in a pan, add the marinated mushrooms, season with the salt and pepper to taste and fry for 4 to 5 minutes. Fold in the cream and parsley and simmer, over a low heat, for 15 to 25 minutes, stirring occasionally, until the sauce is creamy.
Serves 4

Mushrooms Gourmet Style; Mushroom Sauce
on lamb cutlets; Mushrooms in Garlic Cream

NOTE: A delicious accompaniment to serve with steaks, chops and fish.

INDEX

188

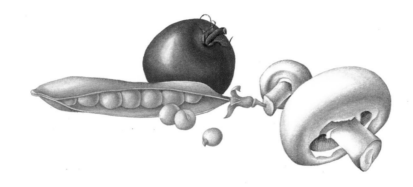

ACKNOWLEDGMENTS
Photography by Paul Williams
Photographic stylist: Penny Markham
Food prepared by Carol Bowen and Clare Ferguson
Illustrations by Valerie Murrell and
Jim Channell of Linden Artists